THE CHASE
Career of the
Compulsive Gambler

HENRY R. LESIEUR

Schenkman Publishing Company, Inc.

326 new copy 20001 champion

Copyright © 1984

Schenkman Publishing Company, Inc.
190 Concord Ave.
Cambridge, MA 02138

Library of Congress Cataloging in Publication Data

Lesieur, Henry R.
  The chase: career of the compulsive gambler.

  Bibliography: p.
  Includes index.
  1. Gamblers. 2. Gamblers—Psychology.
3. Compulsive behavior. I. Title.
HV6713.L45   1984   364.1'72   84-10533
ISBN 0-87047-000-0
ISBN 0-87047-001-9 (pbk.)

Printed in the United States of America.

Henry R. Lesieur received his introduction to gambling while working at a gas station on the major route to a race track. During the five years he spent there as a senior in high school and undergraduate in college, he got to know jockeys, trainers, owners, bookmakers, and gamblers of all types. This left him with a keen interest in gamblers and a recognition that gambling is not equal to organized crime. Since then, he has spent several years observing Gamblers Anonymous groups and interviewing gamblers in order to write this book. Dr. Lesieur is now an associate professor in the department of Sociology and Anthropology at St. John's University, Jamaica, New York, 11439.

To Helen

Contents

Author's Note

As a senior in high school and undergraduate in college I worked at a gas station on the major route to a race track. In the five years working there I encountered many different gamblers.

Some of the gamblers who used to hang around this gas station were "holding their own" (losing money but not chasing). Some of them would "hold action" for a few customers, and at times if the horse was "too hot," I would be sent over to put the action in with the local bookmaker and would occasionally put a few dollars in for myself.

What had impressed me the most about those years was that "gamblers die broke," "you can win a race, but you can't beat the races," "I bet on a horse but it's still running," and "I'm overdue [for a winner]." In addition to this, I saw evidence of some common means of getting money for gambling. A gambler would come in and ask if he could pay the bill with a check always larger than the bill (the answer was a definite no); alternatively he would ask me to give him money on his credit card. As I was about to make out the bill, the gambler would ask me to add ten, fifteen, or twenty dollars onto it, give him the cash, and possibly give me a dollar for doing him the favor. And other gamblers would come in with tires, batteries, watches, shirts, and other hot items for sale.

Later on, in graduate school, the only reference I saw to gambling as a form of deviant behavior was in relation to organized crime. While I sensed that the local bookmakers were pooled into an organized network, the "degenerate gamblers" I knew were "degenerate" because they lost money gambling and would resort to shady business and other practices as a result (for example, several of these "degenerate gamblers" were "honest John"-type used-car salesmen, including one of the local tire and battery "fences"). In a sense, most of the textbooks and readers in the sociology of deviance grossly misrepresented the gambling world.[1] I gradually forgot about the gamblers until I saw a television special on Gamblers Anonymous. This rekindled earlier memories and I decided to do a master's thesis on the organization (Lesieur, 1973).

At the first meeting of Gamblers Anonymous I attended I experienced a sort of culture shock. There were people talking about loan sharks coming after them, fraudulent loans (I found it hard to believe that people could have more than ten loans at the same time), losing a personal business, and discussion of suicide. There were people there who had not gambled in three years and another who had lottery tickets in his pocket and had just placed a bet with the bookmaker.

Given this shock and the inadequacy of the criminology books I had read, I knew immediately that I had to learn more about the career and illegal behavior patterns of compulsive gamblers. *The Chase* is the result of this exploration.

I would like to thank Peter Park for his persistent questions about the whereabouts of the ever-elusive theoretical model. His suggestion about dialectics and feedback eventually put many disparate ideas all together. It was Rob Faulkner who read a student's field notes and talked about wanting to "be there." Without this the notes would still have consisted of the sorry state of one and two pages of comments for each three hours of observation. Rob also insisted on clarifying the sequential model that he knew was here somewhere. It is Tony Harris I thank for pressures to quantify—turn "some" and "many" into numbers and develop the tables that clarify this work. I would also like to thank Peter d'Errico for reading and commenting on all of this, as well as Joe Sheley, who pointed out some problems with Chapter VIII in an earlier stage. Most important of all, however, are the Gamblers Anonymous members who started all this off and commented on portions of the work, and non-Gamblers Anonymous members including the prisoners, students, people at the golf course, wives of the gamblers, and all the others who helped me probe into their lives. As I mentioned to them, their anonymity is preserved.

The following people helped or attempted to help me gain interviews in the criminal justice system: Sheriff John Boyle of the Hampshire County Jail, Vincent Colagiovanni, Richard Greene, Richard Gaskell, Arthur Fortier, Joseph Morgan, Carla Ledin, Lucille Calabrese, Tom Dempsey, Bob Hines and Mary Flanigan of Rhode Island probation and parole, and Warden Wager and Gordon Pitman of F.C.I. in Danbury, Connecticut.

In addition, I received a small grant from the Social and Demographic Research Institute at the University of Massachusetts, which enabled me to hire a secretary to transcribe the last few interviews and make a few more trips to reinterview some key informants.

The writings of a naïve author were gone over with a fine-tooth comb by Elizabeth Knappman and Joan Kass at Anchor Press/Doubleday. Thanks to them, this product is not as redundant as it was. The end product was made more interesting as a result.

Last, but not least, I would like to say one thing to Helen, my wife: It's your turn. I dedicate this book to you with all my love.

Foreword

The Chase is far and away the finest sociological study done on the Pathological (compulsive) Gambler. It is scientific with a disarming simplicity which gives an informative and impressive body of knowledge for all mental health professionals and laymen.

Henry R. Lesieur has written a fundamental study on pathological gambling. His perceptions, insights and concepts are based on an open-minded scientific approach. The reader of this book will recognize the uniqueness of the solid premises. The threads of psychological perspectives, and the touch of the compassionate investigator, are very evident. *The Chase* is a basic contribution to the understanding of a complex disorder. My personal work in the treatment of the pathological gambler has been clarified, stimulated and challenged by Dr. Lesieur's studies.

This book is a worthy start to desperately needed work on a baffling disorder. Dr. Lesieur has captured the critical element of the pathology of the pathological gambler—the mad diminishing spiral of options involved in the chase. And he has done his job brilliantly.

ROBERT L. CUSTER, M.D.

Preface to the Second Edition

The first edition of *The Chase* appeared in 1977. During the writing of that original edition, two extremely important developments were occurring about which I was oblivious at the time. These were the establishment of a treatment center for compulsive gamblers at the Veteran's Administration Hospital in Brecksville, Ohio, and the establishment of the National Council on Compulsive Gambling. As I was a graduate student at the time, I did not know about the first and I would have been opposed to the second had I known about it then. In my student days, I was convinced that there was no such thing as mental illness; this was because of the influence of the "labeling" school of deviance. At best, mental illness was a "label" which enabled the medical establishment to justify its control over and attempts to modify the behavior of deviants. My feeling was that while the model had its uses for some people, by no means would embracing it really help people in the long run. My views were to be transformed.

When I took a position at St. John's University, I went into OTB one day to look around and saw a sign that had the National Council on Compulsive Gambling headquarters phone number on it. It was in New York. Out of curiosity, I dialed the number and decided to see what the organization was all about.

When I arrived at the Council, I met Monsignor Dunne. He was a person with a tremendous amount of compassion for the compulsive gambler and he advocated the medical model. What surprised me was that Msgr. Dunne is not a psychoanalyst and hence had no economic motivation to embrace the idea. At the Council, I also met people there who had read this book in its first edition and who thought it was a true contribution to the understanding of problem gambling. Here were psychologists and psychiatrists who found my views to be very useful to them in their practice. I found that essentially, there was no incompatibility between the sociological and the medical positions.

My transformation from someone who disbelieves in the medical model to one who now endorses it (albeit, with some reservations as spelled out in Chapter XI) took the following form. Over the years through my affiliation with the Council first as an observer, then a member of the education and research committees and finally as a member of the advisory board, I met psychologists, social workers, psychiatrists and others connected with the medical model. I found that they were compassionate persons who knew in their own mind that what they were doing was helpful to the gamblers, alcoholics and others they were treating. In addition, I met literally hundreds of gamblers who praised the work that these professionals were doing. I heard statements like: "Dr. Kramer saved my life." "If it wasn't for Dr. Taber, I would have killed myself two years ago."

What is it about the medical model that does these things? First of all, patients confront their fate and come to see they have a problem that is affecting their lives and the lives of others around them. Secondly, the therapists use group counseling procedures which aid the gamblers in overcoming their denial that they have a problem. Thirdly, these practitioners serve as an alternative to Gamblers Anonymous which some pathological gamblers view negatively. Thus, a consequence of the medical model is that it provides an alternative approach to helping persons who need help. From the testimony of the gamblers with whom I have had contact, this alternative help is greatly appreciated.

It took me several years to recognize that, on balance, the medical model has helped hundreds if not thousands of gamblers. Even if they are not "sick" in the philosophical sense of the term, calling them sick makes sense when it comes to attempting to alter their destructive behavior patterns. The gamblers can use the illness label to help them rationalize the illegal, unethical and otherwise destructive things that they do. As several gamblers whom I have come to know in New York have told me: "I am not responsible for the things I did. I was sick at the time." They say this at the same time that they are busy making restitution for the things they did. This is a curious combination of "escape" and simultaneous acceptance of responsibility.

The Chase documents the relation between compulsive gambling and crime. The medical model is that it is a form of crime control; this is a benefit. People who join Gamblers Anonymous and who go to professional counselors cut down the number of crimes that they commit. While sociologists may criticize psychologists, psychiatrists and social workers for engaging in medicalization, they would be hard put to create a program for crime control which is as effective given the present state of knowledge about pathological gambling.

The last chapter of the book addresses several issues concerning sociologists and the medical model. In addition, it puts forth a functional analysis of pathological gambling as part of the attempt to address medical issues. Finally, the last chapter uses material in this book as well as current research to evaluate the diagnostic criteria for pathological gambling as established in the Diagnostic and Statistical Manual of the American Psychiatric Association.

I should like to thank the following for their relentless attack on my views concerning the medical model of pathological gambling: Monsignor Joseph Dunne, Dr. Alida Glen, Dr. Julian Taber, Dr. Robert Custer, Dr. Valerie Lorenz, Mary Prendergast, Irving Sachar, Ruth Sachar, and Arnie Wexler. The questions and probings of these people also influenced me to become the editor of the new journal being published by the National Council on Compulsive Gambling—the *Journal of Gambling Behavior and Pathology.*

Those who would like further information about pathological gambling should write to the National Council on Compulsive Gambling, c/o John Jay College of Criminal Justice, 444 West 56th Street, Room 3207 South, New York, New York 10019. Additional information is obtainable through the National Foundation for the Study and Treatment of Pathological Gambling, American Medical Association Building, 1101

Vermont Avenue, N.W., Washington, D.C. 20005 or call (202) 789-1666. The author himself can be reached at the Department of Sociology and Anthropology, St. John's University, Jamaica, New York 11432, (212) 990-6161.

Introduction

In many barrooms, poolrooms, bowling alleys, and casinos, and at many golf courses and race tracks, there are groups of men who engage in seemingly illogical behavior. They "chase." That is, they gamble and lose yet continue to gamble some more in order to "get even." The more money that is lost, the more intense the "chase." Another name for the "chase" is compulsive gambling. *Compulsive gamblers* are those people who through the chase become trapped in a self-enclosed system of option usage and involvement.

The "chase" is only one aspect of *involvement in compulsive gambling*. At the same time, the gambler acquires a fascination with the excitement of gambling, and increased debt, and a desire to resolve that debt by gambling. He uses more and more *options* to get money when gambling fails, including everything from the paycheck and "stealing a little from the cookie jar" to use of such lending institutions as banks and loan sharks, to burglary and armed robbery.

What is ironic is that increasing debt *reduces the options* available for resolving that debt. Once an option has been employed to its fullest it is exhausted. If he owes one thousand dollars to the bookmaker by noon tomorrow, there may be only a few options left. The gambler may try gambling with another bookmaker or he may try doing something illegal that he can rationalize.

Increased involvement and reduced options interact as a *spiral. As involvement increases, the options available are steadily used up and a spiral is created,* something like a cone.

The Spirals

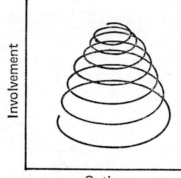

INVOLVEMENT

A gambler gets more and more involved as he gets deeper and deeper into debt and the stakes he wagers climb. At the same time, *he becomes more engrossed in the action and intensity of the chase.* He becomes more deeply *committed* to gambling as the only way out. Now, a person becomes committed to one activity when he involves "other interests of his, originally extraneous to the action he has engaged in, directly in that action. . . ." (Becker, 1960: 35–36)

In the case of a compulsive gambler, personal and financial problems induce this commitment. For instance, a bookmaker may want his money, a finance company or loan shark may start putting on pressure, a wife may find out about hidden debts if the lending institution sends an overdue notice or phones the house, or the gambler must cover illegal activity such as a bad check or embezzlement. He borrows money and hence includes others in his ventures, telling himself he will get even in the end. Because he is committed, the gambler engages in increasingly more serious activities in order to finance his gambling. Yet the gambler tells everyone that gambling is entertainment.

OPTIONS

During their spiraling career, compulsive gamblers use various options to finance their gambling or recoup losses. They can use their paycheck; "borrow" from the joint savings account; borrow from friends, relatives, and lending institutions; become bookmakers or numbers runners; hustle suckers at pool, bowling, golf, cards, or dice; write bad checks; or engage in other legal or illegal activity. Each of these options has a theoretical upper limit of obtainable money. For example, gambling friends have only so much money. They may be able to lend out one hundred dollars, but they may be in financial trouble themselves. The hustler may have only so many suckers he can hustle out of money; the lending institution may stop credit; and the checking account may be closed. Alternatively, the cookie jar may not contain the amount of money needed. As a result, with increased involvement the gambler will have to resort to other, more serious options.

The options the gambler uses cover roughly six areas: family, occupation, the gambling setting and gambling friends, bookmaking, lending institutions, and crime.

Since a compulsive gambler uses up his financial resources to recover his losses, he is constantly in search of money: he owes money to progressively more people and finds more ways of "juggling money" from person to person. Because of increasing pressures to pay debts (both on self-esteem and externally imposed pressures such as bank and loan-shark tactics), the compulsive gambler gambles to a much greater extent. He "chases" faster and faster.

At the same time, the gambler engages in other, interlocking activities. He must conceal loss, get money, conceal the fact that he has gotten the money, and then gamble again. Periodically, if he is married, his wife may find out about the loans he has and he may quit gambling as a result. Alternatively he may quit on his own. His avenues for funding may become dried up and new sources may be used. With each new source used comes a constriction of the remaining possibilities. It is because of this constriction that the compulsive gambler's career looks like a spiral rather than a cycle.

Gambling starts as an adventure, but soon losses demand that the gambler find ways to recoup them. The options he uses, however, reflect back on his career. Borrowed money must be returned, and the quickest way to do so is by gambling. Gambling in turn produces greater losses, which produce more option usage, and so on. As a result, the gambler becomes increasingly committed to compulsive gambling.

THE CAREER FOCUS

Compulsive gamblers have sequential *careers*, much as doctors, lawyers, or thieves. Their careers involve learning the "trade" from other gamblers: how to place a bet, how to handicap, how to get loans, and for more than half, how to get to the loan shark, steal, swindle, and otherwise support an increasingly expensive habit. Their career, like any other, includes

> "a series of statuses and clearly defined offices . . . typical sequences of position, achievement, responsibility, and even of adventure. . . . Subjectively, a career is the moving perspective in which the person sees his life as a whole and interprets the meaning of his various attributes, actions, and the things which happen to him." (Hughes, 1958: 63)

"Success" in any career is *contingent* upon a variety of factors.[1] For the compulsive gambler, having access to credit is one such contingency. This is of prime importance early on in the career, just as getting into debt is a prime mover in the chase. Getting married is another. Marriage produces a strain on finances and increased pressure to relieve that strain by gambling, and the effect is greater the lower down we go in social class. In the pages that follow we will discuss important influences in the compulsive gambler's career: marital status, degree of supervision in occupation, extent of involvement in gambling circles (from loner to group-oriented),

credit and its determinants, social class, personal value structure, and the ability to "manipulate" money.

The career emphasis is on *becoming deviant* as a *social*
process with definite sequential stages. It is also concerned
with how compulsive gambling is done and what it is like to
be a compulsive gambler. This book can be conceived of as a
recipe. "Here is how it can be done, says the recipe, *if
perchance you should want to*" (Matza, 1969: 110).[2] The
process and what it means to be a compulsive gambler is
easier to see by looking at specific gamblers.

THE LONER

For Ken (age fifty-six, married) the most important career influence was that he gambled alone. Yet for a loner he
had the most "successful" career of any gambler I knew. Ken
graduated from high school in 1936 and went to college from
1936 to 1937 for a year as a physical education major. While
in high school he played cards occasionally for very low
stakes on Sunday because there was nothing else to do. He
did the same in college.

In 1937 he went to work in the service department of an
auto company, running errands. From 1939 to 1941 he
worked in the parts department of that firm, until he was
drafted into the infantry. From 1942 until 1945 he was in the
Air Force. During this time he played cards only several
times a month and went to the races on a few occasions. In
1943 Ken got married.

In 1946 a friend introduced him to his uncle, a "connected" bookmaker, with inside knowledge about horse races.
With this stimulation Ken rapidly became interested in horses
and continued even after his friend's uncle's information went
sour. He started working as an auto salesman in the same
year. From 1946 to 1953 he continued going to the races but
gradually eased away from his friends as he got one loan
after another (his first loan was in 1947). During this time
he also started depleting a joint bank account.

In 1953 Ken "dropped the horses like a hotcake" when an
old friend introduced him to sports. From this period on he
bet horses only "once a year or something" and became an

absolute loner. He hid his sports betting from everyone he possibly could. In the same year, he started "bouncing" checks and continued it until 1956, when the account was closed. After this he forged his wife's name to several checks, but he was so easily discovered (by his wife) that it didn't happen often. At around this time he switched jobs to another auto firm and began delivering special-delivery mail at night for the post office to earn extra money. As a car salesman, Ken had a lot of knowledge of credit-bureau information and lending procedures. He put this to good use in getting loans for himself, until he had eleven bank, loan company, and credit-union loans. In the late 1950s, after his wife found out about "another loan," with the urging of both his wife and brother he went to see a doctor (not a psychiatrist). This resulted in his quitting gambling for one and a half years. He eventually returned to gambling by way of Suffolk Downs race track and then back to sports.

Again his debts increased (he had not paid off all his loans during the abstinence); and he continued to use his job as a resource for money. In the early 1960s he had exhausted relatives and friends and began using other people's cars to get loans. He would sell someone's car and instead of paying off the balance on the car, as he promised the owner, he would keep the payment book and make monthly payments (in a sense, he would sell mortgaged property). He again changed jobs and worked for another auto sales firm as a salesman. In the mid 1960s he began "selling" non-existent cars. He would turn in a "client's" name (whom he had checked for credit references) and the "serial number" of the "car." He would keep the loan and make the payments in person. By 1971 he had finally reached a point where the financial pressures (from both bookmakers and seventeen lending institutions) and fear of being discovered and sent to prison drove him to Gamblers Anonymous. He says he hasn't gambled since then.

THE GROUP-ORIENTED GAMBLER

On the other hand, Joe represents many of the working-class gamblers who hung around clubs or bars after work.

There were other gamblers around to rely on when things got rough. Despite this extra help, Joe was not in a position where he could use his work as effectively as Ken. In addition, he was not as resourceful. He also demonstrates that not all is smooth with the bookmakers in the sample. Despite all his troubles, however, he never violated his personal moral and ethical principles, something that several of those who gambled for a longer period of time than he eventually did. Had Joe continued gambling, he *might* have turned to passing bad checks, stealing from work, and perhaps even armed robbery, as others have done before him.

Joe, age thirty-three, was introduced to cards in his teens and became involved in weekly poker and setback (hi, low, Jack) games in high school, where he hung around with other guys who also drank and "chased broads." This became a weekly poker game in his late teens, which was just an enjoyable night out. After high school (and a six-month stint in the Army Reserve) he got a job in a grocery store and eventually became a meatcutter. At around the same time, in 1958, he was married. He used to hang around a luncheonette, where he was introduced to the local bookmaker and started picking one half of daily doubles with a friend who picked the other half. This led to a regular relationship with the bookie.

Like many of his working-class friends, he began to hang around a local "gin mill," where he started betting baseball with the in-house bookmaker and played softball with the other guys. In his midtwenties gambling was an enjoyment. When he lost more than he had, he would "steal a little bit of the grocery money," and later he started to "sneak a little loan" to recover from the "mistakes." Most of these were from loan companies—one from a loan shark. His friends at the gin mill had suggestions about where to get money, and he in turn gave them hints. In addition to the "sneaked" loans he periodically went to his working wife and asked her for money, each time with a promise (sometimes in all honesty) that he would quit gambling. After their savings were gone, he went to her to cosign loans (he says about 65 per cent of his loans his wife knew about—35 per cent were "sneaked"). While most of his gambling was sports-oriented (he became involved in betting *all* sports the bookmaker would handle), he also played cards and went to the track occasionally.

In 1970 he had about two thousand dollars in loans from lending institutions. At that time he received an offer from a friend to become a partner in a bookmaking operation. Joe agreed (it was a good offer: the friend was banking the business and taking all the initial risks). Around this period, Joe stopped hanging around the gin mill (he had to be home to handle the phone calls). He still maintained contact with gambling friends on a mutual consultation basis. After a year of bookmaking, Joe had removed his debts and was clearing a profit. At this time, however, the partner decided to get out of the business and Joe took over. In baseball season of 1971 he was "clobbered" and the profits he had won were eaten up. In football he was "buried" in the first three weeks. On top of this, several customers "hung him up" (failed to pay). The end result was that Joe felt pressured into paying the *layoff man*[3] by taking out a loan. "Everything went sour" after this. He started chasing the thirty-five hundred dollars he had borrowed in order to "get even." He started "hanging up" bookmakers himself. In addition, he took out more loans (some with the suggestions of gambling friends as to where to go) and started asking his wife to cosign again. He eventually obtained five different loans and a total debt of approximately eight thousand dollars. In 1972–73 he borrowed money from his brother-in-law and borrowed on his life insurance; also, a good friend took out a loan in his own name and Joe made the payments. It was also during this time that he contemplated stealing and suicide. In late 1973 he and his wife sold their house and he went to Gamblers Anonymous.

THE ACTION MAN

Finally, Jerry illustrates the gambler who is part of an "action system" of compulsive gamblers. This system is the most significant aspect of his career. Jerry's intensive involvement in all types of gambling is characteristic of the system, as is an attitude of helping each other out of jams. Jerry also illustrates the world of the "professional gamblers," with its disdain for conventional work, and status attainment as "good manipulators" or "good movers" of people (suckers) and money. While Jerry was not the best "mover" interviewed, he was an average hustler.

Jerry, age thirty-three, started gambling in high school on pickup basketball games. He and his friends would bet against other basketball players on another team. At around the same time, he was introduced to card playing (poker, setback, gin rummy) and football tickets (parlay cards). In his senior year in high school he started going to the track. All during this time, he hung around with more and more gambling friends, and also was introduced to drugs (codeine). In high school he bet just what he had in his pocket. After high school Jerry went into the Army and became a clerk-typist. In the Army he became addicted to heroin and gambled more often out of sheer boredom. Card and crap games became a regular routine, as did betting with bookmakers on horses and sporting events. At times his cards supported his heroin habit, and this and other forms of gambling increased as a result. During his stay in the service, he became linked up with another gambler and they pooled resources in order to book horses (Kentucky Derby and other main events) and sports. His Army career was cut short (1959–62) after he and a fellow addict were arrested on eighteen counts of breaking and entering into drugstores. The break-ins were drug-related.

After Jerry left the service he went to college for a year, taking accounting and salesmanship. He supported himself as a bartender and by selling parlay cards. At about this time he was introduced to "action" bowling. He was hanging around good bowlers in a league and started betting on them. Gradually he became introduced to the "action system" of bowling, pool, cards in cars in the parking lot, and listening to the in-house radio for sports results. (An action system is a setting in which almost any kind of action can be found on a given day.) All of this included being on the inside in the hustler's world, handicapping, developing systems, and having betting partnerships with fellow hustlers in action games (pool and bowling) and going with them to tournaments, race tracks, and sporting events.

In 1964 Jerry took out his first loan. He had quit heroin "cold turkey" and gotten married. Part of the loan was for furniture and five hundred dollars extra was "to have money in my pocket to bet with." He had a loan on and off (pay it back, make it out again, over and over) until he quit gambling, in 1974. He found out from fellow gamblers that he could "rehash" (refinance) it while the loan was still on. This loan was just a minor problem in an otherwise clear image of himself as a "professional gambler."

The more Jerry got into gambling the more he started to conceive of himself as a "gambler." He quit several jobs (his most common occupations were preorder soda salesman (1963–67) and insurance salesman (1967–72) for "quite a few" companies). He also worked part time selling aluminum siding for a fellow gambler from 1962 to 1973. If he felt like leaving a job to go to the track he would. Most of the time he would go with other gamblers, but he occasionally went alone. For the most part the money for his gambling came from hustling, loans from fellow gamblers, and work. By the late 1960s or early 1970 (he forgets which) he "started losin' bad." He decided to take action on sports as a bookmaker. He gradually developed twenty-nine steady customers. In the same year, he accumulated another loan and started using three checking accounts as a way to create money when the need arose. He continued to use his gambling friends as a resource for funding whenever he was broke and they had money. Also, during this year he started borrowing periodically from his parents, up to one hundred dollars each time, and from friends at work.

His financial problem continued to mount. He was now almost totally obsessed with paying his debts through gambling. Very little time was spent at home, and jobs were quit with ease to go to the track. Gambling friends introduced him to "oxies,"[4] and he got a siding loan with the help of his gambling employer despite his lack of home ownership. In 1972 he quit work totally and gambled full time (resuming work in 1973 as a postal clerk), hustling in the morning at pool or bowling, the track or more hustling in the afternoon, and maybe a stag party or watching sports at night. During this year and the next he started "doing bags" (cheating other hustlers in bowling matches), fencing stolen goods, and swindling suckers. One scheme, for example, involved printing up stag-party tickets, selling them, and then not holding the party. At around this time he seriously contemplated robbing a bookmaker or a crap game but didn't do it. In late 1973 there was no way he could pay his debts, he realized what he had put his family through (he had four children by this time), and he seriously contemplated suicide. He decided to run away instead, to get a job in Arizona, where his wife could live without harassment from loan-company officials and bookmakers. He made it to New York City, where he went to a Gamblers Anonymous meeting.

No vignette can tell the whole story. The rest of this book will attempt to describe the world of the gambler as he sees it.

## CHAPTER I

The Chase: "Putting Good Money After Bad"

The "chase" begins when a gambler bets either to pay every-day bills that are due or to "get even" from a fall. A gambler can chase on a short- or a long-term basis. Those who are locked into the long-term chase are compulsive gamblers.

It is the chase that provides the initial push for the spiral the gambler becomes committed to and that gives the spiral velocity.

SHORT-TERM CHASE AND FEATURES OF CHASING

Whether a gambler will chase depends on the attitude that he takes with him to the event. Is the event just "entertainment" that is expected to cost money? Is the gambling situation one in which the individual expects to win? Rationalizations for short-term loss are filled with the entertainment idea. After all, gambling *is* entertaining and most forms of entertainment cost money. What happens in those situations in which the gambler *expects* to win, yet loses? He chases.

Short-term chases occur in two types of situations: In the first case the gambler is attempting to pay everyday bills by gambling; this brings on a "get even" philosophy. In the second case the gambler starts out with a certain amount of money but loses more than was expected and attempts to "get even" as a result.

In the first situation the individual is starting from behind. This effort frequently brings on a chase-type situation. Since the bills that you desire to pay are added on, if losses come they seem greater and the desire to recover more intense. This is brought out in an interview with a college student and ex-hustler.

> You go down [to the race track] with the intention, say, of "I need one hundred fifty tomorrow for the insurance on my car." You have forty dollars in your pocket and you lose that forty and then you borrow twenty-five to go back tomorrow and you're lookin' to make that one hundred fifty plus the forty so that's one hundred ninety plus the twenty-five you borrowed that's two hundred fifteen. And then you lose that twenty-five and you go borrow fifty, and you just get into a wicked rut. Eventually you usually bail out after.
>
> Q. How did you "bail out" [get out of debt]?
> A. Well, I've always been a pretty lucky gambler, because I think you have to have luck to win. Usually when I'm down, I've never got myself into that much. Usually when my luck is going real bad everywhere I always go back to the sure things, like working every day.

The work he refers to is bartending. His pool-hustling days were over. He could no longer get matches in his home town.

The effort to use gambling to pay bills would obviously be attempted only by those in financial trouble, most commonly the students and lower- and working-class gamblers[1] in the sample. When it occurred among the middle-class gamblers, it was more common early in their career.

The second type of situation that induces the chase is a product of the gambling setting itself and the structure of relationships involved. Each player thinks he is smarter than the other players (or at least not the worst player). Since most people think of themselves as smarter than average, and the "average" person is losing, then it seems only logical that they will win. Competition develops between self and the "average sucker." A loss means that you are just as bad or possibly worse; this loss is a blow to personal self-esteem as well as finances. After a loss, the individual thinks negatively of himself. The only way to regain his positive image is winning back what was lost. When you fail, it is hard to hold back the temptation to get even, as in doubling up sports bets or looking for the long shot that will pay off what you need to get even at the track.

The chase is based on various get-even strategies in the gambling situation. First, there are forms of betting that automatically encourage getting even. These are coupled with group expectations that you don't quit a loser. Second, there are doubling-up strategies and last-ditch efforts that are not built into the game and that may or may not have peer-group support.

The opportunity to get even is built into many forms of gambling. All one has to do is listen to the words "Let it ride" and "Double or nothing" in crap shooting to realize that this is built into that game. Other games and their variations also have built in get-even or double-up elements. Some of the more popular forms of juvenile and college poker games have this element.

> Man-mouse. Two cards the best poker hand. This was, like, the tops. What happens is the best poker hand, the best pair, would win. You would go "man" if you had a good hand and you would go "mouse" if you didn't. If you went "man" and you lost to another player, you would have to match the pot. If there were three kids that went "man," two would have to match the pot while the third took the pot that was there. The only way to win was if you were the only one who went "man" and everyone else went "mouse." When the pot was up to fifteen–twenty bucks you would be taking a pretty good risk because you would have to match it if you lost. Match the ante plus the pot.
>
> Q. What is three-card murder?
> A. You get three cards and you just make your best poker game out of them. And the person that loses has to pay the pot.

The key element here and in several other games is to match the pot (put in the same amount that is already on the table) if you lose. In these games the pot gets higher than it normally does in other poker games. This makes the game more exciting, and as a result games like this are often favored for the last hand of the night.

In some cases doubling up is allowed in order to make the game more interesting, as in the following discussion of blackjack games.

> When one man got down he would get to the point where he'd owe ten when we had started playing for quarters and see he wasn't making any headway this way and he would say, let's play for a dollar a hand, huh, and we'd say sure if I was up and we would play for a dollar a hand. And they'd get; a lot of times I would clean them out of everything they had, you know. That's when they would get desperate, this would happen to me, you know, I didn't win *all* the time. And we would get to five dollars, "Let's play for five dollars a hand." Sometimes we'd play for ten a hand. I can remember people owing me hundreds of dollars."
> Q. At what age was this?
> A. Fourteen–fifteen. I'd go for, you know, twenty-five dollars a hand, you know. They'd lose; all right, we'd go for fifty dollars. They'd win and we would be even and I'd say that's all right. That's enough. It always happens that way, you know. People always want to get *even*.

Strategies that *can* be used to chase are built into what bookmakers call the "junk." "Junk action" is favored because of the higher payoff it offers. While these strategies are not synonymous with the chase, they can be used to try to get even from *past* losses (losses prior to betting the "junk") because of the higher payoff. The following is a rendition of the parlay, bird cage, "if" bet, and "if and reverse":

> Q. How do you figure a bird cage or a parlay?
> A. Well, a parlay, all the money from one goes on the other. A bird cage is just three parlays. If you

got three horses. Say you had three horses, one, two, and three. Three different races. A parlay, first horse pays four dollars, you got a two-dollar bet. The four dollars would go on the second race. This is a parlay now.

Q. Right.

A. Four dollars would go on the second horse, he pays four dollars. You had two tickets going on it, that's eight dollars, right?

Q. OK.

A. Now, the third horse wins and pays four dollars; you had four tickets on him, four two-dollar tickets. Sixteen dollars, that's a parlay.

Q. Right.

A. Now, a bird cage, you got three horses. Three separate bets. You got number one with number two. You got number two with number three. A parlay, all three have to win. In a bird cage, any two out of three wins, you collect. You got three separate bets. Three parlays. You got two-dollar parlay; it only costs you two dollars but they all got to win. A bird cage would cost you six dollars. This is 'cause you have three bets. Any two of them win, you got a two-dollar win parlay.

Q. Did you ever have anything complicated, like reverses or anything like that?

A. They don't take them no more. They used to be "if" bets. If and reverse. Ah, some people never even heard of them now. Ah, you got two horses, one in the second race and one in the ninth race. I want two dollars in the second race: "if" onto the ninth race. If he wins and pays ten, I got eight comin' here and ten comin' here. Eighteen dollars. That's an if bet. They don't take 'em no more.

Q. What's the reverse?

A. Now, if all reverse. If I have the second race and the ninth race. Right? All right. I want if and reverse on the second and ninth; that is going to cost me four dollars, right?

Q. OK.

A. I got two to win on the second and two to win on the ninth. Now it is going to go forwards and backwards. Now, number two wins and pays ten dollars. I got ten coming. They are going to take two off that and put on nine. Now, that gives me four dollars going on nine, 'cause I had two originally, right?

Q. Right.

A. If nine wins I put two more going back on the first one, which is going to give me another ten dollars.

The "figuring," or calculation, of these bets is so complicated that most bookmakers no longer take "if-and-reverse" bets. Most now take parlays and bird cages in horses (plus possibly what the track handles, such as quinellas, perfectas, doubles, and twin doubles) and parlays, bird cages, and round robins in sports. Parlays, because of the progressive-betting element, are very popular.

Games of skill also include built-in doubling-up strategies. The most prominent here is what is called the press and double press in the Nassau golf games (or Texas and press at other golf courses). Golf is an eighteen-hole game. The Nassau divides the game into three segments: front nine, back nine, and the whole game. Each segment is bet on. The betting gets rather complicated and is determined by how many holes each has won.

Q. What is a press and a double press? How does that work?

A. You've got nine holes. You start out and you lose the first two holes. You press. [That is, the person who is down two has the option.] You double the bet. Say you start playing a dollar Nassau. So you start the first nine. The first two holes you lost, and you are two down. So you've lost, basically you've lost a dollar, if you don't win another hole through the nine. You press because you may win a hole and have the rest of them. You won one press and you lost the first two holes so you come out even, right?

Q. So, in other words, you are compressing the first two holes into one hole.

A. Right. So, if you lose two more holes you are four down and two down, right? If you lose six holes in a row you are three down, two down, and four down.

Q. So how does it, ah, moneywise, how does it work?

A. Well, say if I went out and lost the first and I was playing against you. Playing a dollar Nassau, right?

Q. Right. You lost the first two holes.

A. I lost the first two holes and I press you. In other words, I am playing you for another dollar.

Q. We have a two-dollar bet.

A. That's right. I lose the next two holes. I press you. In other words, I am playing you for another dollar.

Q. We have a two-dollar bet.

A. That's right. I lose the next two holes. I press you another dollar. We have a three-dollar bet. Now we have played six holes, right? There are only nine holes. I have lost the first bet because I can't get six up on three holes. The second bet has gone by because I am four down on that one and there are only three holes left. [In other words, the first press was a new start over again. The first press was a new bet. This time the bet was for the third through ninth holes.] So, no matter what happens I am out two dollars. I double press the last bet. In other words, I double up on the last holes. If you keep losing holes you keep losing. If you win a few holes you get even.

The front nine includes automatic presses (in other words start over again); the back nine includes automatic double presses (start over again but double up each time a player gets two down).

Get-even strategies that are not built into the game also exist. The last event typically has an important significance for "catching up," "getting even," or "getting cured" (from being sick about losses). The last race at the track, for example, has special significance. In this race people bet on long shots (horses that run at twenty to one or greater odds and will have a greater payoff if they win, in an attempt to get even).[2]

> I would go for the long shots in the last race. To try and get even. You hit it a couple a times where it makes the whole day, which was a disaster, a good day, you know.

> If I had twenty bucks I could probably say: "I could take the twenty bucks, lay it on this horse. He is two to one, I'll get back sixty dollars. He will pay sixty dollars. I'll get back sixty dollars." *But,* "What the hell am I going to do with sixty dollars!" Bet it on this one, say he is . . . thirty or thirty-five to one. . . . Last race is the get-even race. It is like the Monday-night ball game, man, you know. It is *get-even time.* And I used to think, and I still do: The people are lookin' to get that money that they lost in the course of the day.

Similar things happen in Monday-night football betting (the last event in a week of football betting) and the last hand in a night of playing cards.

While the above strategies make up much of chasing on a short-term basis, the chase does not just exist out there. It is learned from other gamblers and frequently has peer-group support. This is especially so in gambling consultation groups and partnerships, in which all it takes is for one person to suggest a "martingale" (a system of doubling your bets until you win) or winning it all back in one swoop.

> Went to the ball park one day and saw the Red Sox play and they were putrid. We bet twenty dollars, twenty-five dollars, on them. They were horrid. We

were there and we said, "They are going on a slump. They will be terrible for a few weeks; let's bet against them." We bet against them and they went on an eight-game winning streak. We used the logic, "They can't continue to win, let's just continue to double our bets. We'll break even eventually." So we bet and bet and bet and we came to the end of the week and lost, ah, four grand.

The chase has its limits. The house may have a maximum bet and the bookie may shut you off after a certain number of doubling episodes. Whether he does this or not will depend on his working capital and the size of your credit line.

The chase, in addition to becoming ritualized, is also supported by past experience. Given the very nature of gambling (i.e., the relatively unpredictable nature of the outcome, which varies depending on the event), handicapping, the turn of the card, the events of ball games, and sheer luck, among other factors, get the gambler out of ruts. All is not bad. Experience after experience tells you that luck reverses very rapidly in most forms of gambling. Games have their ups and their downs; all you have to do is hang in there and the up situation will eventually surface. In card playing and crap shooting, this is so frequent as to be uncanny.

Now, with me, I'd start out and I'd be breaking just about even for a couple of hours, and then I'd either get hot and be up about fifty dollars in the end or I'd be cold and be down fifty dollars. It depends, like the last card game I played, it was about two or three weeks ago, and I went into the game with sixty dollars. I was up twenty dollars for a while, then breaking even; all of a sudden I was down eighty dollars. That meant I had to borrow twenty dollars from someone at the table there, which I did; and I kept on playing, because to get into the game I had to borrow some money from friends in the [fraternity] house here. And I kept on playing. Then, all of a sudden, I got hot; within a half hour I was exactly even, so I got out of the game.

I had been playing for a long time, ah, in these games, certain kids would be, myself and someone else, would be way behind and they'd borrow money. Like, professional gamblers, I understand, would never do this, but they'd say, "Hey, look, give me five dollars so I can play." The thing is that that can turn around in another forty-five minutes, where you're the guy who's got nothing and I'm loaded.

The lesson is *very* clear: chasing is worth it. Not only is chasing worth it, but it is worth borrowing in order to be able to do it. By doubling up or increasing your bets or just hanging in there, you should be able to break even or come out on top. This is true in *all* forms of gambling, be it the commodities market, football, numbers, dogs, horses, trotters, whatever.

Chasing is a short-term phenomenon. People will gamble for a day or so and try to get even at the end of this period. Many gamblers chase on a day-to-day basis. After the day, however, they will usually forget about their losses. Of the seventy gamblers I interviewed, twenty were not compulsive gamblers although several chased on a short-term basis every now and then. Of these situations, they stated, "I lost my head several times at the track," and "It is hard to control yourself." Despite occasional loss of control, they adhered to a gambling philosophy that concerns the chase and gambling with affordable (entertainment) money only.

It's a hell of a lot of fun when you win, and if you have the right attitude you can be a good loser, too. If you get into a life-and-death situation, then you're in a lot of trouble. You can come out on the death side of the situation. I don't think I'd ever get into that type of situation. I wouldn't gamble with anything I couldn't afford to lose.

> I figure that if I go to the track and I lose, that's gone. Tomorrow is another day. Don't chase. Don't put good money after bad. It's gone, it's gone.

Gamblers seem to pick up this philosophy from other gamblers, parents, brothers. While this is a mark of the non-compulsive gambler, compulsive gambling should really be viewed as a continuum of increasing involvement.

Most gamblers can be placed on the *continuum* on either side of a dividing line between compulsive and non-compulsive gambling. However, some gamblers straddle this borderline.[3] They lose control periodically and their losses have repercussions: heavy debts which they must finance through loans or other, less legal means. But while their gambling had this serious effect, they always regained control; they were engaged in the short- not long-term chase.

LONG-TERM CHASE

By long-term is meant the *linking* of periods of short-term chasing. The compulsive gambler violates the major philosophical canons of the non-compulsive gambler: he gambles with more than he can afford to lose, *and* he does *not* forget losses once they happen. Instead of saying, "It's gone, it's gone," the compulsive gambler says, "I'll get 'em tomorrow."

> To go to the track to get back what I lost. Not to win it just back for the day before but to win it *all* back. Being from day one. Just to say: "Fuck this track. I got my money back and I am going to walk away." Never walk away.

By jumping over into a new series of gambling (tomorrow at the track or next week in sports betting), the individual automatically puts himself into a position similar to the short-term chaser who wants to pay a debt. He starts with a net loss that has to be regained.

The long-term chase is what some gamblers call "plunging" and Devereux calls the "circle of despair":

> As his losses accumulate, the gambler finds himself

drawn into what we may call a "circle of despair."
He has lost more than he expected, or intended perhaps more than he can afford. He sees himself getting in deeper and deeper; yet if he quits now, all
this is irretrievably lost. The only way to get it back
is to keep on playing. "You can't win if you don't
bet," as the bookmakers repeatedly advise. Hence,
to keep on going appears as the lesser of two evils.
(1949: 729)

After discussing the circle of despair, Devereux talks of
stress in the choice between two evils. The choice is between
an evil that is *contingent* on a future event (which, of
course, the gambler feels he can handicap) and a *certain* evil
of loss of money and reputation. Choosing the future event
temporarily relieves the stress created by the certainty of
heavy loss.

The long-term chase[4] has essentially three stages: threat,
encapsulation, and closure. The first step in the chase, the
threat, is dual: financial and personal. The *financial threat* is
typically the product of loans that have to be paid. Gamblers
feel that the way to get the money is by more gambling, and
this produces a spiral of more debts and gambling to relieve
the debts. The *personal threat* is a product of potential embarrassment and losing of face if the gambling losses are ever
made public. As a result, lies are relied upon, and "the deeper
into the gambling spiral a man gets, the greater the amount of
information he must conceal." (Livingston, 1974: 82) The
losses are an "unsharable secret," devastating to one's integrity
if made known. This fear of exposure brings on a desire to
eliminate the problem by gambling, and redeeming the tar-
nished self-image.

Eventually, given the nature of the endeavor, if the gambler gambles long enough and with enough money, he will
go a bit "overboard." At first, for most gamblers, the losses
can be absorbed with "entertainment money" or by "borrowing" a little out of the cookie jar or other sources without
anyone knowing. Then things "get out of hand." The chase is
taken one step too far. The ready resources are no longer capable of supporting the loss. The loss is now outside of per-

sonal resources. If you are married, the spouse should be (but is rarely) told, because the loss bites into the paycheck. The money to pay off the bookie or to cover up at home must be obtained from an impersonal source: a bank, credit union, or loan company. Interpreted in the following way, all is not bad, though, because this was just one small "mistake," and it will not happen in the prospective future, *or* you have just hit a small "losing streak" and you are *bound* to get out next week and pay off the loan.

> When I was in my mid-twenties, ah, to me gambling was an enjoyment, say I would bet within my means. Say, like, if I was, ah, like, it would be an every-night affair, you would bet five times or a twelve-dollar parlay. At the end of the week you would lose a hundred, win a hundred, you know. That's all you had in your pocket. If that's all you had in your pocket and you blew it, you steal a little bit of the grocery money. If that's all you had was a hundred bucks and you blew [it], you would say that's it, you know, until next week. Fresh money and next week you start again; maybe next week will be better. Well, if you did go a little bit overboard you say I will sneak a two- or three-hundred-dollar loan; you go to the bank; you pick up two or three hundred dollars; you get more ammunition and you try another week. . . . You know, you win eighty or ninety and that would be it. In your middle twenties, especially *my* middle twenties, I would go to the race track, make a little hit, go back and bet a little baseball, football, whatever the season is. And, ah, I used to control myself.

The first loans are typically thought of in this fashion. They are temporary, stopgap measures, until you get back on your feet. "Control" is seen as still there. The loan is seen as an investment of sorts in the continuation of fun. In a way, most gamblers stumble into debt and then recover. The number of stumbles and recoveries will depend on the skill, the luck, the credit, and the resources of the gambler. The poorer the gambler *and* the poorer the luck (after all, luck is involved and fresh situations *do* occur), the quicker the gambler will fall into the long-term chase. The lower the credit of the gambler, the less likely that the long-term chase will occur.

For most, the loans become a turning point in their careers. The debts become insurmountable blows to self-esteem and handicapping abilities, as well as blows to finances and the regard of family and friends. They are the proof that you are not "better than the average." The desire to avoid personal self-labeling acts as a major impetus to the long-term chase.

The second step in the chase is encapsulation, or what several interviewees regarded as engrossment. Engrossment *is* the long-term chase in an abbreviated time span.

Once the gambler becomes enmeshed in linking periods of chasing, the process of getting even is all he thinks about when he reflects on his total situation. Therefore he concentrates on each immediate situation and the next bet he will make. The time span is shortened to the short-term chase and the specific event he is in. To think beyond the short term is painful. Concentration is so intense that almost all else is blocked out. It is a "twilight zone" or "dream world." It is this element that gives rise to the "escape" theories in the literature. (Bloch, 1951: Tec, 1964) There *is* an escape. The question is whether this escape is away from poverty and boredom or is a product of intense concentration on the present action in order to escape from the larger problems that result from gambling.

Despite being enmeshed in the long-term chase, the gambler concentrates on one day (if horses) or week (if sports) at a time. When he thinks of the long term, he focuses on streaks. Despite the fact that he is in a losing streak, for the present he suppresses the possibility of losing. The emphasis is on the here and now: action and *winning*.

Q. Did you often chase losses?
A. Oh, did I chase! I chased 'em up one side and down the other.
Q. What would be a typical situation?
A. Well, in the sports area, losing five hundred on

Saturday and betting fifteen hundred dollars on Sunday. By the time the day was over maybe chasing the five hundred dollars I lost on Saturday and maybe the grand I lost the first games on Sunday. Always. Always because there was a chance that you might break even, or you might make five dollars or a hundred dollars. The idea of paying on Monday never struck you on Saturday and Sunday, when you were gettin' down. Chased every weekend. I don't know anybody that was a compulsive gambler that didn't chase constantly. Classic example in cards is writing bad checks. What could be more of a chase, writing a bad check to get cash to stay in the game. . . .

Losing was not possible. You were going to come out that night a winner. . . . You are not in reality. No part of reality. So, if you blew a thousand dollars and you had a bad check for five hundred dollars and it is Thursday night, the check is not going to hit the bank until Friday; it is not going to clear until the following Monday; that's an eternity. From Thursday night to Monday was more time than there was. So, you know, it didn't have the impact that it would normally have, because that day was never going to come. If it did you were going to be a winner anyway, so why worry about it?

The long-term chase is played in every gambling situation. Each day at cards, at the track, the casino, or each week of sports becomes a separate sequence in which the focus is coming out even or possibly ahead. For some gamblers, each day or week is like a new start, a new lease on life, in which all they have to do is be careful.

What I used to try to do was during the week I used to say to myself, "OK, now, I don't want to get bombed and could lose a couple thousand for the week." I wanted to start smart, so the first bet I would make is maybe a two-hundred-dollar bet.

This is what I considered then a small bet. Now, if I win the bet I'm two hundred dollars ahead. So what I like to do is build it up. If I get ahead about eight hundred dollars, nine hundred dollars, or one thousand dollars, I'll make bigger bets. And this is what I used to do. Well, if I didn't win and I was losing, because there were many times when I was gone into a Friday or Saturday minus one thousand dollars, minus fifteen hundred dollars, I would double the bet of fifteen hundred dollars in order to try to win back the fifteen hundred dollars.

After the gambler feels a sense of threat and becomes encapsulated, he experiences what Lofland calls *closure*. (1969: 61)[5] Closure, the third step in the intensified career of the gambler, seems another way of saying that the gambler is in a self-enclosed system. Gambling both creates the problem and is a way of resolving that problem. The easiest way out, it seems, is the same way you get in: gamble. The following comments are illustrative:

When you are down ten grand, it's worth risking a few hundred to turn the corner, isn't it?

I needed money and this was the only way to get money.

Getting even seemed to be a goal, an objective that almost forced you to want to find the easiest way of making that money, which is the same way you lost it.

In the same manner, the gambler experiences a rise in stakes as he gets deeper into gambling. It occurs in doubling-up strategies and the realization that pre-existing losses are so bad that one can no longer "get bailed" (that is, become free of debt) by being a "nickel and dime" (small-time) bettor. "You can't win big by bettin' small."

The irony of the rising-stakes game is that the deeper the gambler gets in debt the higher the stakes rise and the further into debt the gambler gets when he loses. Another irony is that rising stakes in one form of gambling typically produce an increase in other types of wagering. The philosophy consonant with this is of the form: "Why be a small-time horse bettor when you're bettin' sports for thousands?" The same rationale is used for transferral to all other activities.

> When you start betting hundreds and thousands on the side (by betting with other foursomes), the Nassau in golf can increase, because now you start playing with the fellas that play the big ones, because of the feeling that, well, why would you play a five-dollar Nassau; go out there for four hours to win thirty to forty dollars when you are shootin', ah, five hundred on a game. So, ah, you try to correlate them and say . . . try to win two or three hundred here. Maybe with the side bets you can accumulate five hundred here. . . . It's, ah, silly to be betting big amounts on one thing and, ah, then going along and playing for a little thing on the side. . . . Oh, yeh, cards went along with it. Yeh, you would be playing for more there, too. I'd play at the golf club and I would also play at the bridge club and seek out games at other clubs and whatever. I always had to have something going. This is the way I went. I just got more and more involved in betting and I would go anywhere to bet. Occasional junkets to Las Vegas, that was all part of the deal.

As in the above interview, the gambler frequently searches out more interesting and lucrative games consonant with his skill. However, that introduction is not always favorable. The junkets to Las Vegas were devastating for this gambler, as were the dice games that another bettor got introduced to.

> At this point the setback [hi, low, jack] was not furious; football and all the sports were, but the setback was mostly small. Before long I succeeded in getting the card stakes blown all out of proportion.

I was betting hundreds in a night on sports and here we were playing half and a dollar or one and one setback. So I got the setback up to a reasonable level . . . and I got introduced to some successful businessmen here in town that were making some substantial amounts of dough and who played in a Thursday-night "Bible class," they called it. This was a Thursday-night poker game which rotated between five houses. Poker game, and they played setback sometimes. That was a steep poker game; that was five and ten. The ante was a buck; they played seven-card stud; five dollars on any card; raise any time; ten dollars on any pair and the last card. That was a heavy poker game. . . . And I made a ton of money playing poker and threw it all away shooting crap.

If the stakes stayed at "reasonable" levels and did not get "blown all out of proportion," problems that resulted later would not have been as bad. The rising-stakes game occurs at *all* stages of the gambler's career. It is also typically a very gradual occurrence. One does not go from sharing a two-dollar bet with a friend to putting five hundred to one thousand dollars on a race overnight. It is a slow process. The process is made easier by the seemingly insignificant raises that occur in the betting.

When you initially win when you bet fifty dollars and you bet more when you win, you know, you are at a point when two hundred dollars is not any different than three hundred dollars. It really isn't, it is a paper bet. And you can say there is no difference between a three and a five (or between a five and a six and so on).

Like the short-term chase, the long-term chase is based on experience, either personal or from hearing about other gamblers who have "turned the corner" on a losing streak. All you have to do is just hang in there and invest just a few

more dollars or utilize the credit from the bookmaker for all
it is worth to get out of a binding situation.

> I can remember a situation, one time, where I was,
> ah, this is back in sixty-seven or so, I think I
> had debts of maybe three–four thousand dollars. I
> had no money; I owed the bookie twelve hundred
> dollars; I did not want to ask my mother for the
> money. I was, I figured I was pretty, I was pretty, I
> did not have the guts to go to the banks again and I
> remember calling another bookie and betting wildly
> and winning to the point where I won within about
> three weeks, ah, you know, the two thousand dol-
> lars that I owed the bookie. I remember stalling the
> other bookie. I solved a desperate situation, and it's
> incredible the number of times *it* would turn out, it
> would be successful.

The further "plunging," reckless abandon to get even, works
temporarily for many of the compulsive gamblers. They sur-
vive the present crisis only to get into another. Their debts are
constantly bobbing up and down, yet continue to spiral upward.

Another feature of the self-enclosed system is that if the
gambler engages in more than one form of gambling, losses in
one form may be recovered in another, or vice versa.

> I made sometimes three hundred dollars, four hun-
> dred dollars, five hundred dollars a week at cards.
> And then of course that money would go; I'd lose it
> all at the race track.

> I would make it in baseball, but I would lose it in
> the horses, or football, or basketball.

In this context, the race track has a special appeal. It offers
the chance of winning big money, thus being able to recover
losses all at once.

> I played until I took such a beating that there was

no way I could get my money back at the card
game. They was too small. The money that is at the
track is unlimited. The card game, they come in the
game with only so much. . . . It is impossible to
get what I am looking for, what I lost in a lifetime.
There is no card game or dice game that has that
amount there. . . . If you get lucky you are only
going to get peanuts back. At a track or with a
bookie it's unlimited. And a bookie isn't, because
one bookie took off and he owed me two thousand.

I went there [the track] only because I was barreled in so bad that it was the only place that I
could think of that I could get ten-to-one odds.

Q. Did you ever go there systematically?

A. No, even in the worst part of my career, the
only time I ever went to the race track was in utter
desperation. I can remember, oh, the time I borrowed one thousand dollars. . . . I can remember,
ah, I blew virtually all of it on the seventh race,
which was a sure thing. The jockey dropped the
whip. The horse was running in the lead and all of
a sudden I see the jockey came in third and I blew
the grand. I had saved up most of the one thousand
dollars for the seventh race because that was the
reason I was going. It was going to pay me a short
price, but enough to get me bailed.

Getting "bailed," getting even, being free of debt is an inducement for the chase. All it takes to be free is to invest just
a little more. Of course, the deeper in debt and the more severe the threat the greater the desperation to get out of debt.
William Hoffman, Jr., author of an autobiographical account,
The Loser, illustrates the self-enclosed system in full speed:

The hell! It's just that winning the money is the answer. You gotta redeem those checks. Soon! You'll
probably get probation instead of jail if you can
redeem them quick enough. . . . I searched my

mind for a solution and the answer was always the same: Win the money. (1968: 39 and 98)

Once caught in the bind of the self-enclosed system, gambling loses some of its pleasure for those who are caught the deepest. Getting money becomes so much of an obsession that the "action" is not fun any more. All the pressures mount, and everybody that is important knows you have a problem.

It got to a point, you know, where, where everybody, you know, my mother and father, found out; and, ah, it was at the point where it wasn't any fun trying to win any more. It was just, ah, at the point where again when I was gamblin' there was two teams playing. I knew whatever team I played was going to lose.

Not only is it no longer fun, but the idea that you can win becomes questionable. You start to feel that you are a loser, and the actions you take have a quality of desperation and powerlessness.

I knew I was a loser; when I was driving in [to the track] . . . I knew I was going to blow the dough. I had a hard time even dreaming to myself that I was going to win.

Then came the feeling . . . of uneasiness within myself; a feeling of, probably you might call it of impending doom or disaster, that I had never had before. There was no way that I wasn't going to blow everything.

Despite desperation, there is still that glimmer of hope that gambling will resolve the situation. The possibility of making a "hit" makes all the work and effort that goes into the system worthwhile.

It's one crisis after another, and you gamble to get

even. . . . One big hit, make that one big hit, and pay off the debts and never gamble again, and live a normal life. It never happens, but that's what you think.

I can remember there were times when I went up there almost knowing that I was gonna lose, or going with the feeling, "Oh, God, I've got to make some money." My luck was bad, and I just can't lose again; but I still kept going. . . . What the hell! You're gonna make a big killing. Hearing about this guy who made a killing and that guy who hit the daily double, eventually more and more ideas enter the mind.

This dream of the almost impossible actuality happening is what keeps the gambler going in the hope that he will gain back his self-esteem. There is still that glimmer of hope that he will no longer be a loser; overnight he can suddenly be transformed into the winner that he knows he is, after all.

## CHAPTER II

Action

Everyone who gambles (from the penny poker player to the compulsive gambler) is embroiled in a desire for *action*—preparation, "getting down," the engrossment of the setting itself, and the results.

The world view of the gambler has a seasonal bent, particularly in terms of the anticipation of an upcoming "meet" (the span of time allotted by the state when a track will be having thoroughbred or harness racing) or an upcoming "season" of betting on a particular sport. The first day is one that is not to be missed, as well as the last and such special events as the Kentucky Derby and the Superbowl. Attention is intense for these days. Despite the existence of these annual cycles and special days, typically gambling is *not* thought of seasonally. The major orientation is the day at the track, the night of poker, or a whole week of sports betting strung together.

A gambler's life is a continuous stringing together of action. Each event (be it a race, a sporting event, or a hand of poker) is tied to other events to form a unified whole. A gambler doesn't think of just one hand of poker but of a whole night strung together, not of one sports event but of a whole week of sports betting.

The compulsive gamblers in the group below were predominantly involved in sports and race-track events. Twelve out of fifty were involved in only one form of gambling. Most of the compulsive gamblers (thirty-eight out of fifty) were involved in more than one activity. Of these, twenty-three continuously pursued more than one type of gambling.

Cards only	1
Cards and golf sequenced	1
Cards predominantly but gradually moving to sports or horses only	4
Sports only	6
Sports and cards sequenced	7
Sports predominant—others sequenced	2
Sports and others occasionally	6
Horses only	5
Horses and others occasionally	5
Horses predominantly—others sequenced	13
Total number of compulsive gamblers	50

For example, one played golf every afternoon and, after golf, played gin rummy. During the winter he would play only gin rummy and occasionally (say, at an Elks barbecue) would shoot craps. Many of the horse players who sequenced went from the race track to card games several times a week or alternatively went to *two* tracks (one in the afternoon and one at night) and *then* a card or crap game. In these cases the different forms of gambling become molded into a whole in the eyes of the gambler. While varying styles of action are participated in, much of the gamblers' lives are similar in that they orient themselves around action. Before getting into action the gamblers prepared for it by handicapping; developing systems; hedging bets; using superstition, luck or hunches; and possibly resorting to inside information. After the gambler is prepared, he must "get down." In order to do this he has to get to where the action is. Once in action, the gambler experiences the excitement and engrossment of being in action itself. After the results are in, the gambler must cope with the results both on an interpersonal and a personal level.

PREPARATION

The gambler prepares in many ways for the action. The majority of his efforts, however, revolve around betting strategies. He may handicap without systems, develop systems, rely on "tips" and inside information, subscribe to betting services, pay touts, hedge his bets, or rely on luck, chance, hunches, or skill. These things he may do alone or with others. If he does them with others, he will be involved in consultation groups, partnerships, or just rely on their "hot tips," skill, or cheating abilities. Preparation occurs constantly and takes many forms, from the clockwork of a system that works by itself to the vagaries of chance and the tote board. Gamblers use many forms of betting strategies.[1] These must be seen in their setting. The tactics are used alone, with friends, or in partnership, with each social organization having a structure and rationale.[2]

The most commonly used strategy is handicapping. Handicapping, as a way of choosing selections, involves the massive expenditure of time, concentration, and energy, although the actual amount varies tremendously. For those gamblers who thought of themselves as "professional gamblers," handicapping was their major form of work when contemplating sports or track animals. For a few, the handicapping incorporated looking at the newspaper once a day and keeping up with the sports world; but for most it included thinking about the teams, the weather, trying to balance one team or horse against the other. As they became more involved in the chase, they spent more and more time handicapping, since they felt that this was all that had to be corrected for the losing streak to turn the corner.

Handicapping as an activity is usually fluid and freewheeling. The following interview excerpts give an idea of some of the factors that are involved. They are as varied as the gamblers themselves.

Sports:

> I would write, analyze, look up their records. I'd—I would start to check how this team did against this team for the last ten years. Does this team have a jinx against this team? What about the home field? All this stuff. The wheels would start turning. I had no set formula. I would, I would look at many factors and draw out conclusions.

> I was a great believer in what you'd call team spirit. If a team was on the road and they got their brains beat in, next week. As an example, let's say Oak-

land. Oakland got beat on the road. Coming home next week, they're playing Kansas City and Kansas City just won four ball games in a row. And I knew Kansas City was gonna be a favorite. I'd bet my balls or whatever I had, three hundred, four hundred, five hundred. If I could get— I love rivalry and I love catching home teams when they were dogs—underdogs. And I bet that way. I try to read into their minds, will they be up to the game? I made a fortune on one team that way, six weeks in a row. Patriots beat the spread six weeks in a row. Even when they were playing good, they couldn't win. But they were beat. This year they beat it and I got murdered.

The Race Track:

Well, ah, when I am down there I also notice things. You know, different moves, the horse gets blocked. Saddle slipped, lost his whip, different things. Maybe I see a horse may need a little extra distance, six–seven furlongs, seven and one half furlongs. You know, if a horse is used to seven, you know, and, ah, then I can say that maybe he needs a six. He is a front runner. Needs six furlongs. Also I see moves. When a horse tries, goes out for the lead. Give you an example: A horse goes out to the lead and he dies at the halfway mark, three-quarter-pole, and he goes up a class the next time out, most likely he will win. If he goes up like a couple a thousand the horse will win the race, most likely. You know, a lot of things, come from behind, you know, a horse needs more distance, you know. It depends on the jockey, too.

Once a certain amount of information is amassed on a specific team or race-track animal, the team and, more likely, the track animal will be "followed" because it is "due" or "long overdue" or on a "hot streak." "Following" horses was typically an adjunct to handicapping.

I began to really understand the moves that these trainers make with their horses. I used to follow a horse for a year, would you believe it? For a year, I would follow a horse for six months, a year, but every time I would wait for a horse, I never had the money to bet it and it always used to win. But when you get the money to play the damn thing it loses. It is beyond me how it works. It seemed like that is the way it is all the time. I am sure you've heard it before.

The number of elements that can be taken into account are not limited to the ones noted above. At the track there are considerations of pedigree, trainer, time trials, morning workout, how the horse (or dog) does on a muddy track, etc., etc., *ad nauseam*. For sports, depending on when and where the event is, there are considerations of the weather, the players' health, "streaks" the team may be on, offense and defense, batting averages, passing abilities, pitching, and so on. The specifications fill volumes of books, back issues of newspapers and magazines, and hours upon hours of poring over statistics. It is not uncommon to hear a bettor say he used to spend well over a dollar a day in newspapers. Some keep these papers on file for later reference (at one house I went to I saw a three-foot-high pile of *Racing Forms,* and folders of sports statistics about two feet high). In fact, a firm indicator of a commitment to quit gambling may involve throwing these things away.

One form of handicapping that stands apart as a subtype is the *system*. All systems involve some form of handicapping, but not all handicapping involves a system. When gamblers talk about "systems," they are typically referring to sports or race-track betting and handicapping.

Race-track bettors will look up past histories, pedigree charts, and other information to create blueprints for future action. Sports bettors develop formulas to determine point spreads and make their own lines in order to compare them with the lines the bookmaker comes out with. They create guidelines that will steer them to the winner. A "system," for the gamblers interviewed, is something that, once developed, can be plugged in and will work by itself.

The development of some systems is simplistic. They are based on betting favorites or underdogs or using a consensus of tout sheets, racing columns, betting services (some of which are daily, others weekly), and reading up on and having recourse to various systems others have developed and sold. These types of systems were more common early in the gambler's career. Once they came to know more about betting, their systems, much like any other form of handicapping, mushroomed in complexity. The sports bettor gets to know what the line is and how to figure out his own point spread.

Early, Simplistic "System":

> I was betting the favorites, and that happened to be a year where the favorites were winning, because it was incredible to me, you know, having no understanding of point spreads or anything like that. I'd look at a team like Greenbay, Baltimore, at that time, or some ragtag club and the point spreads would never enter my mind. All I can remember betting is favorites.

Later, Complex System:

> I would get ready for the next season; no matter what season it was, I would be reading ahead for the next season, to know who's on the team, who's good at what, who's a good passer, who's a good shooter, a good home team, a bad home team. Then I'd read up that night to see if anybody was out. I'd find anything in any paper that would give me an idea of injuries. I would classify this information, and I would knock off games that were tight, and I would figure out my own line for every game. If there were one hundred games that night, I would figure out one hundred lines through a system I devised on my own, figuring what team should get how many points, for the home team, who's really

good at the home team, who's really good at the
home team I'd give 'em ten points, who is fair at
home I'd give 'em five points, who's stunk at home,
I'd give 'em two points only. I figured out on my
own there's just got to be a way you've got to or-
ganize in order to win. You have to plan your work
or work your plan.

Similar patterns apply for horse-racing "systems." In these
cases, a formula once created is applied by rote. Little or no
divergence is allowed. A system is played, once it is worked
out. If the system doesn't work, then it is reviewed or dis-
carded. A major characteristic of "systems" players is that
they are constantly going through cycles of development and
casting aside of systems. The dream exists for a perfect "system"—something that exists only in the imagination. As a result, it is easy to change the system and feel that this is what
it will take to turn the corner on a losing streak or make one
a millionaire, only to find out that even this new system has a
few flaws that have to be worked out.

If you ask most gamblers if they had a "system," they
would tell you no. Some gamblers will tell you that that is too
much work. "I couldn't be bothered with that kind of shit."
In addition, most of the gamblers like the freedom that handicapping without a system affords. To them handicapping is
a lot of work, but it is also fun.

God, there's nothing I love better than staying up
all night and studying the relative positions and
abilities of the teams and comparing points and
then coming up with my choices and then, you
know, getting everything set up for the games.

There is a *hierarchy in handicapping* that has a pattern. As
a gambler becomes introduced to a new form of gambling, he
will rely heavily on the handicapping abilities and systems of
others. After all, they know more about these activities than
he does. As he gets more experienced at handicapping, he will
develop his own strategies and come to see them as better
than those of others. Of course, this depends on the personal

confidence that is *perceived* and *not* whether this is true in fact. If he still relies on others, it is only as a check on his personal handicapping and to find out if they see something he doesn't see or have some inside information he doesn't have. If he has had some bad experiences with others (which is almost inevitable), he will come to rely on their abilities less and less and come to define his own as better than theirs.

The hierarchy applies for each new form of betting the gambler tries. As a result, a gambler can accept consultation from others in one activity, yet rely on his own skills in other activities.

A horse handicapper uses someone else's system for sports:

I used to read, handicap them, but I didn't have no systems or nothing like that . . . [here he described his handicapping work]. I used to analyze them myself. I like to pick a lot of out-of-town horses. Them out-of-town horses are pretty good. Mostly, with sports, I used to go along with that fuckin' book. They used to have a book where a guy picks games, you know. I used to buy three or four handicappers. I used to judge which one picks the same team the most, you know. Used to bet that. Whichever they liked the most.

Q. You were subscribing to some form of betting service?

A. Right.

A football systems player uses someone else's system for the horses:

And I had to chase that football money with other forms of gambling. A place you can get a lot of money is at the track, so I bought Larry Wilbough's system on handicapping horses. I made almost one thousand dollars the first week. And I did that for a while until I had something like twenty-three races in seconds [his choices came in second] in 15 seconds. I went down the drain there.

Nearly all compulsive gamblers handicap in some fashion. This convinces them (along with early successes) that they are "smarter than the average." With increasing loss, it is to this that gamblers turn to "turn the corner" on a losing streak. As a result, statements like "You're running around like a maniac" are common. Getting papers, preparing by using one of a million handicapping methods, finding out the weather and other important information in order to be able to make a selection take considerable time and energy. The deeper in debt the gambler gets, the more he feels he must put in extra time to discover his mistakes and change his method of handicapping in order to resolve those financial problems, which seem to occur with more and more frequency.

Another aid for handicapping is the *hedge*.[3] This is a form of insurance against total disaster. It is an actual bet. In sports, it may take the form of purchasing a parlay card. At the race track, it may mean placing more than one bet in a particular race—one for the "tip" and another for the horse that was handicapped. A very popular form of this is "wheeling the double." In this case, one of the horses that is running in the double (the first and second races) is felt to be a sure thing. This horse is bet with all the horses in the other race that are felt to "have a prayer."

The "bird cage" and "boxing" numbers follow the same principle. The "bird cage" is three parlays overlapping one another. Boxing numbers includes all possible combinations of three numbers. For example: 821, 812, 182, 128, 281, and 218. In both instances, one's chances are increased by increasing the complexity of betting. (While this may be true, all hedges cost more.)

The most common forms of betting involve preparation, and it is these forms of betting that make the gambler think he is smarter than the average bettor. While gamblers rely on handicapping or inside information, they also use *superstition, luck,* or *hunch betting.* Few gamblers don't study at all and rely totally on information and hunch betting.

> Never read a form. The only form I read would be
> the paper—the program that you buy. I never went

by forms. I never read the *Armstrong,* the *Green Sheet,* or anything like that.

Q. You're the first person I've talked to who's never read the *Form* [laughter].

A. . . . I used to bet on a number or a name and that's all. In other words, I didn't care; my money would be wagered on a horse two to one or on a horse one hundred to one.

I never read a *Telegraph* in my life; I wouldn't even look at a *Telegraph,* but if you tell me something I'd listen to you. Some kink maybe ain't got a shot to win, I'd blow five hundred dollars. Honest, I never read the papers. I don't even know how to read a *Telegraph.* I just pick up a paper and pick something I like and play it.

The use of luck and hunch betting and superstition are most often intermingled with systems and handicapping. They are mixed in two ways: as an aid to handicapping when the gambler doesn't know what to bet yet feels he has to have "something going," and as a way of "insuring" the bet by doing certain things like being in the bathroom listening to a ball game because that is where he won thirty-eight hundred dollars the last time, wearing good luck charms and unwashed shirts (because, for example, one man noticed he had ketchup on his shirt when he won a double at the track).[4]

Luck and hunch as an aid in selection:

If I see a car from New York, I'll bet the Giants tomorrow. If I don't see it, that's a bad omen. Don't bet 'em. Sick.

Q. Were you more likely to do that at certain times than at others?

A. You mean bet on ball games?

Q. No, bet for seemingly strange reasons.

A. That was strictly on ball games—if there were two teams that I didn't know who to bet, you understand. It was mostly at work. . . . And I have

when I say hundreds, I've got thousands of IBM
printouts. So I pull a rack out, they're all alpha-
betical by name but not by state and city, if Chicago's playing Detroit, the first one I come to that's
the one I play—Chicago? That's my bet. And I'd
bet 'em! I would bet 'em; that's how insane I was.
And I bet 'em big—you know, fifty bucks on 'em.
I'd bet 'em.

Superstition as insurance after selection:

Q. Have you ever developed any systems?
A. Oh! I don't even wanna get involved in that.
Christ, we'll be here all night. Systems, when you
talk about systems, you know, I think about being
superstitious, ya know. I used to have superstitions
about systems. I had to be at a certain place at a
certain time doing a certain thing, ya know. It was
incredible. I've had a lot of systems. Like, for example on a *Telegraph* speed, rating, class, weight, everything, you know. It was so many things it was
incredible. I ran out of systems, know what I mean.
This is when I became superstitious. At the track I
had to be leaning against a pole with my legs
crossed, winking a certain way, because this is what
happened when I had a certain winner, you know.
It was just incredible.

While superstition is used as an *aid* and *insurance,* it is
rarely the primary means of selection. There is a tendency to
degrade those who use only luck or superstition.[5] The only
exception is with games of pure chance, like numbers, in
which the dream you had last night, the time your baby was
born (and the weight), the age of children, or anything else
is of central importance. Nothing seems to surpass the fascination with luck among craps and numbers players.[6]

Despite the use of this superstition, there is still the tendency to justify betting on games of chance. Whenever GA
members mention betting on numbers, they speak in such

terms as "I got so whacked out, I was even bettin' numbers."
Other justifications were also used.

> I wasn't trying to do something wrong. I was only
> trying to do in the best interest of me and the fam-
> ily. I mean, how the hell can I bet one hundred dol-
> lars on a number and have the odds 999 to one if I
> didn't think it was right. 'Cause, logically speaking,
> logically it is impossible. I mean, that's the most
> stupidest thing a guy can do. Betting one hundred
> dollars on something that's 999 to one. But if you
> *believed* in it, it wasn't stupid. If you *really believed*
> that you were going to hit it, it wasn't stupid. You
> know? 'Cause you figured, not that you figured, that
> you believed that sooner or later you were going to
> hit it. That's how wrapped up, involved you get in
> things like this. When you bet whatever you bet,
> you believe . . . that's in the best interest for you.

While most gamblers handicap, they also take advantage of
hot tips and *inside information* whenever they can get it. This
is more common among race-track (usually thoroughbred)
bettors than sports bettors. The nature and quality of the information received varies with the source. One of the gamblers was a groom at the race track on and off for a while. He
would get tips from other grooms and vice versa. Some of
this information involved the kind of shoes worn by the
horses, medication, and so on.

For the sports bettors there is the possibility they will hear
first hand about *"point shaving"* (the deliberate reduction in
scoring by ball players) or they may even attempt to initiate
it, as one person did. More probably, they will hear other useful information, which may range from injuries to a player's
getting arrested the day of the game.[7]

As for the horseplayers, one must understand information
hierarchies and rumor mills. As far as inside knowledge goes,
owners and trainers are seen to have the most, followed by
jockeys, and then the network of gamblers that surround
them. The farther down this pyramid-like structure one goes,

the less trustworthy and more rumor-like the information becomes. There is a massive rumor mill at the race track.

One of the stories told by a horse man attests to this rumor process. At a Gamblers Anonymous meeting one of the members recollected a story about a "hot tip." He had gotten a tip from a friend but figured it wasn't worth anything, given the source it came from. After he got the tip, he went to buy a hot dog. The woman at the stand asked him who he liked so he told her #6, which was the number the friend had told him. After he bought the hot dog he got a tip from a trainer that he was "going" with #8 (that is, the trainer was going to tell the jockey to try to win). He went in line to bet #8 when a friend came up to him and told him to bet #6; he had a "hot tip." He figured that maybe the horse had a shot, because this person had good sources, so he put money on #6 as well as #8 (he was "hedging"). After he placed the bet, he asked his friend where he got the information from about #6. His friend said, "Oh, I got it from the hot-dog lady."

Not all the information is of the hot-dog-lady type. Some that is obtained is of real value (though *most* is not). While for most of the gamblers good inside information is not a regular occurrence, for some it is almost a daily thing. I knew two persons who were privy to many "bagged" races (fixed —they were "in the bag") and got interested in horses that way. But bagged races are rare. The most common form of tip is that the trainer is "going" with the horse. When this "sure thing" occurs, every available penny is scraped together to make sure the opportunity is not wasted. Good inside information rarely occurs during every race. Even those who tried to rely only on this reverted to handicapping for other races.

Betting strategies and other forms of preparation take place in social settings. Depending on whether the gamblers are loners, group-oriented, or subculturally oriented in their gambling habits, they engage in consultation and partnerships to a greater or lesser degree. Consultation with friends is more common than preparing alone, which is, in turn, more frequent than the gambling partnership.

Gambling with the help of friends is the most common

preparation strategy. Gambling associates are used as sources of information by other gamblers. Consultation on horses ("Who do you like?") or sports ("What do you think?" "Dallas by six?") is a frequent phenomenon.

Constant consultation frequently occurs in long-standing friendship groups. The most frequent pattern is the use of other gamblers as polling devices from which you can get a reading, which you don't have to follow if you don't want to.

> **Q.** Did you used to discuss this stuff, you know, the bets you were going to make, with your friends?
> **A.** Yeh. Well, I had a couple of them who would call me and say who do you like today. I'd say I like the Brooklyn Dodgers and they liked the Red Sox. We'd talk it over.

Usually gamblers seek the advice of winners. This is true when they bet on sports and at the track.

Baseball:

> It was 1951 when I was betting baseball. I had a fantastic year: I thought I was the world's greatest handicapper. I figured I couldn't lose; I knew too much about the sport. So I start— ah, I was hanging around with a couple of friends of mine. They used to call me every day. "Who you bettin', who you bettin'?" That year, in 1951, I predicted the winner in the pennant; this was the New York Giants, when they beat the Brooklyn Dodgers . . . [and] they were a long shot. Like . . . the year before I'm picking them to pick up the pennant next year. Well, when this happened, everybody said: "Boy, that [name], what a handicapper! He picked the New York Giants; how did they even win?" You know, it was like I was in the limelight.

Horses:

> At one time, I hit upon a system of betting a number of horses in combination. For three straight

days I won the daily double, and in the next five
days at least one of my choices won while the other
finished second or third. Each of these bets, however, was only for fifty cents and thus the net profit
on each day was between five and ten dollars, and
after the first three days I lost. For this eight-day
period I was operating at a loss, and yet for the
next few weeks I was consulted by other bettors and
kidded by the bookies as being "too good." One
even joked about barring me. (Zola, 1967: 385)

Consultation episodes are frequently efforts to confirm personal choice. If, however, a friend can convince you that he
has knowledge you don't have or "saw" something you didn't
see, you may change your mind prior to betting on the event.
This, of course, becomes a factor in later rationalization.
Here the blame can be foisted onto the person with the extra
knowledge or inside information. Comments such as "I
shouldn't have listened to my friends" and "Without my
friends I was a pretty good handicapper" are frequent. This
may even be a rationale for becoming a loner. This, along
with the desire to keep winnings rather than loan them out,
and the stigma of being a loser are the most common reasons
for gambling alone after having been a group-oriented gambler. This was especially true of race-track gamblers.

I was a loner most of the times. Except in playing
cards, and once in a while I would go to the track
with a few fellas. Didn't come out too good. With a
bunch of fellas I lost. I would change my mind. I
would end up playing their horses and lose.

I started out with people but I couldn't be bothered
with them because, ah, they don't know what they
were doing. They used to distract my thinking. So I
used to go alone. I'd meet people down there. You
know, I never hanged out with them. . . . I used to
run away from people. They used to break my
chops. "Who do you like? Who do you like?" You

know, I don't want to hear their story. You know,
maybe they say they got a tip. Tired of this shit, the
tips.

Most of the loners do not consult with others.[8] When they
do, it is either a desperation move or a halfhearted effort that
is, in the actual betting, more frequently ignored than not.

> Q. Were you ever involved with any other people
> who were betting sports?
> A. . . . Oh, yeh, I've spoken to other people. There
> is a friend in Cincinnati who I used to consult with
> occasionally about football. And basketball, there
> was a guy at work I might talk to now and then
> about their thinking. Rarely influenced my betting.

The loners decide that they are smarter than their friends
when it comes to the activity in question.

The third and least-frequent form of preparation is the involvement in *gambling partnerships*. Gambling partnerships
are of several varieties. They vary with the type of gambling
under consideration as well as whether money is involved.
They are generally of two varieties: total deference and
pooled intellectual resources.

In the first situation, one individual defers to the better
handicapper. This is more frequent earlier in the gambler's
career than later, because he gets to feel he is smarter than
the others and as a result doesn't need to defer. What happens
more frequently later is that an individual will defer to someone with "inside information" or a "hot tip." In this instance
resources may be pooled on an event basis, or each may go it
alone.

Another case of total deference involves the skills of a
player (or hustler) and his "backer" (alternatively called
the "banker"). This arises more often in games of skill such
as pool, bowling, and cards, but it also exists where one handicapper feels the other is better at the dogs, trotters, horses, or
sports. In games of skill there either is a hustle (see Polsky,
1969: 50–52) or an attempt at a hustle. The following is an
example of an attempt.

The most prestigious duckpin bowling league in the state bowled on Thursday night. My average was, you know, 108, 110, 112, in that area; but I had 130-plus bowling friends. . . . One other guy, who was an older guy and a compulsive gambler for some fourteen years, he was the bowling half of the team, and I was the bankrolling half. But he'd get into double matches, taking a weaker partner, and end up slightly overmatched. Enough, but not enough to change the percentages. I got eaten up alive. Part of that was my football money. I was unconsciously lucky at first in football.

This relationship is very tenuous. "Almost always the hustler (or the person that thinks he is a hustler) has no standing agreement with the backer." (Polsky, 1969: 51)

A second form of partnership is the working agreement in which intellectual resources are collectivized for material gain. This type of partnership need not involve the pooling of *financial* resources but always contains the combination of betting strategies. The *handicapping abilities* of both (or three) are pooled in order to come out with better picks for the day. These partnerships usually develop among handicapping equals or near equals who come upon the idea that two heads are better than one. By using the consensus idea they can both benefit.

Most partnerships are not business relationships. They involve only the pooling of intellectual resources with the understanding that they will bet alike. In several partnerships, there was sharing of telephone bills or the expense of touting services. Very few actually pooled monetary resources. Where finances are combined, problems often result. Disagreements may occur or one partner may blow the resources.

We used to meet every Sunday and plan our attack for the day. And on Saturday (or Sunday, we used to meet both days), we used to decide how much we would bet that day. Just what teams, you know; we had three guys, so we had to decide two out of three as to what teams. This was our system. The

system was working real good until one of the guys
that we were betting with decided that the system
wasn't good enough, so he bet on a Saturday night.
He blew our eighteen hundred dollars in that night
and that blew our partnership, corporation, whatever you want to call it.

Q. How long did this partnership last?

A. The partnership was about two months.

The partnership, as in any case in which business associates
disagree on strategy, will eventually be disbanded or will file
bankruptcy, as in the above example.

GETTING DOWN—"NEITHER RAIN, NOR SLEET, NOR SNOW . . ."

Once the person has prepared for action by obtaining inside information, handicapping, or just having hunches or superstitions, he must "get down." Getting to where the action
is may be a simple process for the gambler involved in a network of gambling friends. Despite the word "action," there
is frequently a ritual that can be followed for the gambler,
with a game at a certain place and time every night of the
week. Monday night may be at the Elks Lodge, Tuesday may
mean the organized game, and so on throughout the week,
with every week being the same.

Every now and then there will be a stag party or an Elks
barbecue where he can get into the action. A similar thing occurs for the sports bettor who buys the newspapers, makes his
selection, and then "gets the lines" at six o'clock every night
and at twelve-thirty on weekends.[9] After he gets the lines on
the games to be played that day, he makes his final decision
and then calls the bookie again to place his bet. Where he
calls from will depend on his location every day. It may be at
home or at a hangout, bar, or action setting.

For some, the local *hangout* or bar will serve ritualistic
purposes. Most of these hangouts also double as bookie joints
and alleviate that problem as well. Hanging around the local
bar is *most common early in the career of the gambler*[10] unless there are other compulsive gamblers there or it is a hangout for hustlers or cheats and he is one. In these cases he

will continue to frequent the establishment on a regular basis. If he is a good card player, he may alternatively see the hangout as a place where he can recoup losses from his other activities.

Some settings are literally action systems, in which almost any kind of action can be found on a given day. If the action cannot be found, it can be invented. In the following case the place was a series of bowling alley-poolroom complexes (with one as a center).

So a typical day would be that I would leave the house for work at eight and do my job until eleven or twelve. I'd get the *Form;* talk things over with the fellows; sometimes actually take off for the track if we could leave early enough to get there and there were enough guys who wanted to go. . . . Play cards in the car on the way up and back. Go to various places in [city] where there's a poker game every night of the week and play all night. . . . Sometimes we would just bet with the bookmaker. I'd play pinochle in the afternoon or poker or blackjack or shoot pool or play chess. They had all these things at the bowling center. . . . If there wasn't any form of gambling we could get involved with, we made something. We even played Stratego for money. We've done everything. We've played Monopoly for real money; we've done that too. We were a group of hard-core compulsive gamblers.[11]

The most important aspect of all is the large group of fellow compulsive gamblers who could possibly be convinced to do any one of a variety of things that involved gambling.

In addition to the hangout and the action system, many gamblers become regular race-track attendees at various points in their lives.[12] The track may pose a special problem: getting there.

Getting to the action is usually no problem. For the routine-oriented gambler, the action is there every week. For the person in the hangout or action system, all he has to do is go to the focus of activity. For many, getting to the action may mean just sitting in front of the TV or radio alone or with a group of friends. The only problems are the wife and work. Besides the hassles of home and work, the gambler may have problems with distance. He may get out of work late and then go out to the track, his major problem being that in order to get to the track he may encounter obstacles. His auto may be in a sad state of repair. (A story at a GA meeting that is certain to get laughs is the description of going to the track in a beat-up jalopy with bald tires, wheels wobbling, smoke coming out the rear, and tailpipes singing away, at 90–100 miles an hour.) If, however, the gambler is convinced that this is the day he will "get bailed," nothing will deter him from his task—neither rain, nor sleet, nor snow, and so on, as the story goes.

> Now it's, like, I *gotta* have the money and I *gotta* go. That's the difference now than it was years back. Now it's, like, I *have* to go. And I used to get mad if I . . . I used to run eighty miles an hour to get there and if I missed the first race I would be mad. You know, at myself. You know, and I got nine more to go, heh, heh. And then nine more after that, heh.
>
> Q. You mean at night?
> A. Yeh. And then go to the card game.
> Q. What would you do when the tracks were closed?
> A. I would always gamble. If the tracks are closed for the horses, the trotters are open almost all year round. They used to close for Christmas; they don't close no more. I went there in blizzards and everything. It used to be snowing out and cold as a bastard. Used to get snow piled on the track and they used to move it away.

> I remember going to the track, this is right after we got married. I had my brother's car at the time. It was a Mercury, and it was the beginning of November, it was at Suffolk; the other side of Boston.

[Wife] and I were going to go to the track, and then we talked my sister into going, and she was pregnant at the time. It was cold out. So the three of us were going to go to the track. So I picked my sister up and we were on our way, and we were on the highway about thirty miles out of [city], and the top of the convertible ripped right across the top; it just ripped, you know, worn out. And here it was cold outside, my sister's pregnant, and the thing is ripped. And we're still going. I said we're still going; we'll fix it. We finally stopped on the side of the road and [wife] and my sister had pins and we pinned it. Then we were about twenty miles from the track, the thing come right off, right off the car. But we went to the track, and then the canvas is off the car, lying on the back, and we're at the track. At the track we bet and then we come out. Then I realized what really happened. The thing is out, and I was only worried about getting to the track. We stopped at a store and bought needles and thread and we sewed the thing, and we made it home. But this was something that— you know, I didn't care about anyone else in the car as long as I got where I was going. The summertime would have been nice with the convertible top down, but not in the winter.

While every track gambler has stories like this (including getting into accidents because the mind was at the track), the more common occurrence is to try to leave work or home early enough so there is no rush.

Any bettor who has surmounted the problems listed above will have very little difficulty placing the bets. Problems arise if the bookmaker gets arrested, the track closes for some reason, or not enough people get together for the poker game that was slated for the afternoon. These only rarely occur, and they are not insurmountable problems. Most of the gamblers had more than one bookmaker; there are usually other tracks running, and other poker games.

IN ACTION

"Action" he can obtain slouched in bed, phone at the ear. "Action" he can get hunched over a kidney-shaped blackjack table, immobile, signaling hits with the flick of a finger. Action. Supposedly the word speaks to the process of betting. I suspect it speaks more deeply to what happens within the gambler. He places the bet, juices flow, he feels really alive: action. When the bet is on, his existence is confirmed. (Trippett, 1970: 39)[13]

"Action" activities (activities in which the risk of loss is possibly avoidable) include gambling, being on a high wire, being a policeman or a miner, etc. Here action is taken on for its own sake.

All compulsive gamblers (and many non-compulsive gamblers) talk of the action aspect of gambling. It is described in terms of "getting my rocks off," "adrenalin flowing," and most often compared to sexual excitement.

I loved that thrill. I loved gettin' in bed with Marilyn Monroe at Lincoln Downs. I loved gettin' in bed with Raquel Welch at Rockin'ham. I loved gettin' in bed with Lena Horne at Suffolk Downs. If you are gettin' my viewpoint.

This tension comes to be described in terms that evoke physiological states of agony and ecstasy.[14] There is a tempest brewing within the event. Each win is described in terms of being a "high," and each loss is a "downer" or "depressing." These are *emotional* rather than purely economic terms and states.

The nature of this action has an uncanny similarity to "tolerance" among alcohol, barbiturate, and narcotics addicts. Once the "high" of a five-hundred-dollar event has been reached, the two-dollar bet no longer achieves the desired effect.[15]

The excitement to a compulsive gambler is just un-believable. He can count it in so many ways, you can stretch it out, you want to, ah, comes down to the last minute or so. It depends on a basket being scored or a touchdown being pushed across, a point missed or something like that. Then it becomes the ultimate, the extreme in excitement because you don't lose; you've had the fun in action down to the very end of the game, and whatever you bet, five hundred dollars or five thousand dollars, it hinges on the last few minutes of the game. As soon as the game is over you go down, because you've ex-perienced everything in that moment. It becomes an obsession of reaching for that high; but you reach for it so much that the bets get bigger and bigger in order to supplement the, ah, extreme emotion.

Q. It takes more money to, ah . . .

A. It did for me. I don't know if it did for others, but this is one of the symptoms for me. Once you've progressed to betting thousands, you can't go back to betting hundreds and getting a kick out of it.

After the gambler has purchased papers, gotten to the set-ting with money in hand (or has enough credit with the bookmaker), he will place his bet and is ready for the action.

If he is committed to the full-fledged chase, he will be try-ing to "get even" constantly. Getting even implies betting more events or betting heavier amounts of money. The only way to actually bet more games at once in sports and still fol-low them is to watch more than one TV and/or listen to more than one radio. Most of the sports bettors wind up "bet-ting every game on the board" and as a result spend much of game time switching dials to listen to the games and get scores. Similar things can occur if you are at work and have bet the horse race and want to listen to it.

He may also wish to have as much action going as possible. This may mean betting sports and the horses and having a number going for good measure, all at once. At least two peo-ple went as far as being at the track and listening to the radio for sports results at the same time. One person at a Gamblers Anonymous meeting recalled being thrown out of a poker game because he would go to the radio at a quarter of and a quarter past the hour to get scores and listen to a basketball game he had going at the same time. I saw the same thing at a bowling alley. There were several gamblers who were constantly leaving the lanes to catch the scores from the in-house radio. In addition to this, the proprietor of the lanes broadcast scores on the loudspeaker after each quarter.

Once the gambler is sitting down at the card game, in front of the TV(s), at the track, or involved in some other form of gambling, he typically becomes oblivious to his surroundings and concerned with the action itself. This is much more intense when the gambler is involved in the full-blown chase, in which there are more events to be watched and more desperation to get even.

> From six-thirty on I'd get my line, bet who I wanted. Then you'd listen to a lot of games. I had two televisions going on on whatever day there was two sports, on two different channels. I'd have two games going on; I had the earphones on for the radio; and another radio station on another one. I'd be listening to all four of them, and I could hear all four of them at the same time. . . . Never home to see the wife or kids. When I was home I wasn't really with 'em. I was here physically but mentally I was a million miles away. I'd make 'em go out of the house. "Get the hell out of here, I want to listen to the game." The kids made noise, like all kids do; you don't see it as that. You feel like they are interfering with you. They are in front of the TV set, it is a key play, even if it is a lousy play, it is a key play, always a key play. They got in your way. You don't want 'em in here, you want 'em out of here.

This constant obsession with the action occurs at home, work, or wherever the gambler happens to be. Many who are at home were like "mummies." Like the previous gambler, they are there physically but a million miles away mentally.

This engrossment includes wanting to stay in the action, once it has started, even to the extent of putting personal property and well-being in danger as a result. One person wound up in the hospital after the ship he was in was torpedoed in World War II. He was in a crap game and making a comeback from a losing streak when general quarters were sounded. He yelled, "It's only a drill!" Everyone left but him. In going (reluctantly) to his station, he was injured when a torpedo struck the ship. Another person's car was on fire, but he, too, was about to make a comeback. His reluctance to check out the fire cost him money.

I can remember one night at the club, a pretty rough night. I was in one of my losing nights, and we heard fire engines right outside. I looked at my hand and I said, "Sit down, if the place is on fire they will come and tell you about it." I had three kings in my hand. And finally somebody opened the door and called down cellar and said, "[name], your car is on fire." "Fire!" I says, "Oh, brother." First hand I get tonight and the car is on fire. I said the hell with it. So I ended up losing that hand; the guy beat me out with a flush. I say that is pretty good and then it dawns on me that I don't have fire insurance. By the time I get upstairs, get out on the street, it was a convertible, the roof was down, the fireman used an ax to open up the hood; the only thing he had to do was reach inside the door and release the hood release. He smashed my hood and grill and everything else with a hammer and ax, a fire ax. Here I am with no insurance. If I had ran out as soon as someone had said that my car was on fire, I would have saved all that damage. Three kings was more important than letting my car burn. As you think back and think of the silly things you do in life, that is one of them. That day cost me, I don't know how much I lost in the card game. I know I lost fifty bucks for the wire [burned in the fire] or so and it cost me another hundred and a half to get my car going.

While this type of incident occurs, what is more frequent is the attempt to continue gambling rather than quit. The continuation is either to maintain a winning streak or to get out of a losing streak. In many cases the continuation becomes habitual. A day of golf is followed by gin rummy; a day at the track is sequenced by an "express" to another track or a night of poker.[16]

COPING WITH THE RESULTS

After the action is over, there is a obsession with getting results. If at all possible the gambler gets the results during the event. If that is not feasible, then he attempts to listen through static on the radio. All possible means are used to get the results.

This obsession with scores and action is quite common once the gambler has gone "gonzo." There are stories of squeezing out scores (this is a popular procedure whereby the newspaper is bought and the gambler puts his hand over the number, racing and/or sports results and slowly "squeezes out" the results by moving his hand a little at a time until the full results are revealed), waiting until 2 A.M. to get West Coast games and scores, going to the railroad station at 11:30 every night for the race results. Many of the gamblers stated that they couldn't sleep until they got the race or sports results. For those who could sleep, the first act of the day was getting the newspaper for the results.

After the results are in or the card game, crap game, or racing day is over, there are several possibilities for the gambler. He can win, break even, or lose. *Breaking even* for the day is avoided at all cost. This is accomplished quite easily. Instead of wagering on six events in an afternoon, the gambler will wager on five or seven. Alternatively, he can wager on six but have a parlay card going at the same time. Breaking even makes for a wasted day (for this reason, having a game fall right on the point spread is worse than losing). While this is so, the prime reason for betting an odd number of games is the gambler's desire to come out *ahead* rather than be in the same position he started at. On the last race, for example, wagers are made so it is not possible to break even. If the gambler came with one thousand dollars and now has twelve hundred, he will bet either one hundred or three hundred dollars but not two hundred.

A gambler clearly prefers to win. Winning means that he can make a payment on a loan or pay ahead so there will not be any pressure; he can pay off people he owes money to in order to keep these avenues open; or he can buy back personal property from the pawn shop. Alternatively he can do other things with the money: reinvest it in gambling (the most common use of all), spend it wildly (most did *not*), engage in "share the wealth" sessions with friends—buying meals or drinks (those who conceive of themselves as big shots do this type of thing).

Winning also reaffirms the gambler's handicapping abilities, and it gives vent to fantasies of what can be if this turns into a "streak." (Many think of nice cars, world cruises, mink coats, and friends at their feet.)

> Big-shot ego, that big-shot image. . . . I used to say, "Someday I am going to own a Cadillac and it is going to be powder blue with clouds." And it was. The first car I owned was powder blue and the clouds was the oil blowing out of the back. It lasted twenty-nine days and it burned eight quarts of oil in two days. That was my life.

The gambler never wins enough, because it is never enough to get the gambler even. The joys of victory may relieve pressure and tension by allowing the gambler to pay off those people who are demanding money, but they are never enough.

> Greed. That's the main. A gambler never has enough. You walk out of the track and you hit 'em for a thousand. You could have made three if you weren't such an idiot. If you had bet this one instead of that one. Any gambler I've met is a tremendously greedy person when it comes to money.

What the gambler wants are winnings that will free him from debt, pay off everyone owed, and have some left over to

fulfill fantasies. This has not happened to any of the compulsive gamblers I interviewed. They frequently continued their
winning streak (for anywhere from a few days to years)
and never won enough to pay back all debts. Almost inevitably the streak turned and they lost.

All but two of the compulsive gamblers I interviewed bet
on race-track or sporting events. In these cases, the gambler is
working against the odds. Gambling entrepreneurs take cuts
that eat away at winnings: race tracks take anywhere from 13
to 20 per cent, bookmakers take a "vigorish" of either 10 or
20 per cent added onto the bet as a handling fee, which is
payable if the bet is lost, and house-run games take a percentage that varies depending on whether it is a legally oper-
ated casino, a game run by organized crime syndicates, a
"gambling club," or a private party "chopping the pot."[17] In
addition to the vigorish (interest or fee) charged by these
entrepreneurs, gamblers must also confront hustlers and
cheats in games of skill. (These factors defeated the two
compulsive gamblers who were not sports or track bettors and
helped "bury" six of those who played cards or dice as well
as bet sports or track animals.) It is little wonder, then, that
once involved in gambling, only those with an edge win in the
long run. This included hustlers, cheats, percentage card
players, the entrepreneurs themselves, and those who have inside knowledge and bet only when they have this.[18]

While gamblers commonly lose because of the vigorish
charged, most studies of gambling and gamblers show that in
order for a person to continue gambling at a regular pace, the
losses *must* be rationalized in some fashion.[19]

One can blame either oneself or others for the loss. The
latter is more common and ranges from scapegoating and
stereotyping of individuals and events, for example

> You could play the horses for twenty years and still
> not know how much of a chance you have because
> most of 'em are crooked

to blaming specific individuals, as certain gamblers blamed
specific jockeys by name, or coaches, or players. There are
suggestions of payola, point shaving to meet the spread, fixed

races, the jockey may drop the whip, or a dog may get closed out on the first turn, or some other "that bastard . . ." and "Why me? Why did he do it for me?" types of complaints.

The external fault may also be put squarely on no one but chance, a bad turn of the cards or dice. As everyone knows, even the good players have their bad days. "It just wasn't in the cards." "Hey, what can you do? When yah ain't got it, you ain't got it." In some situations this bad luck may be vocalized as a product of the dealer or bookie who is himself just bad luck. A study of Gardena, California, poker clubs illustrates this point:

> The manners of good winning and good losing call for losses to be blamed on bad luck. The managers and dealers assiduously promote this practice to "cool out" the losers, even though it means that the dealer himself becomes the ultimate target of the loser's rage. Since he deals the cards, enforces the rules, and acts as mediator (between winners and losers), he is the visible representation of the luck of the game. Sometimes heavy losers hurl insults at the dealers. (Martinez and La Franchi, 1969: 32)

Blaming stereotypes and persons is more frequent among horse and sports bettors, and blaming chance or bad luck is more common among card and dice players.

Blaming himself for a loss usually takes the form of realizing he has made a "mistake." The "mistake" can easily be rectified by changing strategy.

> With me, I was convinced that I had a knack of picking winners. Ah, I, ah, I, ah, just felt that why pass up an opportunity, I guess. After a while, of course, I started to lose; and, ah, this was difficult to, ah, accept, really. It was a difficult thing to accept, but then I said, well, this is, ah, something's wrong. I would go back to looking at those things a little more carefully, a little more closely. And, ah, I would start in again and maybe would hit a cycle where I would win for a while.

This is much like the horseplayer who "sees" something he didn't see the first time around and therefore can "rationally cope" with the loss.

> The past fifteen years of my gambling, I was either at one track and the bookie or two tracks and the bookie. So much time went into gambling research. Not only the picking the animals but looking at my mistakes till four in the morning.
> **Q.** You'd rationalize your mistakes.
> **A.** Sure. You'd rerun your races. What I should have done if I saw this or if I saw that. Research.

If the individual sees this "mistake" and others are around, he will use the "mistake" as a way of accounting for the loss. If no one else is around, he will look at the "mistake" and call himself a fool for not noticing that earlier. He tells himself that the *next* time will be different because "I have learned my lesson. It won't happen again." The fact that others also make the same type of mistakes may make it easier to accept this minor fault. This is more so the more one is involved with others. As Livingston says, "The resulting atmosphere can resemble a culture of losers, where jokes about losers and near-misses abound. Losers also have a collection of sardonic remarks about their losses, the horses they bet, and so on." (1974: 68)

While the gamblers attempt to maintain face in front of others through lies and avoidance, they still have to face themselves. *Denial of incompetence* was the major strategy used. The gamblers had to deny to themselves that they were not "smarter than the average bettor." Being confronted with loss was proof that they were not as smart as they thought. If losses persisted, the gamblers could then latch onto "losing streak" explanations. In this case, "bad luck" is temporary and "something must happen" to "turn the streak." Group support for this notion comes in the form of "everything comes in cycles." Gamblers refer to themselves as being on a yo-yo or a roller coaster and view the present bad streak as a little longer than the last one, but eventually it, too, will turn for the better.

However, once the loss or debt becomes large enough, denial becomes difficult. One way to ease the loss of self-regard is to impute a *Jekyll and Hyde* character. Gambling losses can be attributed to a second person: the Hyde in a Jekyll and Hyde personality. In this sense, the gambler perceives that the "real me" is a winner, while that other person is a loser. The other person is the one that goes "bingy," "cuckoo," "nuts," or "crazy." Temporarily the individual feels out of character.

> I always lower myself, because, ah, actually it's a double conflict. It's like a man with two lives. In other words, when I'm gambling and losing my money I'm a different person. I'm back to the original person I am. I don't know if you can understand that or have an idea of what I'm trying to say.

The real person is a "handicapper" who is "smarter than the average" gambler. Sooner or later, the losing streak will turn and reveal his true self. All the gamblers have a basic unwillingness to admit that there is something wrong, that their gambling is out of control or that they are "sick."

> When I was going down is when I really punished myself, being the so-called idiot for doing the things I did, you know. Because I looked at myself as not doing things compulsively but doing things *stupid*.

## CHAPTER III

The Family

A gambler must contend with his parents while single and with his wife while married.[1] The relationship is both an embarrassing and an exploitive one. He loses money and must get it somewhere; frequently he will use family or parental resources in order to do so. Since his subjectively held motive is to continue gambling without interference from others, he will lie in order to conceal the loss. The procedures the gambler uses to conceal loss and the consequences of this concealment for both his personal actions and the actions of those around him are as complex as they are fascinating.

The gambler's family forces him constantly to think of the repercussions of his actions on the home front. He knows that if he loses money it is at their expense. He also knows that if his wife (or parents if not married) finds out, there will be an explosion and arguments, and his life will be miserable for a while. As a result he conceals the losses and further escalates his gambling in order to get rid of the ugly evidence, be it golf clubs he has to get out of the pawn shop, a slowly disappearing joint bank account he has to fill, or some other source of discovery that has to be made right.

The impact of the family is felt at *unpredictable* points in the spiraling career. However, such family resources as bank accounts are likely to be used up early in the gambler's married life. He will accelerate his gambling to recoup these prior to discovery. Later on, he will have loans out and will again escalate the spiral in order to recover losses. The family (especially his wife) will enter at this point, because he fears their discovery of the loans. Escalation up the spiral is interlocked with the use of family resources, as the gambling both produces and is produced by family considerations.

BEFORE MARRIAGE: THE SINGLE LIFE

Gambling while single is distinctly different from gambling while married. For the single person there is no one to *account* to for the time and the money spent gambling; no one, that is, except the parents, girl friend, and gambling buddies. The addition of a wife brings forth incredibly complex *consequences* in terms of money loss. However, to assume that all the gambler's problems start with marriage would be a grave error.

If the gambler is not winning early in his gambling career, the losses will have repercussions for the rest of his life. These repercussions mainly involve getting to know what losing *means*.

It does not take long for the average gambler to know what it means to lose. Loss has two different meanings for the young gambler. The first is its effect on respectability, and the second is the consequences lack of money has for normal living. Starting with the effect on respectability, we can see that it has two bases: moral condemnation of gambling and a patronizing attitude toward loss and losers as "stupid," "fools," "idiots," "dumbbells," "morons," "foolhardy," etc.

From the interviews, the gamblers perceive that others have a dual attitude toward gambling. Either people agree that gambling is OK or they do not. The question of legality or illegality is typically overlooked, and the major question is one of morality.[2] The following interview illustrates the duality that gamblers recognized as common in the attitudes of others toward them. The gamblers found that they could discuss gambling with those who say it is OK, but not with those who condemn it.

Q. Is gambling affecting your reputation?
A. This I say with absolute honesty and sincerity, that as far as my reputation is concerned, the people that I worked with did not know that I was a

gambler. I didn't tell people that I was a gambler, that I had to work with.

Q. Why not?

A. Well, I guess, ah, even though I myself don't think there is anything wrong with gambling, I know a lot of people, you know, didn't look favorably upon this. Being a public school teacher, I figured that I had better not reveal this to them. They would not have, if I said that I won two grand last week, wouldn't have impressed them at all. They would look at, you know, I know I was . . . I think I knew well enough that that wasn't something that would go over that well. So, therefore, I didn't mention it. However, there was another, and I didn't really chum around with gamblers. I was a loner type of gambler. There was this one bar that I used to go into occasionally, maybe once a week for a couple of drinks, usually on Friday, and I would run into certain people and I might discuss a little bit there. That was apart from, that was not a place that these people would go to. In fact, it was up in [City A] and these other people were in [City B]. So, I mean, it was another life, so to speak. I didn't hang around there too often, but once a week I would drop in and Tuesday night or so I would go to pay the bookie or to collect. The people in there knew me as a gambler, but they didn't know me as a teacher.

So, as far as my reputation was concerned, my reputation amongst, ah, even my brothers did not know I was a gambler, nor did any of my relatives. My mother did not want them to know, either. I think my mother did tell one brother, which, later on, somewhere along the line, and he knew. But over all, it didn't, as far as my job is concerned, people that knew me for the last fifteen years that I have been teaching school in [state]. You ask them am I a compulsive gambler, they would look at you like you were a nut. They would even be surprised that I ever gambled.

Among those who agree that it is all right to gamble, there arises the second aspect of the effect on respectability: the patronizing attitude toward losers. Unlike those who condemn gambling, they feel it is all right to gamble so long as you are winning, or, at the very least, not losing. The gambler encounters this attitude, like the dualism, early in life, as it ranges from the sophisticated views of parents to the sheer protestations of common sense that cry out against seemingly irrational and foolish acts. Some parents have gambled in the past and know what "suckers," "marks," and "fish" are. They have nothing against gambling, so long as their son is a hustler and not hustled.

> **Q.** Would gambling ever conflict with your home life at all?
> **A.** Oh, yeh, I can remember my mother getting a little pissed off when I went to the track like three or four nights in a row. Because I used to borrow her car to go, heh, heh. Occasionally when I was on a losing streak or something, ah, and she overheard that I owed money to my brother and she'd say: "Are you guys gambling again?" Stuff like that, and she'd tell my father, stuff like that. But my father never really, my father was real strange about it. He wouldn't mind one bit us gambling as long as we were winning, but as soon as he heard we were fish he would immediately get down on ya for gambling, but as long as he heard you were winning things were fine and dandy.

Other parents frown on losing because of the money involved and may exhort the son against the gambling compulsion, which they define as a form of sickness.

Because of the patronizing attitude attached to loss, the gambler will start to lie in order to save himself from the sermon. He already knows that on this occasion he was, and will be seen as, foolish, dumb, stupid, and an idiot. He doesn't want to be reminded of it and as a result will engage in deception and avoidance. Three forms of deception become common: the flat-out lie; partial failure to inform (avoid

conversations, situations, etc. that would inform—especially
as to the exact amount of loss); and total avoidance of potentially explosive situations. The following interview excerpts
with a college student (whom I predict is on his way to a
very disastrous gambling career) illustrate all three forms of
deception and avoidance.

> **Q.** Did you lie to people about your gambling?
> **A.** One time, my parents came right out and asked
> me if I was gambling, 'cause they couldn't explain
> where my check had gone, you know. It hadn't
> gone to gambling; I had just blown it, but they said,
> "Are you gambling?" and I said, "No, I am not
> gambling." But my girl friend knew I was gam-
> bling.
> **Q.** Did she know the full extent of your gambling?
> **A.** I used to lie about the amounts, heh, heh. I
> wouldn't want to tell her about that.
> **Q.** Why not?
> **A.** She would think I was a fool.

In a different situation, here is an illustration of the avoidance
process in which he avoids going home by calling a friend.

> What happened was that Monday night was the last
> chance because football just happened on weekends.
> One night I was faced with taking a loss of one
> hundred fifty dollars, which I was down paying the
> bookie that week, *or* risk it on a football game,
> Miami and Pittsburgh. I bet on Miami, they had to
> win by four, they won by three. They had a thirty-
> to-three lead at the half. I ended up losing one hun-
> dred eighty dollars on that, 'cause of the vig (in
> this case the thirty-dollar fee the bookmaker charged
> to handle the bet). So I was out three hundred thirty
> for the week. I had to get up that money in three
> days. I had to pay the bookmaker on Thurs-
> day. . . . So I was out three hundred thirty and,
> ah, I had the money in the bank at home but there
> was no way I could go home and say, "Hi, Mom

and Dad, I'm here to get my bankbook, you know."
So I had to call on my good friend again, the one
that first gotten me into gambling, and I had to explain the circumstances to him, and I told him I
would give him the money when I went home on
vacation in two weeks, you know. Said, "All right,
if you are really sure that you can get me the
money in two weeks, you know. I'll mail you a
money order for three hundred thirty," heh, heh,
heh, so I paid the bookie.

All of the gamblers who had losses experienced the patronizing attitudes. Usually the lies and avoidance are for
losses, but if gambling itself becomes associated with the
losses, then that will be hidden as well, as in the case above.

The second meaning of loss is the practical consequences
for normal living. Having less money as a result of loss means
that you cannot buy luxuries or go out an extra night during
the week. If you want to do these things, you have to borrow
or restrict your activities.

Sometimes I would lose money that I was going to
go out with, but then, when I go out, I would just
have a couple a dollars. I would just have enough
for a couple a drinks. Just stretch it out. Stuff like
that. Or if I didn't have the money to go out I
would borrow it. I didn't drink that much, so if I go
out, just have two or three drinks just to, you know,
talk to different people; have a couple a drinks; go
home; stuff like that.

If the single gambler lives with his parents, losses will have
repercussions only for luxuries. If the gambler is living apart
from his parents (that is, living alone or with friends), food,
rent, and other bills may be put in jeopardy.

Q. You said that you borrowed from friends and
relatives and gambling friends.
A. I never really borrowed from my parents. That
was my money that was sent to me [from his bank

account], you know, to do what I wanted to do. I didn't tell them what I wanted it for. I told them it was grocery money. I had an allowance, and this allowance would come and instead of going out and buying the groceries, I'd eat TV dinners all week and give the rest to the bookie.

My senior year in college, either one half of my meals was macaroni and ketchup, that's when I was losing. I'd have macaroni and ketchup and water for supper, and that's when my money— I'd have many weekends I wouldn't have a dime in my pocket, no money for food or anything.

For the single person living alone there are far fewer hassles than for the married person. He has no one to account to but himself. If he feels like being a track bum or playing cards five, six, seven nights a week, he can without someone else's complaining about his absence. In addition, he has to account only to those he gambles with and borrowed from. Despite this seemingly idyllic setting for the gambler, most I have encountered (partially because of Gamblers Anonymous bias and partially a product of the instincts of man) have been married.

THE MARRIED LIFE

Getting married can cause trouble for a gambler. More than half of the married gamblers I interviewed believed that their gambling became worse right after they married. While most of their personal funds were going to gambling and other forms of entertainment (taking the girl friend out, etc.) prior to marriage, now some of this money must be diverted to the household. Of course, with increased responsibility and added expenses, it may only have seemed that getting married worsened the situation. When financial crises arise, gambling is often used as an added source of income to help stiffen an already sagging budget. Losses that could be hidden easily when single must now be accounted for in some fashion. The pay has to be made up if lost. This crisis may induce the gambler to get his first loan. Once this occurs successfully, the paycheck is used, and only later does the gambler worry about how to hide its use so his wife will not know.

Q. How did the stakes increase?
A. The stakes increased after I got out of the service. I was married and my wife would say, "There is not enough money coming in the house." Then I started playing the horses. The first month, I grabbed the mailman before he got to the house with my check and I lost my check. I said, "Gees, I got to get this money back." And I was talking to a friend of mine. He says, "I don't have it but I know a friend of mine who is a manager of a loan company and he can get you a loan if you want." I said, "Beautiful." And that's how I started to really go gonzo.

Patterns of exploitation

Once gamblers find themselves in a chase situation and have to get money, they exploit every avenue possible for doing so. In the process, they take advantage of their wives. How well the gambler can exploit her depends on *her* situation. The irony of the exploitation is that it depends on *trust*.

Monetary exploitation is of two types—direct and indirect. *Direct monetary exploitation* implies the use of directly *accountable* money and is avoided at all costs, yet does occur. Accountable money is money that is needed for the house. It includes the rent money, food money, etc. It also includes money that is jointly owned by the husband and wife: money from checking accounts, bank books, savings bonds, and insurance policies as well as jointly owned property such as the car, furniture, etc. *Indirect monetary exploitation* involves the use of entertainment money, funds from part-time jobs (which most gamblers have had at various points in their lives), and overtime money. These funds can be seen as the "husband's" money. This image, of course, is a product of exploitation of females by males in our society, and *all* the married gamblers I interviewed were involved in it.

The indirect exploitation was taken for granted by the husbands. This is partially because most of the part-time jobs and overtime that the gamblers had were to pay off loans, to rectify the effects of direct exploitation, or to gamble with, rather than being conceived of as household money.

> Well, I used gambling, I felt I wasn't making enough money, which I was. At the time, it was good money. Ah, I was always short of money, always, I felt. Not knowing that gambling was draining it all, that I made. I always had those other jobs after I got married. Figured that I wasn't making enough money, but I was. Always had fifty to one hundred dollars on me all the time when I was twenty years old and on. You know, that wouldn't be used for the house, that would be used for the gambling. I would never use it as an expenditure for the house.

The degree and extent of direct monetary exploitation by the gambler is seen as the source of the "problem" that develops. If the exploitation was only indirect, there would have been few if any complaints. The "problem," however, at least in the interview, develops when direct exploitation is involved.

Several patterns of exploitation develop among the gamblers with respect to the paycheck, as shown below.

Wife not working	
Use of paycheck, and disaster	5
Use of pay or alternative sources, and concealment	20
Wife working	
Wife hands over check	3
Wife keeps check	7
Total number of married gamblers (2 cases—missing data)	35

The first form of exploiting pay is the use of the paycheck to gamble, followed by disastrous results—having no money and having to borrow from parents or in-laws. In this case, the gambler may come to depend on the parents or in-laws for support. This pattern existed for five gamblers. Their employment records were rocky and they had monetary problems without adding gambling as a source of worry. Two out of the five men had periods of non-employment stretching for months at a time. During these spans, both became dependent on their parents for support. The other three cases would go to their parents after they had blown their pay, and a crisis of major proportions would erupt. This pattern is also involved with failure to pay other bills in the house, and failure to buy clothes and other necessities. The following excerpts are illustrative of this pattern:

> If I won, that wouldn't make it any better, because then I would go on to something else. I would save it all for cards. I've never bought her anything in the last few years. Nothing. No clothes. Never bought myself any clothes. . . . I would never spend money. I have not paid a doctor bill in three years. 'Cause I figured them son-of-a-bitches make fifty thousand dollars a year and I needed the money, so. Cards came first, and I needed my paycheck for Sunday-night card games. . . .
> Q. Did you ever have trouble getting money?
> A. Oh, yeh. All the time. Usually I came out of it somehow. I would take money instead of buying. I would go two months without buying food, three months without buying food. My father-in-law would buy it or he would pay my rent for me. I must owe him two to three thousand dollars actually . . . they were always supporting me. Buyin' us food. They were supporting my wife for three years, since I got married.

If the husband is losing his paycheck, the wife may try to get it as soon as possible. She might meet him at work in order to get the check. If she has the paycheck, she may not need to go to her parents for support. However, getting the paycheck or part of it became hell for a few women and for one in particular.

In other words, ah, the rent was always paid. Just so we wouldn't get kicked out of the house. That was the one thing that was paid. My wife made sure of it, because the landlord was downstairs. But, other than that, my wife walked through a snowstorm to get five dollars once, and I remember that I gave her the money and she had to walk five miles back because I wasn't about to give her a ride, because I was into a poker game. . . . If there is a knock on the door and it is your wife and she says: "I know he is in there."

Q. What would happen then?

A. That happened a few times, and after that, ah . . . nothing. I would leave the game and I would have to say, "Why did you bother me?" "We got no milk in the house and the baby needs milk. You haven't been home." Again I would give her a few dollars and I would leave her.

The second pattern of exploitation involves the use of the paycheck or other income resources to gamble. The majority of the gamblers rarely, if ever, lost a pay. Having no food and not being able to pay the rent was never a problem for the bulk of the gamblers. The following was a frequent comment:

I always kept, you know, we never were without money for food, for shelter. My wife lives very frugally. She was never without the things she needed, the necessities of life. In other words, if she said I need twenty dollars I always had the twenty dollars to give her. We never reached the point where I don't have or where I said you can't have it or anything like that.

If the gamblers lost all or part of their pay, they tried to hide this from their wives both to maintain respectability in their eyes and to avoid a potential fight. There are three ways they hid this loss: *first,* by claiming they were winning, breaking even, or just losing an affordable amount.

Q. Were you losing quite a bit of money when you were playing rumere?[3]

A. Oh, yeh, I used to get barreled in. Not into rumere but, ah, the sports end of it—basketball. I was a constant loser. You know, you'd win on occasion, but I was a constant loser. So every April I would start out owing a considerable amount of money, and she [wife] had no income at that time. I used to lie to her and say I won five hundred dollars playing rumere. Maybe I didn't even play rumere. Maybe it was borrowing one thousand dollars and giving her the money to run the house. It was one of those kinds of deals.

Secondly, the gambler can reduce the amount of money coming in by lying to his spouse about the true extent of earnings or by "creating" bills. These actions are all the more effective when the wife thoroughly trusts the husband. How he accomplishes this will depend on his occupation. If he has a job with a steady income, he will not be as free to hold back money as he would in an occupation with a fluctuating income. Self-employment and jobs with commission-based salaries enable the gambler to engage in "withholding" without the wife's knowledge. The case of a writer ("office man" —which I will explain in the chapter on bookmaking) and a car salesman below show the advantages of fluctuating income in this regard.

Now, my wife and I, we got into a hassle on this income thing. When I was working in the office [as a writer], I remember earning as high as maybe five hundred dollars or six hundred dollars a week. Of course, what I told my wife I was earning was different. She didn't know. I didn't give her all the money, and she always was under the impression that I was earning two hundred dollars a week or two hundred fifty dollars, because I was keeping this other money for my gambling habits. But I went maybe as long as a year and a half where I earned, you know, some serious money.

I made some decent money selling cars, but my wife never saw it. As far as she was concerned, I wasn't doing too well selling cars. When income tax comes around I was doing better than she thought I was. If I made one hundred fifty, two hundred dollars that week, I would give her one hundred, you know.

In those cases in which the pay is accountable, the alternatives are limited, but the husband still has several usable tactics: the creation of "bills" and new "deductions." The results are similar, only the methods used are different.

Well, I used to say to her I'm gonna have the car fixed or something. And she'd say, well bring it down to the mechanic and see what's wrong with it. So I used to take it down to the garage where I knew the mechanic and say, hey, ah, make me out a bill for about fifty dollars because, you know, I need some money. So he would make me out a bill for a new oil pump or something. She didn't know anything about cars. Next time, I'd bring it back to the guy and had a water pump put in for fifty dollars or, you know, I'd take fifty dollars out of my pay to pay the guy.

"Deductions" are more likely to occur if a certain portion of the pay is deducted by the credit union at work. The lie here is a distortion of a basic truth rather than a total fabrication.

I think I went to the teacher's credit union and that was, ah, no sweat. . . . So they deduct it out of your pay. Lot of lying usually, though, when you are married. Had to lie a lot. Real bad.
Q. What do you mean? Typical lie.
A. Like, your wife will wonder why your check isn't as high this month or this week. You make up some story. They deducted this out and you know. They trust you. That type of thing. That kind of hurts, too. You know, this person has all the trust in

the world in you and you're lying. You could say
the sky is falling and they believe you.

The *third* tactic occurs in the act of "borrowing" to hide
accountable losses. A gambler thinks he is "buying time" by
using this strategy. So he will "borrow" from family resources (bankbook, savings bonds, life insurance), from
friends, or banks and loan companies. This money, in turn, is
given to the wife as a "pay."

This "pay" provides a perfect rationalization for exploitation, because, after all, he is a good breadwinner. The following interview is illustrative. This person had several loans
out his wife knew nothing about, yet he could rationalize his
losses by references to the paycheck and failure to totally
exploit his wife.

I would give my wife the paycheck, but then I'd be
all day Thursday trying to figure out a way to pay
the bookies. But she always got a paycheck. Just
for one reason—to make her think I wasn't doing
anything wrong.

The third and fourth patterns of exploitation involve the
working wife. The third pattern makes heavy use of her loy-
alty to her husband. She hands over her paycheck to him and
he proceeds to swallow that up as well as his own. Here, as
above, the gambler may take out loans in order to hide the
exploitation. The husband is looked on as the money manager and the wife trusts his money-managing capacities. He
convinces her that everything will be OK just as long as she
hands the money over to him. All he is accountable for is to
see that the house is running OK and there is enough money
for a few extras.

This pattern exists only early on in the marriage, and if the
wife continues to work will transfer to the fourth pattern of
exploitation, in which the wife's pay is used for the support of
the family while much of the husband's salary goes towards
gambling. The third pattern involves trust of the husband,
while the fourth does not. The fourth pattern develops only
after the wife's trust is destroyed, when she finds out that the

bank account her husband was supposed to be putting the money into doesn't exist. With this go her dreams of owning a house or doing whatever she had planned on doing with this money. She begins to protect herself. In the case of the pay, the wife demands accountability for the paycheck. If it is her pay that is involved, she will invariably take full control over it.

The paycheck may be the major source of money for the gambler, but it is not the only one. He will also "borrow" from joint resources (where they may exist) "temporarily" and with the firm belief that he will put it back before his wife finds out. If he goes into the bank account, it is slowly drained, five and ten dollars at a time. Before he knows it, he is taking it out at a faster rate, until it is finally depleted. Five of the gamblers recounted stories similar to this, but I am fairly certain there were more untold stories that went along these lines:

> My wife had saved a little bit of money. She had worked in a shop during the war, a plane factory. She had big plans for me. She said that she had saved the money for me to go into something, some kind of business, something. And, ah, she had bonds and stuff. For quite a while, without her knowing, I was cashing the bonds, slowly, losing the money she had saved, slowly.
> Q. In order to gamble?
> A. In order to gamble, right.

The "borrowing" of joint resources is not the only means of directly exploiting the family. Fifty per cent of the gamblers had sold real estate or personal property to finance their gambling. This property ranged from records to coins to stocks to automobiles, and four sold their houses to pay off gambling debts. Whether the property is one's own set of golf clubs or the wife's wedding ring, there are repercussions for the family finances. About half of these sales involved the pawnshop. Again, as in the case with the bankbooks, the intention is to buy back the items as soon as possible so they will not be noticed as missing.

There is a difference between those who sell items of personal property and those who do not. Those who do, *tend* to be lower in financial status than those who do not, and have lower- and working-class occupations. The mostly middle-class gamblers who do not sell personal property tend to believe that they have nothing of value to sell. A typical response to Gamblers Anonymous question #11: Have you ever sold any real or personal property to finance gambling? was "I didn't have any real or personal property." They felt that their debts were greater than their assets, so why bother? Those that did sell personal property tended to attempt to sell everything in sight whenever they could. The following are some other responses to Gamblers Anonymous question #11:

Sold my tools, sold my car, sold my camera, sold my wristwatch. Sold personal things, antiques that I brought from Europe. I sold them for gambling. A stamp collection. Yes, I sold everything.

Anything I could—pawnshops; watches.
Q. Do you remember the first time that happened?
A. No, not really. I don't know if it was a pawnshop or I sold something to somebody else. I know I sold a lot of things. I must have sold about five hundred dollars worth of silver coins. If I had kept them today, they'd probably be worth a few dollars. The series jumped up an awful lot. And gold pieces that I thought as ridiculous. I had a gold piece for sixty dollars and sold it for sixty-six dollars; now it's worth one hundred sixty. Not one hundred sixty but two hundred sixty-five dollars, a twenty-dollar gold piece. If I hadn't sold them all to finance my gambling, I'd be quite a wealthy man today.

I sold my car one time, which my wife didn't know. . . . Some friends on my wife's side had won a car on a raffle, and they had this car. It was a 1940 Chevy. My wife bought it with her saved money, I remember. I sold that, and I disappeared for a week. I went to New York, and came back when I was broke.

Q. Was there anything else you sold?

A. Yeh, there was watches. . . . I remember going in and charging a new watch and going down to the pawnshop and pawning it for ten dollars, and I paid maybe fifty dollars for the watch. And, ah, I never go back, 'cause I didn't care. I'd pay a buck or two a week on the watch. I never go back and say, well, I got that ten dollars now so I'll go back and get that fifty-dollar watch. When I was in the service I remember going back on the train. I lost all the money I had and when I got to Seattle I pawned my watch. There are a lot of things, but I can't remember.

The list of items for those gamblers is so long that several stated they did it so often and sold so many things that they cannot remember the number of times or the circumstances and instead related stories they could recall similar to the ones above. The stories they remembered are the ones with the greatest repercussions, like the car.

Nothing can surpass in magnitude the sale of a house or bankruptcy in its exploitative impact.[4] Here, all that the wife has dreamed about must crumble under her feet. There are indications that this is a "joint" decision of both husband and wife. Both house sale and bankruptcy are last-resort measures that are intended to help the gambler get out of debt and give him a new start.

Since direct exploitation of the sort described above is more easily discovered and therefore liable to accountability, most husbands relied on loans from various sources (friends, banks, relatives, etc.) rather than promote potential disaster. The wife need *never* know about these loans, and a confrontation can be avoided.

Hiding loans

All but two of the gamblers I interviewed borrowed money from somewhere. Since they did not want their wives to find out, much energy was expended hiding the loans and keeping their wives from finding out about them. Primarily the gamblers relied on confidential loans to keep their wives in the dark. This wife attests to the power of this strategy:

> I didn't have any idea that he took out these loans. And he made agreements that they were confidential loans. Some of them would just not call the house. How could you suspect?

A similar thing occurs when the gambler borrows from friends and relatives.

> I don't know if your husbands ever did this, but mine, he would borrow money from people, he would tell them either that his wife was sick or something. "Please don't tell my wife, 'cause she is so nervous," you know; "don't call her, because she'll be, she'll get so upset." Poor guy has been trying to get his money for, like, six months from [husband], so he calls me: "Your husband. . . ."

Once the gambler has defaulted on the loan, and he knows that there will be knocking at the door, he can try to keep his wife from finding out. The payment books can be put behind the tiles in the bathroom, in the garage, or in any other convenient hiding place so the wife will not accidentally find them while cleaning or whatever. In addition to worrying about accidents, the gambler must worry about the collection agents' informing his wife. He can meet the mailman every day or have a post-office box where his mail can be sent. In addition, he can answer the phone.

> The thing that would always bother me was the mailman and late notices, payment due and things like that. So I finally had a deal with the mailman where he would hold my mail, if, ah, I would go out and look for him, but if I didn't find him he would hold it. Christmas I used to give him a

twenty-dollar bill. And, ah, I was very fortunate, 'cause my wife was the type who never ran to the mailbox. In fact, you know, she very seldom would go to the mailbox, but I still didn't want it to be the one day I would get caught. I, I couldn't get home in time, she would get home from work and she would stop and pick the mail up. It was just like answering the telephone; I was very fortunate at that. She'll never run to the phone when I'm here; she'll never answer the phone. While I was here it was OK. I could answer the phone and be talking to somebody and the guy could be threatening me at the other end of the phone and finally, when he hangs up, I could still be talking to him, nobody on the other end, and say: "OK, John, sure, don't worry about it. I'll see what I can do for you." She would say: "What was that?" I would say: "Oh, a guy looking for a job."

Discovery patterns

Discovery occurs in three types of situations: "getting jammed up," "facing the music," and "getting caught." Any one of these three situations can initiate the discovery process.

Discovery can be initiated by "closure,"[5] or what the gamblers call getting "jammed up." Getting jammed up occurs for several reasons, most frequently inability to pay loans. The loans that have been accrued are now larger than the spare money, part-time-job money, and "moved" or "juggled" money the gambler can gather together. He can think of no new avenues for getting money.

The second way of getting jammed up is the immediate need to pay off the bookmaker, because here the credit line must be kept open. Again we are in a state of closure, although the gambler could easily not pay the bookmaker and know he is in no danger (for all practical purposes we will assume that "Joe" the gambler is gambling with an "unconnected" (not mob-controlled) bookmaker, which was true of 90 per cent of all bookmakers in the areas I researched). If the credit line is not kept open, the gambler cannot get even. Given the situation of the chase, the pressure to get even at any cost produces an artificial situation of being jammed up.

A final source of getting jammed up is the fear of going to jail. In reality, the individual realizes that all he has to do is burglarize, rob, embezzle, or whatever, but *at this time* his moral stance and fear of the consequences prevent his taking the step needed to resolve closure. This occurs after the first two types of closure. For some gamblers it never occurs at all, because the closure they have is the fear of going to another bank and being turned down.

The end result of any of these closure states is that the gambler feels that there is no other place to go, and his wife or parents are seen as a potential source of money to clear up the problems that he is having. This type of initiator may be the first form utilized by the gambler. The parents or wife are approached in order to bail him out[6] of the jam. That appears to be the only other reasonable alternative. The gamblers with middle-class parents were able to use this resource more than working-class gamblers. The parents can be relied upon to relieve the immediate situation when single and even after marriage.

> I am certain that if push came to shove I could always create the proper environment to get bailed out. Again, that again is part of the problem. You know, my parents just, particularly my mother, [gave him money] exceeding whatever the demand was . . . , if I played my cards right and manipulated them properly I would get what I want.

Alternatively, the married gambler may feel he can go to his wife and ask her for the money. She may be working and putting the paycheck in her own account or they may have some other resources he can latch onto with her permission.

"Facing the music" occurs when the gambler is without pay or is entering an encounter without money that was expected. He has squandered the vacation money, honeymoon money, or furniture money and now must face the "music" (alternatively called "raucous chatter" or "bitching and moaning").

For those gamblers who married having a loan out (15 per cent), life was miserable from the start. They were constantly put under stress by financial circumstances and especially from the fact that they had told their wives that they "would never gamble again." "Facing the music" and "seeing if she'll still marry me" may be the first introduction to discovery and repentance for the gambler.

> I started at the finance company in September, so it [the gambling] must have been pretty doggone heavy, because I had my first bath [he had heavy losses] in betting in February of the following year. I had gotten in very heavily and I owed a fair amount of money, and I was planning to be married. My wife in the meantime was working at the hospital and saving like a rabbit. Of course, I'm blowin' it as fast as I am making it. So I got in and I think I owed about, the sequence of it I am trying to figure out, the first one I think must have been maybe twelve hundred dollars. It seems like that was the figure, which at that time to me was a ton of money.
>
> Q. This is when you were working for the finance company?
>
> A. Yeh. And I had to face up to my wife along about March or April that there was no dough. I had been squandering it like a madman, ah, and if she still wanted to marry me I still wanted to marry her. I was truly sorry. It would never happen again. So, yeh, it was just before I got married. It seemed like twelve hundred dollars. So that consolidation loan, and then it was all straightened out. That must have been February or March of the year that I was married. I was married in June. It didn't take me long to recover from the trauma. I got over the guilt feelings, because I was right back at it right after. To the point where I was—by the time I had gotten married I had blown tons of dough, beyond what I had just straightened out.[7]

When the gambler gets jammed up or must face the music, he may have hours, days, or even weeks to prepare a proper scenario for deceit. This scenario will lessen the amount of "raucous chatter" he has to listen to. He can broach the topic gently and lessen the shock to his wife or parents. As a result, more concessions will be won in his efforts to maintain respectability and continue exploitation. There will be no (or less) social stigma attached to the act if it can be attributed to an "acceptable" cause. He can say he was "swindled" in a card game, he lent out money to someone who isn't paying, or he cosigned a loan, which he now has to pay because his friend has defaulted on it. Some were quite successful at externalizing the debts, as shown by this wife.

> For seventeen years, all the loans that we ever had and if I ever made a list it would go around . . . it was always 'cause business was bad, somebody didn't pay him. . . . He brought me a paycheck every week. We never went without. The lights were never turned off; we always had food. There was never any problem. But, for his gambling, for him to take days off from work when he said he was working, he would have to make it up somehow. He would say that this customer didn't pay him, he had to go take out a loan, and I always accepted it till I found out it was gamblin', you know. That's the reason why. And no matter how many times I confronted him with this and said: "That's why you have the loan, 'cause of gamblin', you know." "No, it was because I didn't have the money to bring home." "Why didn't you have the money to bring home? It was 'cause you were gambling instead of working, so you didn't have the money to bring home." And he'd always twist it, and after a while you think you are going nuts up here.

It is interesting to note that when people get jammed up, they will attempt to avoid or diminish penitence by using "the Mafia" as a resource. Since "everyone knows" that there are hit men behind every tree waiting to murder anyone who fails to pay, this resource is quite popular and effective.

> The only person that really went out was my father. Initially I would start out with stories, my first year when I really panicked, I thought up stories that I had knocked up some girl or something. . . . Finally, I had to tell him I had been involved in gambling, guys were going to kill me unless I could come up with this money, so it was a matter of maybe seven hundred dollars and one thousand dollars that my father gave me in terms of money.

Similar stories are used when approaching friends and relatives. Some of the gamblers were good manipulators, capable of "creating the proper environment" so that others (usually parents or spouse) would bail them out.

The third and most common form of discovery is to *"get caught"* by the wife or parents. Getting caught implies some previous form of deception and that a crisis of major proportions is now on the scene. Getting caught can occur when a bank sends an overdue notice in the mail or a loan company calls to ask why payment is late. Someone could call up twenty or so times to see if the husband was home and the wife may finally get up the nerve to ask what he *really* wanted; the end result would be the revelation of a new loan by another friend. For several of the wives, the frequency and intensity of the calls and harassment from creditors was tremendous. The calls are made to the home, but the husband is nowhere to be found.

> People would knock on the door and say I'm sending your husband to jail. He came in my store and ordered whiskey and he's not paying for it. And it was the constant threats she had. Harassment from the finance companies; they used to come and say he obtained this loan under false pretenses and they'd say he has to pay this money. It was a constant calling and people coming to the door. Now, at this time she's got five kids, and she was deathly

afraid, because she didn't know who the hell was coming to the door.

Alternatively, the wife may find out by accident. "Accidental" discoveries occur when the wife finds a loan payment book, an empty bankbook, or evidence that the insurance policy is no longer in force. In some cases the circumstances of the accident are bizarre, to say the least. For example, one of the gamblers recounted the story about the telephone man who had to go into the bathroom to repair the phone. It seems there was a short in the wires inside the walls. When the repairman took out some tiles in the bathroom, money and payment books flowed out of the hole in the wall. After this, "all hell broke loose" (alternatively called "the walls caved in" or "the roof fell in"), and an argument ensued. None of the gamblers or wives stated that the wife had found out in any other way. As one wife said: "You didn't want to know. You wanted to trust him."

Unlike the two previous situations—getting jammed up and facing the music—the husband is at a definite disadvantage when he "gets caught." His wife has not cooled off. In fact her blood is boiling. The most common reaction of the husband when confronted with his misdeed is to deny or formulate an "account" for the loan, missing bankbook, or other sources of financial difficulty. Unlike the situation in which the gambler has the upper hand, now his wife has it. In addition to the accounts discussed under jamming up and facing the music, a bold-faced denial is attempted. The denial is an attempt to remove the cause of the trouble. If the wife has such verifying information as the stub from the loan-company payment or the emptied bankbook, the denial fails. If the wife doesn't have it, there is a doubt planted in her mind. The following interview is illustrative of the use of the bold-faced lie to forestall penitence. In a sense, there is an effort to deny that correction is necessary.

Q. Your wife would find out periodically?
A. Right.
Q. How would she typically find out?
A. She got a phone call, you know, if you are late

with the finance company, if you don't, if you purposely don't call them, naturally they are going to call you. They have employees working there that are trying to make a name for themselves, so they don't care. They call your place where you work or they call your home. That's how I got nabbed a lot of times, by not calling them up and they would call the house. She would want to know why they were and what I owed them. I would tell her: "I don't have no loans." I tried to lie my way out of it. That was until she actually presented the book. They'd send you a little stub with the amount due and the day it was due. That's how I got caught.

Further lies of this sort are "There must be some kind of a mistake" or "What the hell is going on here?—that bank . . . I'll sue. . . ." "Give me that notice. I'll give them a piece of my mind, trying to pull some kind of shit like this. . . ." Of course, the more frequently this happens the less likely the wife will be conned into believing her husband.

During discovery, the husband must reply to his wife in some manner, usually *combat and resignation*.[8] If a husband is calm, he will become resigned to the wife's hollering and just sit back and take it on the chin. If he is aggressive, there may be a knock-down, drag-out fight. Sometimes, however, a person who is normally combative with his wife (such as arguing to get out of the house) may become resigned to having gotten caught:

First wife: And they get mad and say: "I don't want to talk to you about it. You are blaming me, right?"

Second wife: No, my husband used to never get mad. I used to get "You're right, you're right." And then I used to end up screaming "I don't want to be right. I want to be wrong once in a while." I wouldn't get any satisfaction. "You're right, you're . . ." If he would be confronted with something and it was true, you know, and he couldn't

deny it . . . "You're right, you're right." That's the
worst thing in the world.

As part of the process, the wife may help the husband clear
up his debts if possible. She will work to pay them off, cosign
loans, consolidate loans, refinance and get others to cosign as
well. In addition she will help him out of jams by posting bail
or paying off bad checks or stolen money, all in an effort to
keep him out of jail. But she does all these things on condition that he not gamble again.

Discovery-process cycles

Discovery occurs more than once in the career of the gambler. The more frequently he gets caught or jammed up or
has to face the music, the greater the loss of faith and trust by
the non-gambling spouse for the gambling spouse. With each
episode comes a string of broken promises. "I won't gamble
again." "I promise not to use the pay to gamble again." "I
won't do it again." Many times, the promises are made in all
sincerity. The gambler himself may be personally disgusted
with what is going on at the time. He may be "sick and tired
of being sick and tired" (an old AA saying that is also used
by GA members). But with each attempt to quit may come a
series of events that bring on relapse. Later on he will get
jammed up, get caught, or have to face the music, and the
cycle starts over again.

There appears to be no way of accurately predicting which
form of discovery will follow which. The gamblers themselves
frequently don't remember the order in which things occurred. There is some semblance of order, however. If the
gambler is in debt while single, his first cycle will involve getting jammed up and having to go to his parents. Later, if he
gets married with bills, he will face the music. This may be
the only point when he tells his wife the true extent of all his
loans. Later on he may feel that he can handle them. After
facing the music, he will either get caught or feel jammed up.
The greatest variance among the gamblers exists in their perception of feeling jammed up. Those who get jammed up and
go to their wives more frequently have a closer, loving rela-

tionship with the wife. They don't feel threatened going to the wife, and as a result going to her is preferable to certain forms of illegal activity.

Most of the gamblers take loans from behind their wife's back and get caught, then later get jammed up and get caught again and maybe have to face the music at a later date. For several the jam-ups and getting caught are so frequent that they cannot remember every time but say, rather, that "every three years or so . . . ," "every six months . . . ," the cycle would start again.

The gamblers varied in the number of times they were involved in the discovery process. The range involved was from a low of two times to a high of ten. This is because of the varying ages of the gamblers. The younger the gambler the fewer the number of discoveries. For many, five or six times is all the wife could stand. At this point she starts searching out external means of resolving the gambling problem and comes up with Gamblers Anonymous.

The frequency depends on the gambler's ability to get loans, the capacity to hide them from his wife, personal attitude toward illegal behavior (for several hustlers there were no corrective work cycles), and the degree and intensity of gambling.

HIDING GAMBLING

After discovery, a gambler promises not to gamble again. In reality, he is promising not to *exploit* the family again by being foolish, dumb, stupid, and any other negative adjective the wife can think of when she is involved in "raucous chatter." After this, gambling becomes synonymous with exploitation itself and is frowned upon. In many cases, the husband will quit gambling and eventually will relapse. After the gambler has experienced repentance and is back gambling (if he ever quit in the first place), he will feel the necessity to hide gambling itself as a symbol of exploitation. The major strategies employed depend on where the gambler is gambling. If he is gambling at home there are fewer problems than if he gambles elsewhere. With greater pressure on the home front comes a greater tendency to bet with the bookmaker.

My wife was watching me, so I didn't go to the tracks at night or anything, but I have very little freedom. Mostly it was done through the bookie. I had two bookies that I would call up.

There are four basic strategies used to get out of the house to engage in condemned gambling for an extended period of time: sneak out of the house and back in; use stag parties[9] and other social events as an excuse; use work as a resource; and create arguments. If a person is gambling at home, the only problem that he will have is contacting his bookmaker.

Gambling away from home:

I'd get lucky at the track and I'm supposed to be home by six or four, I'd watch another race and get home around seven. I'd call and say I'm working late and won't be home for an hour or so, or I'd lie and say I had car trouble and won't be home on time. All those things.

My wife used to be up at five-fifteen in the morning to go to the hospital. She had to be there at seven and she wanted to have time to eat and whatnot. So all I had to do was be in [from a card game] by five, slip between the sheets. She had long since gone to bed thinking I was out on a business appointment; she would go to bed at ten, ten-thirty. I would get to bed at five; she would get up at five-fifteen with the alarm. As long as I got in before the alarm I was home free.

Gambling at home:

Q. Um, did, ah, you have, ah, typical lines or lies that you would tell her for certain things?
A. Well, let's see. Sundays I had to go out and gas the car, put air in the tires, check the car, change the oil, do something. Something I had to do. I had to do this at one, twelve-thirty. There was always some kind of lie to get to a phone.

Q. You never used to call at home?
A. Oh, yeh, if she was upstairs. Try and sneak a call downstairs, but if she is downstairs, call upstairs. Try and get the line. A lot of times you call and get it wrong. It all goofed up that way.

The telephone creates a major problem for those who gamble at home. The number of telephones in the house can create problems. The gambler above had two phones. Those with only one would either have to leave the house more often to get air in the tires, buy the newspaper or milk, go for a ride with the kids, etc. If he can come up with no other excuse, then there is the old stand-by, the argument with the wife ("tell her her cooking stinks or something").

Fellow gamblers engage in teamwork to further the concealment that the gambler engages in. They develop codes to use over the telephone and lie for one another.

"This is Harry; your husband said he was going to look for a car for me." All the while, once they got on the phone it would be, ah, "What's the line for tomorrow?" "for tonight?" ah, on the other end. And [husband] end would be saying: "I was looking around and I didn't see what you wanted, you know, what kind of car." And the other end: "The Bears are this or that." You know, and all I was getting was the car end but he was getting the line-up. Or what were the hot horses today.

Not only must the proper front be maintained on the phone and everywhere else, the gambler can't get excited over the game, no matter how much money he has riding on it. He must perform at home like an actor on a stage.[10]

I can only say this. I spent more time trying to run around ducking and trying to keep it hidden. I would never make a phone call from the house. I could sit and watch a football game like I had nothing on it. Went cold turkey. They never knew I had a dime on the game or one thousand dollars.

He can't even get excited when he wins. Because of the gambler's story that he will correct his faults, he can no longer go to his wife when he wins great amounts of money, especially if he told her he would not gamble any longer. After so many loans and discoveries of loans and harassment from loan companies, etc., the wife comes to see *all* gambling money as evil and dirty. It has ruined so much of her and her children's past lives that she cannot stand gambling money any longer.

All the above tactics are designed to be able to get even while preventing the wife's "bitching and moaning" and shouts of "Are you gambling again?" "You will do it again," and the "I told you so . . ." arguments that will follow later.

The concealment strategy that the husband engages in occurs at lending institutions that require a cosigner. The husband, knowing that his wife will definitely not approve of the loan, will forge her signature. Some never have to do this, because of business contacts; others do not do it because of moral qualms (besides this, forgery is definitely a criminal fraud); still others get their secretary to sign the wife's name or have a fellow gambler for a cosigner. Despite these possibilities, especially where the house may be involved, the bank will insist on the wife's signature. In this case either the gambler feels jammed up and goes to his wife or else he forges her signature. Signing, once it is done the first time, seems easier the second and thereafter. Besides this, it avoids the "hollering and screaming" that are inevitable should she find out.

Wife on the offensive

A full-fledged spy game of moves and countermoves is in play. The wife comes to feel that she can no longer trust her husband, and as a result she attempts to keep track of time and money and block his future moves. Only rarely does the wife go on the offensive, and this occurs when she can no longer take it. In these instances the wife may call the creditors and tell them the truth; the bookmaker may be warned that she will call the police if he accepts any more action from her husband (at least four did this); others may be called and asked not to gamble with her husband.

I just found out that he was really gambling and he was with a bookie; I found out the bookie's name and I got a letter off to this bookie and explained to him that, uh, that he better not give any credit to my husband. I don't know where I got the nerve at that time, because it was right at the beginning, before anything was really bad. But I did get a letter to him and the bookie called me back.

In one, isolated case, the wife called *all* his creditors, with disastrous results.

For the first time in my life my creditors had cut me off, because my wife had called them up and told them I was sick, that I was a compulsive gambler, and she begged them not to give me any more money. When I found out that she did that, I was furious with her. [Immediately after he found this out] I, ah, was making a drop [in the night deposit box at the bank]. Instead of making the drop I took out my knife and I ripped the bag open and I stole the money out of the bag, and I ran with it. Ran away for about a few days. . . . That was on a Saturday night. And my, ah, naturally Monday when they went to pick up the vault bag, they went and called up my wife and my wife went up and made up the $487 so they wouldn't prosecute me.

Whether the wife becomes fully committed to a spy game, complete with interrogations ("Where the hell have you been for the last hour?"), or to resignation and defeat, the net results are the same. There is a *loss of trust* by the wife with more and more discovery cycles. With more disappointments comes more nagging of the "You did it again; you did it again" type and a loss of love. If she thinks of it, or someone has told her about it, she will demand that he see a clergyman, counselor, or psychiatrist, or go to Gamblers Anonymous.

More than 50 per cent of the GA members that I have encountered were forced there as a condition of their promise to reform.[11] The route to the psychiatrist and other counselors is through the prodding of other people. The move to GA is a product of hearsay and other situational factors. If the husband goes to GA and "hears nothing" (GA jargon), at least the *wife* can attend Gam-Anon, which will give her backbone to think of her family first and think of the loans and problems as his and his alone.

Alternatives to the counselor and GA are separations and divorce. Divorce proceedings are desperate, last-minute attempts to get the husband to quit. Some wives back up threats of divorce by attaching conditions such as attendance at GA meetings and quitting gambling.[12]

Separations were initiated by the husband or the wife. Separations by the wife are less common than those by the husband. Many of the husbands have a dream. The dream goes something like this: The wife walks out of the house never to be seen again. Now there is no more bitching and moaning. There is no longer anyone to account to—what time you come in, whom you see, where you go, and what you do. As one gambler aptly put it, "It would have been a delight." Despite the possible "delight," many gamblers separate from and go back to their wives repeatedly.

> *Wife:* You went on "vacations." You were literally thrown out of the house. You went out bag and baggage. At least fifteen times during our marriage. I used to tell the kids you were away on business when they were small. . . .
>
> **Q.** How did it happen that you used to get out of the house?
>
> **A.** Ah, I wouldn't say anything about the loan, and the loan company would send a notice. She felt that I wasn't being faithful, that there was no honesty between us, that I was still gambling. And she couldn't live under that condition. And, down deep, I didn't care if I left the house or not, because this gave me more time for gambling. I mean that sooner or later she would get over it, after a few weeks. You know, this is the way I was and I

couldn't help it. And, ah, this is what would happen. She'd take me back after a week or two and I'd come back.

Others took off only once or twice, but the effects of separations were the same; freedom to gamble, but the paradox of wanting to be married.

My wife gave me a choice after finding out about a few loans I had plus some money I owed out. She gave me a choice of either stopping (i.e., going to GA) or leaving. And I really did think if I did continue looking for the big hit that I'd make a lot of money and then everything would be all right. It just didn't work out that way.
Q. What did you do then?
A. I really went haywire with my gambling. I had my own time. I didn't have to come home and say I was here or I was there, and I went through a lot of money. I borrowed from a lot of people. And I finally realized that the only place to go was home and try to talk my wife into taking me back.

Most of those who separate[18] do so at the prodding of their wives. Their wives leave, or they are thrown out. For a while they are in their glory, gambling every day. But living in a one-room flat or in a motel becomes depressing. Besides that, there is no one to cook dinner, wash clothes, and do other things that make life more livable.

Some gamblers have neither been separated nor thrown out, but are gone every weekend and are nowhere to be found from Friday after work to Monday or Tuesday morning.

She'd get upset plenty of times when I'd go spend three or four days away without telling her where I was.
Q. How often did that happen?
A. Periodically. Never any plan ahead of time.
Q. What did you do?
A. I'd get caught in a card game, for example, and

I'd finish the card game at ten in the morning and maybe from there we'd go to the track. From the track go to bowling, get in a card game again. One thing led to another, and I'd just not bother to call her and tell her where I was. The only thing she wanted me to do was call her and tell her I was all right. But if I was in a bad mood, I wouldn't even bother to call. It's all fine as you sit here and talk to me and I'm completely quiet and normal. But I wasn't always a quiet and normal person. I was a very intense and very emotional person.

Of the gamblers I interviewed, four became separated from their wives in an effort to run away from the pressing financial problems and impending doom. Two had emotional breakdowns and were hospitalized. One gambler had a history of repeated trips to VA hospitals all over the country, where he felt safe from the "noise" that was imminent back home. Another ran away three different times. Each time was after a bad-check spree. For both, after a while the trips were to another city and a hotel near a race track. The trips became more like the pattern of such other gamblers as William Hoffman, who felt that all he had to do was go somewhere and win back the money that caused all the problems he was having (Hoffman, 1968). In addition to running away from home, they were running toward gambling. All the gamblers in my sample came back; Hoffman didn't.

## CHAPTER IV

Occupation and Gambling

A gambler's job is vital to his gambling career. For instance, jobs that allow more free time and have less supervision permit more handicapping and possibly more gambling. These jobs also increase the gambler's access to money. If he borrows money, he must return it. This is one more pressure to face.

The gambler's use of his job is *exploitative,* because the gambler is benefiting at the expense of the employer or clients. Of course, how "serious" the exploitation is depends on the power of the employer as well as his economic resources.[1] This exploitation takes two forms: temporal and financial.

TIME USAGE AT WORK

The degree and possibility of exploitation of time will reflect several work conditions. First and most important is the degree of supervision the person has on his job. This is less for the self-employed person, the hustler, and the person with an independent occupation than for the individual with a dependent occupation.[2] The second-most-important factor is the degree of gambling that is allowed on the job, as well as the gambling habits of fellow workers.

THE SUPERVISED JOB

The amount of leeway a person has on his job will greatly influence whether he can gamble as much as he would like. The person in charge has control over the amount of the worker's activity.

Most compulsive gamblers lose time from work due to gambling. Most of the use of time at work is of the type in which the employee uses normal work and lunch breaks and normal slackness in the work day to place bets and handicap. Wherever possible this pattern is followed. It is the most common with schoolteachers, millworkers, job-shop employees, meatcutters, and other supervised personnel.[3] The following quotation is from a gambler who said that he had never lost time from work due to gambling.

> I would probably go to the washroom or something like that for a few minutes. Or if, ah, I would have one or two parts of it, what I would do is just take a few pages and mark on how they came in and have those tucked away. When I was alone I'd usually have it tucked away in my pocket and take it out and read it.

Worktime itself may be used to prepare for gambling or to gamble on the job. The lunch hour, coffee breaks, or the time in the men's room can be extended to accommodate the need to handicap. The average time was around fifteen minutes to an hour per day expended in this fashion. One person broke the record with a reported three hours per day (no one else was close). This is possibly an exaggeration.

> People that I used to work with thought that there was something wrong with me because from nine in the morning until twelve I was in the bathroom, you know, looking at those papers where I could have been doing my job the way I should have been doing it. And, you know, here I am just sitting back relaxing because I didn't want to do that job. I wanted to look at the paper to see what was going.

Gamblers also make good use of sick days. Usually they take these after all-night card games. The player either wants to extend the game or is too tired to go to work. As a result, he calls in sick or uses some other equally acceptable excuse (for example, "I am 150 miles away and my car broke down so I will be late"). For some, this is almost a weekly occurrence on Monday morning and possibly Tuesday as well.

Track gamblers left work early to go to the track. There was a horse running that they had been "following" and it was sure to win. All they had to do was go for one race, or go for a race and come back to work. They wouldn't be missed. Either they had others "cover" for them (e.g., He has gone to get supplies or something) or else others would punch the time clock. If the track was too far away, they would call in sick and not go to work at all.

Gambling at work itself (or possibly making book in the shop) will depend on shop rules and the attitudes of the supervisor. I have known no gambler fired for gambling at work, but several said, "If you gambled at [shop name], they would fire you on the spot." Others may work in "casinos" or "gambling havens," where as long as they do their work they can gamble on breaks or time spans between heavy work. Here it is guaranteed that the floor workers are runners for the in-house bookmaker. This latter situation is less common than the first.

Unsupervised work

Getting up in the world has special meaning for the gambler. If he becomes a shop foreman, supervisor, or manager and has to answer to people that aren't situated where he is, there is new opportunity for exploitation. Lack of supervision means more time for handicapping, gambling, and possibly catching up on sleep.[4] This is also the case with salesmen who are on the road, and some truck drivers. In addition, being self-employed and working in an illegal occupation (also, in a sense, being self-employed, unless you work for an organization) provide free time or situations in which free time can be gotten.[5]

These jobs are good for the gambler because they offer the chance to capitalize on "cutting corners" and "hustling" to get the work over with and then go to a card game, bowling alley, golf course, or the track, or listen to a ball game. As long as the work is done (or appears done), there should be no trouble with the higher-ups.

A supervisor, manager, or other potentially "free time" employee can leave work, even if others on the job object, under some pretext in order to gamble or prepare for gambling.

Group supervisor in an aircraft plant:

> I was spending more time on my gambling than I was at my job. Spend the day reading the newspapers and sneak out to the track, the afternoon or something like this. Especially when I got on salary work. I had a company car and took it to the track. That is when the hell started. The lying, cheating, conniving, and all the things that a compulsive gambler does. Taking time off from work, conniving (lying to your boss, telling him you are going to be somewhere and you are not, go to the race track instead, and stuff like that). I mean you are not paying attention to your job.

Manager of a motel:

> Q. Do you lose time from work due to gambling?
> A. Yes. Between running around trying to make connections to make payments to the bookie and getting prepared for a week's business. What I mean by a week's business, buying papers and going away from the job so that no one would see me. Just running away from the actual job just so I could set up the gambling business. I would say that 50 per cent of my time was spent on gambling and 50 per cent of my time was spent on the job.

Salesmen who are on the road have it better still. There is a very minimal possibility that they will be caught at their misdeeds. In addition to this, they can "cut corners" and rush through their jobs in order to be in action.

> I would buzz through my accounts. I wouldn't see

maybe three quarters of them during the week. I
only had ninety stops. I'd see maybe fifty of them, so
I could get done early so I could listen to the ball
game.

Adjusting [insurance] claims I'm out on the road—
in the office one day a week, out on the road four
days a week. It's awful easy to find a card game in
the afternoon or during the time I'm supposed to be
working. . . . I'd work like hell to get what work I
had to do done, but I'd cut corners on jobs, cut
corners on investigation; there's an awful lot of
ways to cut corners on that job.

Of those that "work" (given the gamblers' definition of
that term), the ones with their own businesses have it the best
of all. There is no supervision whatsoever except by the wife
and possibly a business associate. Most often, the business
partner gambles as well.[6] All told, 25 per cent of compulsive
gamblers have, at one time or another, been self-employed in
legitimate businesses.

Those with partners who gamble go to the track with them
or play cards at work. Few gamblers feel they must "sneak
out" of this type of work to gamble. Where they do, the situation is closer to the supervised worker. One person I know
had a paperwork partnership in which he "owned" a tropical-
fish business as a front for several bookmakers. In a sense he
was self-employed yet had a boss (one of the bookmakers).
The fish store was close to a major race track, and whenever
there was "something going" that he had been "following" he
would leave the store on some pretext in order to go. He
spoke of "sneaking down" to the track whenever he had to
pick up fish at the nearby airport. In this sense, he was close
to the management types who are allowed some freedom yet
have periodic supervision. In his case supervision increased as
he was pushed out of the partnership because of his gambling.

Gambling takes time. The time that it takes is time that
cannot be devoted to the business. If you want to handicap,
gamble at work, or go to the track or wherever, to gamble,

the business has to be "inconvenienced" in order for you to do it. If it is possible, business appointments will be changed to another time or canceled. About one half of those who are self-employed do the type of thing this hair stylist did:

> I buy the paper in the morning and look 'em up and look [to] see who's going [that is, what horses are running] and if I like something I was all enthusiastic, and say well if it's a slow day today I probably can go there for one race.

Later in the interview I found out how a "slow day" received a push.

> **Q.** Did you lose time from work due to gambling?
> **A.** I did, yes, in a way I did lose time 'cause if I had a custom' [he speaks with an Italian accent] or a custom' call me up and say would you do me up at four o'clock. I would say no I got, ah, I can't take you, something like that. But the reason for that is I wanta go to the races, you see what I mean.

The other half of the self-employed gamblers are more involved in the action. They "inconvenience" their business more and more frequently, from one afternoon a week playing cards to five or four at the track and one at a card game as time goes on. They become like the salesmen "cutting corners" and "rushing through" the job in order to get in action. Most of these develop "morning" businesses. They do their work in the morning (or whatever they can do) and then gamble in the afternoon and night.

Owner of an oil business:

> Being in my own business I would find time two or three hours in the afternoon to play cards. And I tried to get most of my work done before one or two o'clock 'cause I knew the card game was in the afternoon, when all the men would get together, say at somebody's house or in a store or in a gas sta-

tion. I'd be there by two o'clock so I could play to
five or six, 'cause by six I had to be home. So it was
four hours almost every afternoon.

The two check men are just as concerned with rushing
through their "jobs" and getting to the action. They see passing checks solely as a means to an end—getting into action.

> **Q.** Did gambling conflict with your job?
> **A.** My job?
> **Q.** Sure. Passing checks.
> **A.** Sure. If I knew that I could go to three banks, I
> would only go to one. In other words, if I knew that
> I could be guaranteed, say, two thousand dollars
> but in order to get three thousand dollars I have to
> go to two banks, I would only go to one. 'Cause I
> felt that I had enough money to go to the track, and
> I would let that bank go. . . . I know I got to
> travel and it would take me another half hour. Let
> me go to the track.

QUITTING WORK

Many gamblers dream about work. The dream goes as follows: The gambler quits work (or doesn't have to work during the summer) and gambles. He thinks of taking summers
off to just gamble or follow the races or other gambling cir-
cuits. After all, he can make more money gambling in one
day than he can at work in a week or a month. He has possibly done it before. Now that he is gambling full time (and
possibly making book), he will be at ease and without a care
in the world.

> I was winning, you know, work is a pain in the
> neck. I could be out, you know, during the day and
> having a good time and thinking about tonight.
> Here I am only making seventy dollars for the day
> and I am going to be betting fifteen hundred dollars
> for the night. What the hell is the sense of working
> in the day for seventy dollars, you know.

The dream was voiced in various ways by 40 per cent of the compulsive gamblers I interviewed. Many, however, conceive of it as a fantasy that will never be realized. It dawns on the person that his handicapping and playing abilities are not as good as he would like.

> Q. Ever think of quitting work and gambling on your own?
> A. Well, way back you used to have pipe dreams that you wouldn't have to work and you would just gamble. Soon found out that was just a dream.

If his lack of luck or lack of personal capabilities does not dawn on him, then the gambler might alternatively think of the family as a responsibility that holds him back.

> Q. Ah, did you ever see gambling as a profession?
> A. Ah, if I didn't have any other responsibilities right now [wishful thinking?]. I mean if I didn't have no responsibility, then, you know, if I wasn't married maybe I would like that. I would.

> Q. Did you ever see gambling as a profession?
> A. Yeh, I thought about it. I thought I would rather enjoy it. But I couldn't lose my family to, ah, I think if I was single, ah, I would, ah, gamble professionally.

Several say the only reason they work is "I have to have a job because of my wife and kids, but my main interest is gambling."

Twenty-five per cent of those I interviewed have actually gambled full time for various periods of time. For some, this included gambling sprees of a month or two at a time. For others, there was a serious attempt to maintain gambling as a full-time occupation, with work only as a necessary evil.

Most often, gamblers quit work in order to convenience personal betting. The job is looked upon as "a pain in the ass" that is getting in the way of gambling. There may be several days to a month layoff and then another job is found that it is felt will be less of a hassle. Usually there is just a change, with no layover between jobs.

> I quit every job I had. I never got fired.
> Q. Ah, did you ever quit because of gambling?
> A. Yeh. I quit the [aircraft company]. I quit because I figured I would have more time for gamblin'. I quit, ah, let's see, between car sales and managing. Well, managing, I quit that because of gambling. Indirectly I quit because of gambling.

Some gamblers have such a rocky work pattern that they have trouble recalling their job histories.[7] During these periods of spasmodic employment and unemployment, these gamblers had lower-class conceptions of themselves: When I asked them the question, "Did gambling conflict with your work?" I found it was the wrong question to ask. The better question would have been, "Does work conflict with your gambling?"

> Q. Did gambling conflict with your work?
> A. All the time. It took time away from my action. Like, if I was supposed to go into work at eight in the morning and I wanted to go to the race track, that was taking time away from me, you know. I would just *quit* work. I wouldn't care if I was fired or if I quit. If I wanted to go somewhere to gamble I would go. Nothing would hold me back. My wife could tell me you got to go to work. I would say, "Oh, bullshit, I am going gambling." I would go. Nothin' would stop me. Once I had made up my mind to gamble, I would gamble. Nobody, nobody, many people told me, friends, relatives, you can't do that. You just can't do that. I would say, "You are right. I feel bad about it." And then, as soon as they are finished talking to me, then bing, off to the race track or off to the bowling alley or off to somebody's house where you can watch the game without people bothering you. You know, and you would go. . . . I had so many jobs. Part-time jobs,

full-time. I had so many that I don't remember, you know. And if I felt like going to the track, I would just go. Or if I felt like bowling I would bowl. Many times if I was bowling in a match [beginning in the evening] and I am still bowling in the morning. I am not going. Winning or losing it didn't matter, you know. I would stay there until somebody was broke. . . . Quit work on the spot just to go to the track. I must have quit twenty jobs just because I felt like going to the track.

Other gamblers quit work or do not work in conventional, legitimate occupations, so they can gamble full time. They prefer to work as gamblers or in gambling-related jobs. The most preferred occupations are bookmaker and other gambling-related jobs.[8] Gambling is an occupation in which the gamblers do not have to work (as *they* see work). Work is for suckers. Theirs is the world of the "action man," the professional gambler, or the good hustler.

Q. During the three years you were gambling heavily, if I asked you the question "Who am I?" what would you have answered?
A. I would probably say, ah, I would have told 'em I am a person that doesn't have to work and make a good living. I would tell 'em, I am a person that knows how to make money without having to work for it. I am a gambler, I would tell them; I am a professional gambler. I would have told them I am a professional gambler. I would have told them I am a class all by myself and that I don't have to work for a living to make money. I can make it through gambling. I am smarter than most people, I would tell them. I have found a way where I can just bet and make money. That's all I ever thought of them.

Q. While you were gambling did you ever call yourself a gambler? Or did that ever enter your mind?

A. Ah, yeh, I thought I was a pretty good gambler.
Q. What did you think in relation to that?
A. I thought I could make a living at it. You know, work is for suckers. People that work, you know, ah, did things that were out of the ordinary. People that would wash and wax their cars rather than to go to the car wash; they were too cheap. They had no class. They were too cheap to spend that extra deuce. . . . Any time you walk into a poker game or any place where there was a big gambling, where there was gambling cronies around, ah: "Look at [name], he is a gambler." This was a big thing, you know. "Wow, he just made a big score." I considered myself a good gambler. Good hustler. I considered myself a hustler of people.

There is a certain status that goes with being a good hustler, good handicapper, and/or excellent poker player, that these gamblers searched for. Several continuously try to achieve the goal of being a successful professional gambler. In order to do it they quit work.

I always thought that I would be a very successful professional gambler. From the time I was . . . [he quit work many times]. Every time, I'd figure out a system on the [merchant marine] ships. I used to buy two, three years' back issues of *The Racing Form.* At Triangle Publications in New York. . . . I used to study and come up with systems that worked for about seven months and then throw them books overboard. Sell my tools, leave most of my clothes, get the money and go to New York and play the system, and inside of a week or two I am back looking for a job. And just when I have enough money, buy the *same* set of books, same set of *Racing Form,* same systems.

Not all who quit to become professionals are as persistent as the individual above. The steadfast, undying efforts change their nature as time goes on. Many always maintain the dream of being professionals, yet still work. The work patterns will be rocky; if they are not rocky, then work will be inconvenienced slightly in order to accommodate gambling.

EXPLOITATION PATTERNS: FINANCES

Gamblers use their work to get money to gamble with. They often work part-time jobs, overtime, and sometimes two jobs at once in order to gamble or pay gambling debts. In addition to this, they borrow from close friends at work, get advances in their pay, steal money and items for ready cash, and in other ways exploit fellow employees, the boss, customers, and business associates.

Like the exploitation of time, financial exploitation will depend on the degree of supervision that the employee has on the job. It will also depend on opportunity, skill, and awareness. Teachers do not have much opportunity to steal items or money from the job.[9] Many other jobs are so highly supervised that the opportunity is minimized as well.[10] Some forms of exploitation (such as "juggling" accounts) involve a degree of skill that most employees don't possess. Other forms involve contact with customers and the opportunity to violate their trust or take advantage of them.

As in the exploitation of time, legal avenues are attempted before illegal ones. When small amounts of money are involved, fellow workers and customers will be hit up for the money. They will be asked only after gambling friends and other close resources are drained of money. In this connection the borrower offers various reasons prior to borrowing. As one gambler put it at a Gamblers Anonymous meeting: "Think of the ways of asking for money and we have done it." Some of the more common justifications are "something happened to the family," doctor bills, "buy something for the wife's birthday," or just "I'm short," or the use of some other "fault," such as drinking or women. Gambling is mentioned only as the last resort because of the potential sermon that would go along with it. Again, the patronizing rears its head and there is the possibility that others will not give the gambler the money he needs. Also, the gambler feels ashamed to go to fellow employees, and the fear of losing self-esteem is so great that well over half never did. Those that did borrow typically did so in a minor monetary range, from five dollars to twenty-five dollars on the average. In some cases more was lent out, but this was rare.

Some gamblers borrow from "everybody" they can get money from—"no holds barred." Some leave jobs so they won't have to pay debts. They borrow and then quit their jobs after incurring debts over their heads. They owe more than their next paycheck. The pressure gets too great; there appears to be no other avenue open except to quit their jobs, so they quit.

The second-most-common form of borrowing at work is advance payment.[11] Some take an advance on their vacation salary every year for years.

What is avoided at all cost is going to the employer with the problem. Employee theft and embezzlement seem more sensible than going to the boss. Some bosses would not agree with gambling at all. Others would take a highly patronizing and/or untrusting view.[12]

> My boss told me I had the mind of an ant. Then, before you know it, I start gambling again and start losing time from my job. Taking an afternoon off; taking a night off to go to the race track with this man. Before you know it, it was the same thing, borrowing money again. Had a friend of mine sign a loan, in the meantime establishing my credit again, paying. All the time, I'm losing, losing, losing, and finally the man I was working for said I was crazy for doing the things I was doing, 'cause he knew what I was doing.

EMPLOYEE THEFT

Employees can steal either money or salable goods, depending on what is available.

Stealing goods at work is quite a common practice. What is *not* common is pilfering for the sake of resale, as seven gamblers did.[13] Typically researchers talk about the distinction between theft of goods and theft of money. They call one "blue-collar theft" and the other "white-collar theft." While blue-collar theft tends toward goods and white-collar toward money, collar color is just one, minor factor.

The first major factor involved in theft is the conception of what is personal property, what is company property, and what is of uncertain ownership. Those last items are more likely to be stolen, and include those that are thought to be useless for the company but useful personally, items the company made and would let you take home anyway, and small, seemingly valueless property. Some gamblers steal items of uncertain ownership, but these are unrelated to resale. They are of low value and for personal use. Gamblers argue, "Everybody does it." And they deny illegality to the theft of items of uncertain ownership.[14]

The next-most-important factor is surveillance by company personnel (Horning, 1970). In this sense, the degree of supervision should be related to theft of property and money. The right opportunity has to be present. For the interviewees that stole for resale, it was.

> **Q.** Have you ever committed or considered an illegal act to finance your gambling?
> **A.** Yes. I think every compulsive gambler does something illegal. Me, it could have cost me my job at the store; I could have gotten arrested, for a number of different things, like stealing something from the store or giving something away.
> **Q.** How did that happen?
> **A.** Well, I had an opportunity to take something from the store, say a case of canned hams or something, and sell it on the outside, you know, and keep the money. Where, if I ever got caught, it would, you know, be just like stealing one thousand dollars out of the register. It's the same thing . . . you know, the circumstances were just right, where I knew I could get away with it. . . . I really needed the money, you know. I needed the money and the opportunity was there, where I was alone at the time and we had just finished taking inventory

of the merchandise and I knew what was there. It
was just the right opportunity.

This meatcutter stole only once, on a one-shot opportunity
and at the right point in time. The electrician cited below was
freer than the meatcutter and also pilfered more often (although this was not an everyday thing).

> Q. You said that you stole some electrical equip-
> ment; what were the circumstances surrounding
> that?
> A. Just some wire. You know, cable and stuff like
> that. Sold a few cables and stuff like that at ten
> bucks a throw. You know, not enough, probably the
> extent that I have taken over the eight years comes
> to seven or eight hundred dollars. . . . Everybody,
> you know, all electricians do it, you know. When
> you got the opportunity to get equipment, you
> know, whether you need it for yourself or your
> mother or father, you know, you take it. It is very
> accessible. It is very easy.

More persons in unsupervised positions steal than those in
supervised positions.[15] Those who have held supervised and
supervisory jobs at different points in their lives are more
likely to steal at jobs with less surveillance. Those who are in
positions of trust are more likely to violate that trust.

If we look at the offenders from a different vantage point—
style of offense—we get another idea of what these trust
violators were like. There are two types of employee thieves:
those who steal occasionally and those who steal habitually.
The gamblers who steal occasionally are either "hit and run"
offenders or those with restricted opportunity. There are two
kinds of habitual thieves: those who "borrow" ("jugglers")
and those who steal.[16] Four gamblers I interviewed stole on a
"hit and run" basis. One was assistant manager of a shoe
store who stole money out of a vault bag after his wife had
closed off all opportunities for lending by calling up loan
companies. After he stole the money from the vault bag, he
disappeared to race tracks for a while. Two interviewees stole

company checks and ran. One of them just rode around in his car for days; the other went to the track to try to recoup the losses, pay back loans, and pay for the checks as well. The fourth had been accused of stealing from the "hamburger joint" he was managing. He stole from them and then quit the job.

> The only place I nailed was the hamburger joint. They got robbed and I was accused of taking the money, and I didn't. I said that if I am going to be accused of it I nailed 'em, and I beat the lie-detector test with it. And I beat the state lie-detector test. They couldn't prosecute me, nothing; then I quit on them. The owner of the hamburger joint was a crook, anyways. I knew. I used to figure out the payrolls. I knew what the hell he was doing. I wasn't stupid. That's besides the point. Two wrongs don't make a right. I guess I was, ah, justifying to myself. I could have hit him real bad, but I didn't. I thought of a way of doing it. I had it all worked out, but I hit him for a few hundred.

Four gamblers were potentially habitual thieves but had restricted opportunity. Three had stolen only once. The first, a meatcutter, was discussed above under surveillance; the second, head shipper at a foam rubber company, had forged a company official's signature to a check and was caught. He spent six months in prison as a result. The third, a chief engineer in the merchant marine at the time, "had a condenser retooled" that never was retooled in fact. The paper contract made him two thousand dollars, which he used to pay off shipboard debts. He was in the habit of borrowing more than he could afford to pay back; he made most of his gambling money on the black market. A fourth gambler worked as a cook at a race track until he was fired because his boss suspected he and another gambler were teaming up to steal meat (which they were). In each of these cases the gamblers would have become habitual thieves were it not for restricted opportunity.

The first category of habitual thieves is the "juggler." There were six jugglers in the group. They talked of moving money around, rotating money, and juggling it in order to pay off debts they owed through gambling. They were "borrowing" for a week at a time or a month, until the money had to be returned. One was a motel manager who juggled some figures around in the account books in order to straighten out temporary messes whenever they cropped up. The second was a manager of a shoe store who borrowed weekly receipts and played with them.

> I had pretty good access to money. We did our own books. We ran the store as if we owned it. Central Office was in [a distant city]. So I used to take money out of the safe and play with that.
> Q. Do you remember the first time you did that?
> A. Ah, not really; I just remember doing it a lot. I would take next week's receipts and cover this week's. . . .
> Q. Were you ever caught?
> A. Nobody knew about it. No way anybody would ever know about it. I used to take care of the books and I always had the money coverin' me. I never made my deposits until the week after.

The third was a liquor salesman who was "rotating accounts" on his accounts receivable. He was constantly using money from a thirty-day cycle. Money that was "borrowed" had to be replaced in thirty days. In his case there was a mushrooming effect because he was also selling liquor on the side.

> Q. Did you ever take liquor and resell it?
> A. Yeh.
> Q. To other places?
> A. Oh, sure. I'd tell 'em I'm deliverin' it to an account and I wouldn't deliver it; I'd get it stamped. You know, I had accounts who I took care of; I'd give 'em a case once in a while or I'd sell it for a per cent over wholesale to private people. And use

that money to gamble with, too, you know; just rotating money.

Q. What do you mean by "rotating money"?

A. Say you owe one thousand dollars; you have a
thirty-day credit line with your company, you
know, an account does. So I had it to a point where
three times a week I had to take merchandise out to
pay for the merchandise I had taken from the previous thirty days. I had to keep paying it, see, so that
increased.

Q. You mean the amount of merchandise increased
because you had to pay back?

A. Right.

Q. What did you think of the embezzlement?

A. I felt pretty shitty after it was over. But during
it I really honestly thought I would pay 'em back.

The fourth managed a bowling alley and borrowed funds
for a week at a time. The fifth "manipulated" accounts receivable in his oil business. He embezzled from his customers
by failing to credit accounts. The sixth person "borrowed"
from bowling banquet funds. Every year for fifteen years he
would borrow and then return the money just prior to the
banquet. Although he did not steal from work, his pattern
was similar to juggling accounts.[17]

In addition to the borrowing jugglers, there were seven
other habitual employee thieves. They stole without the intention of returning. Three of these habitual thieves stole items
for resale: one repeatedly sold sample cigarettes, a Navy cook
stole meat and butter for black-market sale in World War II,
and an electrician stole and resold wire and other electrical
supplies. Those who stole money over a continuous span of
time included a clerk in a milk store taking receipts without
ringing sales, two who "scalped" and padded their expense
accounts, and an unemployment-compensation worker who
forged compensation checks and cashed them. Two of these
were discovered and fired, and a third was imprisoned.

The actual theft should not be separated from the exploitation of time, discussed earlier. In the following interview excerpt we can see the hustle and cutting corners that denote an

exploitation of time as well as the exploitation of available monetary resources. All must be kept in context. The cigarette salesman had this to say:

> I used to sell to get money to go to the track. You remember the sample cigarettes?
>
> Q. Right.
>
> A. Box of fours. I used to sell them to truckin' outfits, drugstores, and everything for fifty cents a box to get 'em. I'd do that in a day. Ah, I'd fake my report out for [a tobacco-company name]. . . .
>
> Q. What would a typical day be like?
>
> A. I'd rush out; I'd make a few calls in the morning, get twelve or fifteen calls in the morning and then rush here, rush there, and then off to the track. If I had money I wouldn't sell the goods. If I needed money I'd sell cigarette lighters in [city name], sample cigarette lighters [brand name] and, ah, [other brand names]. I don't know if you remember them, maybe that's before your time, but, ah, I'd sell them and I'd sell the little samples of [brand name] or [brand name]. I'd sell them to support my habit and get to the track.

SELF-EMPLOYED GAMBLER AND BUSINESS

The self-employed gambler can use his personal business as a resource for money to gamble with. He, too, can borrow from fellow workers and customers. In addition to this, he can bleed his business of financial resources; he can fail to put money back into it and use the business to get money through business loans (about as ironic as home-improvement loans).

Stealing from accounts and customers is not that common. Borrowing by using all available means is more typical. Again, after all other avenues are closed off, gamblers borrow illegally by failing to pay income taxes on employee withholding, by using client money by failing to credit accounts on time for booking purposes, and by postdating checks for money owed. In the cases in which the account was not credited, some customers ended up paying double invoices. The self-employed persons use their positions of trust to violate that trust. All these cases involve a paperwork theft. In only one case was there a reported theft of cash from a customer. The customer was drunk at the time and wound up paying $30.95 for a pair of $10.95 shoes.

While the self-employed person may be "borrowing" from others in one way or another, even more common is the deterioration of the business through neglect, failure to invest, and draining of resources of the business. More than half of those gamblers with businesses lose them. Several lose more than one business. The following is typical of those who lost their businesses and most of the others who did not.

> I branched out from the family business [building maintenance] in 1960 and started from scratch working alone. And in a period of three years I had fifteen part-time people working, and the business was grossing sixty thousand dollars a year. And gambling just disintegrated it in about a year. . . . You lose accounts by not paying attention 'cause, you know, you're wrapped up in gambling. . . . I wasn't paying attention, 'cause I was gambling and, ah, and I was using all the money that was coming in for gambling. So it had to fold. There was nothing to keep it alive. . . . I was taking the accounts receivable and spending them. I just wasn't putting anything back into the business. I wasn't paying any bills. That's why it folded; I never paid any taxes.

How some of the others did not lose their businesses is a miracle. Only one took care of his business. He used to stay at work while those with "inside information" would go to the track with his money. He quit gambling and joined GA just as the losses were about to eat away at the business. Another (paper wholesaler) had a business that supported itself despite his daily excursions to the golf course and gin-rummy games afterward (he was a sucker of the first order). He had to sell the business, but this was due to the closing of paper mills rather than deterioration. These two gamblers were the only ones not to have any loans. The businesses they owned and personal resources were great enough that they chased losses with their draining bank accounts rather than with loans.

## CHAPTER V

The Bookmaker and His Business Relations

Twenty-four of the compulsive gamblers got involved in book-making and other entrepreneurial activities either as full-time jobs that supplied all their income, as full-time jobs that over-lapped other employment, or as part-time jobs.

Some non-compulsive gambling bookmakers have busi-nesses that are not significantly different from those of com-pulsive gamblers, excluding the effects that compulsive gam-bling has on business. These bookmakers have the same problems with customers and other aspects of work as the compulsive gamblers. Four of these were interviewed.

For these bookmakers, the longest period of employment may be twenty years, the shortest a week, with most hovering around one to three years on and off. Those who sell parlay cards (cards on which a person must choose at least three sports events—all of which must win in order for him to collect), do so for only one or two years. Other activities, such as "chopping the pot" or setting up a gambling club of some sort vary from several months to three years. Bookmakers, runners, and writers have the longest careers, with a three-year average. The types of activities they engage in overlap. Some of the gamblers only "chop the pot," act as numbers or parlay-card runners, or book sports events.[1] Let's look just at bookmaking and related activities.[2]

Briefly, the actors in the bookmaking setup include the cus-tomer, who places his or her bets, and the bookmaker, who "takes the action." The transaction can occur in any one of three ways: over the phone, in person (at a newsstand, in a bar, at work, or at some other busy location), or in a "horse room" (a room with a blackboard with such important information on it as jockeys' names and track conditions, and a cashier's cage). Drinks are also often served on the premises.[3] The bookmakers transact business over the phone or in person. While several of the gamblers bet in horse rooms in the late forties and early fifties, these places are no longer in existence in their area.

The customer can place bets with any of three people: the bookmaker, a runner (agent), or a writer. The bookmaker is the person who sets up the conditions of the bet. These conditions include such factors as size of maximum and minimum bets, whether credit will be allowed, how soon prior to the event the customer must place his bet, the payoff, and the type of "junk action" (for example, parlays, bird cages, and "if and reverses") he will handle.

The bookmaker will have and create problems in his business world, especially in relation to "using" bookmaking as a way of making money. There are two essential distinctions the bookmaker makes in these business problems—those created by customers and those created by the support group.

THE BOOKMAKER AND HIS CUSTOMER

Bookmaking is a two-way street. The prime rule of bookmaker-customer relations is shown in the following quotes from two bookmakers:

> This is how I feel about the whole thing. If a person's willing to gamble with me, he's investing a dollar. If he loses, I keep it. If he wins I should be man enough to pay him. Even if I had to remortgage my home all over again.
> Q. How did you handle credit?
> A. Very seldom I got stiffed. Ah, there was no set amount. I would just say, "You will pay tomorrow, right? If you win this bet I will pay you tomorrow and I expect the same."

This is the prime rule of the relationship. If either reneges, the relationship may end. It is not that simple, however. Other things cloud the issues. A look at the customer or the businessman who fails to pay his end when he loses both clarifies and complicates the issues. The compulsive gambler in the role of customer *often* has money problems. But the compulsive gambler as bookmaker may also have problems.

If the transaction that takes place is a numbers bet or a parlay card, everything will be on a cash basis. With "flats" (thoroughbred horse racing), trotters, and dogs, most betting is cash on the line, but some is on credit. But with sports, the action is over the telephone, and credit is the basis of the relationship. With numbers and off-track betting the major problem that develops arises because the bookmaker may fail to pay. With credit transactions, however, the likelihood that it will be the customer that reneges increases many times.

THE CUSTOMER'S MOVES

The compulsive gambler who contacts the bookmaker will eventually owe him money. If he is new to the business of betting through the bookie, he may have the naïve notion that all bookmakers are organized-crime-oriented bonebreakers who would just as soon break a leg as let a customer pay a week late.[4] Through talking with other friends who bet with bookmakers, however, he soon learns that they are sometimes late in their payments and nothing happens. He finds out that most bookmakers are relatively harmless, and even the ones with a reputation for being bonebreakers (or those who make use of collectors who are "known" bonebreakers) will listen to stories to *buy time*.

The stories that are told to the bookmaker often foist the blame for the lack of funding on other people. Other friends owe the customer money, or the bet itself was for a friend who isn't around. If he is in business, especially as a bookmaker, his customers owe him money. Alternatively he can say that he won money from another bookmaker but *that* bookie owes him the money. All these stories are used in an effort to gain a few days or a week.

I'd tell him that I didn't get any collections that week or someone owed me money. But I'd give him something and I'd get the money this week. I always had to give him some kind of story.

And Monday you would have to go to the bookmaker . . . and tell him a story or you would have to start finagling for loans.

Q. What were some stories you'd tell the bookmaker?

A. Ah, initially [I'd] . . . tell him it was for a friend. This was, you know, a classic story. The guy was up short, although it did happen to me. This guy put in fifteen hundred dollars worth of action with me and he left town one week. Another guy put up three thousand dollars worth of action with me and he didn't pay it. You try every angle, you'd go and say I'm going to get it here and there, anything you could think of.

The money to pay the bookmaker is just around the corner. All he has to do is wait just a little while.

A second, equally popular tactic is to avoid the bookmaker like the plague. Let the bookmaker look for you. When he finally does contact you (which is usually very soon), then you tell him you will meet him someplace. When he gets there you fail to show. Since most bookmakers have regular "meets" with their clients on "straightening-out day" (usually once a week for sports, maybe every day or once a week for horses and dogs), the missed appointment is typically on this day. When the bookmaker calls about the failure to show up for the appointment, the gambler has a ready repertoire of stories. The most common story has something to do with the car. Illnesses in the family and other "enforced" absences are then utilized as available resources for tardiness.

Finally, some people tell their bookmaker the truth. They just do not have the money and he will have to wait. Stories and avoidance are more common tactics. If these fail, however, the gambler can rely on the final resort: "I can't get the money, no way, no how; you'll just have to wait."

What is the rationale behind these tactics? For the compulsive gambler, getting even is the predominate feature of his life. In order to do this, he feels he *must* stay in action. If he doesn't, then all is irretrievably lost. He has a justified fear that if he tells the bookmaker the truth, he will get "shut off." This fear is intensified if he has only one bookmaker he can call (most have more than one). The fear is such that he will commit illegal activities in order to "keep the line open" and be able to bet with the book. As a result, lying to the bookmaker is preferable to the truth.

Most gamblers eventually obtain contact with more than one bookmaker. As a result the individual will be able to use bookie A while bookies B and C are waiting for their money. As one gambler said, he will be able to "play ring around the rosies" with their money. He will be able to *move it around, juggle it,* or *manipulate it,* in some fashion. His prime consideration, however, will be to keep at least one, if not two, *lines open* for betting purposes. This strategy usually develops only well into the career of the gambler, after he has a familiarity with the gambling setting.

The main strategies used involve betting with more than one bookmaker at once. The gambler may win with bookmaker A but lose with bookie B. He will collect rapidly from A and use the money to try to win enough to pay off B. Of course, he is still betting with A and possibly C and using them to try to pay B. The scenario may be as follows. Here I am assuming a daily payoff.

Sunday	Monday	Tuesday	Wednesday
bet with Book A win $500	collect from A and use winnings to catch up with B at the track	bet with A, lose $1000— buy time	cannot bet with A
Book B $1000, lose—buy time	win at the track only $50, but go broke at card game after	cannot bet with B until you pay	use winnings to pay B plus bet with B to catch up with A
Book C—break even		bet with C, win $1000	bet with C to catch up with A

Just as the gambler will use money from one form of gambling to recoup from losses in another, he will use the money won from one bookmaker to recoup from another. Of course, if he loses from all three bookmakers, he will have to go to outside sources if he cannot convince any of them to extend more credit.

Another common strategy in sports betting is to borrow cash from the bookmakers without their knowing it.[5] Let us assume the gambler has credit with two bookmakers and owes a third, or he may owe money somewhere else (a loan payment is due or he owes his bookmaking customers money). He may *deliberately* bet opposite teams on the *same* game with two bookmakers. He knows he will win from one and lose to the other. He will collect from the person he wins from as fast as possible and delay the person he lost from. In a sense he is paying the vigorish to borrow money for a few days to a week. The following is a clear description of the practice.

> Call up two bookmakers and bet the Giants on one bookmaker and St. Louis on another, figuring I had to win one or the other. . . . You're bound to lose one but you pay him later. You collect the money you win, and that's moving money. . . .
>
> Q. That's for sure you're going to lose the vig.
>
> A. "Not only lose the vig, of course you're losing the vig. That's exactly what you're losing is the vig. But you're gaining cash to play with. For example, if I had to pay a bookmaker three thousand dollars Tuesday morning, oh, let's make it Wednesday morning. Say I had to pay a bookmaker three thousand dollars Wednesday morning, and I don't have a dime. And there's a Monday-night game, say the Giants and St. Louis. I'd call one bookmaker and bet the Giants one thousand dollars and call up the other bookmaker and bet St. Louis one thousand dollars. Now I haven't got a penny to my name and I owe three thousand on Wednesday. So I'm gonna lose one and tell him I'm gonna pay him Friday. Collect the one thousand from the one I won. Now,

Tuesday morning I have one thousand in my hand. I still owe eleven hundred dollars and I still owe the three thousand dollars. So I have a thousand in my hand and I owe forty-one hundred. I'm just one hundred dollars worse off than I was the day before. Agree.

Q. Right.

A. I owe three thousand dollars but had zero in my hand. Now I have one thousand dollars in my hand and I can do something with that thousand. I can't go to the track and bet credit. Can't get in a card game on credit. You have cash. Technically you're borrowing one thousand dollars at 10 per cent interest. That's what you're doing. You're borrowing one thousand dollars at 10 per cent interest. You're using that thousand to try and build it back up to forty-one hundred dollars so that you can pay everyone off and you'd be even.

If all else fails and credit is lost with the bookmaker, those with gambling friends can ask their friends if they can bet through them and will reciprocate when the situation is reversed. Every now and then, one friend screws another in this fashion by failing to pay when he loses.

Not only are friends not paid; in many cases bookmakers are not paid. They are "hung up." Those gamblers who bet with many bookmakers have at least two or three they owe money to and have no intention of paying. In many cases they feel the book has "beat" them for enough money. The gambler most likely has other bookmakers he can bet with and does not worry about the ones he owes money to.

A reportedly common strategy for "hanging up" bookmakers is to get introduced to a book, bet with him for a while, and then call him up and ask him if a "friend" can bet through you. You and the "friend" bet simultaneously, maybe on opposite teams a few times as a convincer that the "friend" is real. This "friend" bets for several weeks for small amounts and pays when he loses. You gradually raise the "friend's" bets and when they are as high as desired you collect when he wins but fail to pay when he loses. When the bookmaker comes looking for his money, you say the "friend" has disappeared and "I only knew him from the gin mill."

Those with many gambling friends and those who were bookmakers or otherwise worked in the gambling business tended to "hang up" more often than those who were loners and non-bookmakers. They would bet with the bookmaker. If they won, all was fine; if they lost, they never paid. One gambler put the major criterion of who could be hung up and who could not in a nutshell:

> Like myself, I used to go with the intention of hangin' up bookmakers. Bet with them and not pay them. You know, I did this because I didn't care because they weren't, you know, they weren't any mafia or anything connections in here. If they were, you would think twice before you would do anything like this.

Not paying or being late is only one way in which conflict develops between the bookmaker and his customer. It can also be created in the betting process itself. The customer will try to "beat" the bookmaker in every way possible. The more common methods involve *past-posting, "catching the middle,"* and use of *inside information.*

Past-posting (betting after the results are known) is accomplished in many ways. The most common is the use of errors in the newspaper. Starting times for races or sporting events may be listed wrong. Those bookmakers who are not keen to this can easily be "buried" by their customers. In other cases, the starting times may be correct but, for some reason, changed at the last minute. If the time is moved ahead, the aware gambler can make use of this. A move of ten to fifteen minutes can be crucial in a horse race, as can the difference between the bookmaker's watch and the clock at the race track.

A second popular method of past-posting requires two people: one at the track and a second near a phone booth. Since the results at the race track become official only after two or three minutes, the person at the phone booth can sometimes call in a bet after the race is over but before official time. The arrangements are as varied as the people who try to past-post.[6] Every conceivable means of communication and signals has been used in this effort. This method of past-posting can easily be protected against by the use of the "scratch sheet," which has the post times listed.

Compulsive gamblers who are hustlers use telephone betting services to obtain results rapidly. These are also used to inform the hustler of races that started early. Some have arrangements with officials at the race track to see what time the race began and the results.

"Catching the middle" involves a tactic similar to "borrowing" from the bookmaker without his knowledge. Most frequently this involves the use of the "early line" in sports betting.[7]

> On Tuesday I would try to get an early line. I could never get a line until Wednesday for football, but I could get an early line by using the company WATS line. I would call all my friends across the country to see if I could get an early line. So, what I'd do on Tuesday is make a WATS-line call, two or three. Try to get an early line to see what's happening. Just write 'em down and don't think much about 'em. On Wednesday I'd hit the newsstands and buy a couple of tout sheets, whose predictions I didn't follow but I liked some of the reasons. The statistics in fact were helpful to me. On Wednesday I kind of select from all of the college games. The games I thought there may be an edge, a few pro matches. There would be an indication from the early line; I kind of thought that they would be misnumbered, because of the way the bettors were betting.

An early line serves several purposes for the football bettors, and most of those who bet sports bet football, a fact confirmed by the gamblers and bookmakers. They can use it to compare with one they have made themselves, or can use it to bet early in order to be able to "catch the middle" as the line moves due to public betting patterns. In this instance they would bet with two different bookmakers on the same game. The point spread, after having been moved through public pressure, changes. For example, Team A is favored by 6 points over Team B. The public likes Team A so much that they bet heavily on Team A. The bookmaker changes the line to a 6½-, 7-, or 7½-point spread in the hopes that later customers will bet on Team B. (If they don't and Team A wins by more than six points, he can get "destroyed," put out of business.) He does this (especially the move to 7½) in the hopes that the game will not wind up with Team A winning by 7 points on the nose. The smart gamblers, realizing this, will bet on Team A at the early line (if they like Team A, of course, because if the line doesn't move they are stuck with Team A); and if the line moves to 7½ will bet on Team B with another bookmaker. The worst they can lose is the vigorish (interest) the bookmaker charges as a handling fee. The best they can do is have the game land on 7 points, in which case they "catch the middle" and win both bets—a very rare occurrence.

Inside information is used against bookmakers as well as at the track. Several of the gamblers were privy to fixed races and two had regular relationships with "connected" gamblers who gave them "hot" horses. These gamblers acted as the "connected" gamblers' "beard." A beard is a person who places bets for someone else so other people will not be informed of the arrangements that are occurring.

The customer can also "screw the book" by using newspaper errors and making false claims or distortions of bets made. I will discuss these under the bookmaker's moves.

THE BOOKMAKER'S MOVES

Protecting himself

The bookmaker does not sit idly by as his customers try to take advantage of him. He must protect himself in the wagering and in collection.

In the wagering he must be careful of past-posting, taking

advantage of newspaper errors, use of inside information, and misunderstandings and deceptions in the wagering itself.

The only way a bookmaker can protect himself is to be aware of post times and not accept bets too close to the start of a race. Some bookmakers get beat time after time without wising up to the situation. Most bookmakers, however, are constantly on their guard for these schemes. Those who handle horse and dog racing, naturally, have to be more alert than sports books. The surest means of protection is to check the newspapers the next day for starting times of the previous day. Newspapers do not only have misprints of starting times; they may also quote the wrong payoffs for results in races. The only guard against this is a double check (two papers).

In a further effort to protect themselves, bookmakers will limit their clientele and, at times, the events they will let people bet on. If the customer is consistently winning, he may be "shut off" for a period of time from betting with certain bookmakers. The bookies feel they are being taken advantage of but cannot prove it. Rather than make a big issue of it, they will just suspend betting on the types of events that are being bet on or with the people that are winning too consistently. The bookmaker will also suspend betting on those sports events that are feared fixed or are so unpredictable that he is not able to create a point spread. This happens with expansion teams and exhibition ball games, although some bookmakers will take anything.

While the bookie can be "screwed" by being past-posted or having false information used against him, he can also have trouble because of misunderstandings and deceptions in the wager itself. After the race is over, the customer can claim he bet to show or place, not win. He can claim he bet a certain team with an eleven-point spread rather than the eight points he did bet, or he can say he bet the other way. The most common strategy the bookie must guard against is a customer's claim that he bet more on a winner or less on a loser than he actually did. Most bookmakers will write everything down to avoid misunderstanding. One who transacts in person (usually numbers and horse wagers) may write the bet down, give the bettor a copy, and keep a carbon for himself (if he has a writer, the writer will keep a copy). One who transacts over the phone will usually recite the bet back to the person and then write it down in the office. In addition, the book may use a tape recorder as a record; most, however, do not. The following accounts are rather typical.

Off-track betting:

Every bet was written down, so there was no verbal shit, you know? If a guy said two and two [in the daily double, #2 in the first race and #2 in the second race; five times means that the player wants five $2 "tickets" in the double], you know, five times. It wasn't two and five. You understand? They try that shit, so you write it down. You show it to 'em. If he says two and five, you show it to 'im, and "This is what you give me."

Sports:

Q. What would a typical transaction be like?
A. Somebody would call up; I would tell them what the line was; say it, ah, the Giants are underdogs by seven points. If they wanted the Giants, they would say: "I want the Giants fifty times or one hundred times." I would read it back to them: "You want the Giants, you know, one hundred times, right?" "OK." "You got it." And I would hang up. You know, after this went on for an hour and a half, then I would call all the bets in to the guy. Take them down on paper and then call them in [to his boss].

Knowing that customers will take advantage of him when he is down, we can see the importance of a bookmaker's maintaining adequate records. These records are particularly susceptible when he gets raided. The records may be destroyed, and if his business is large enough he will not be able to remember all the bets he took down. Many of his customers know this and will issue him false claims. Since his greatest resource is his integrity and willingness to pay off when he loses, the bookmaker may feel that he has no other choice than to pay the customers.[8]

Since his business is illegal in most states, the bookmaker does not have the legal right to collect debts. As a result, he must rely on his personal resources in order to collect on money owed. The limits to which he is willing to go will depend on his personality, his connections, the amount of money owed relative to his personal resources, how much money the customer has lost in the past, and the customer's demeanor.

When straightening-out day comes and there is no money forthcoming, the bookmaker will listen to the story the gambler has to say. If there is a no-show and a story after, he may feel incensed but he will usually still listen. Also, he will grant up to a week's extension at a time, during which he expects the customer to come up with the money. Until he comes up with the dough, the gambler is "shut off."

Many customers just avoid the bookmaker, either figuring that they will come up with the money some way and just need time or figuring they do not know where they are going to get it and do not want to confront him. The bookmaker has several options in response to this type of action: he can just leave the person alone and let him continue to avoid, he can wait until he confronts the person accidentally on the street and remind him that he owes money, or he can try to contact the gambler. Most bookmakers rely on the third option for about a week, after which the phone calls and visits will trail off into an accidental-confrontation basis. The extent to which the gambler owes money, the bookmaker's predicament, and the gambler's demeanor (from "Fuck you, I ain't payin'" to "Gees, ah, I overextended myself; I'll try to come up with it this week") will determine the amount of harassment. If he knows where the customer works he will call there. Alternatively he will call the gambler at home. If the amount of money owed is large enough, he may tell the employer, wife, and/or parents of the gambler that he owes money; or he may show up at the gambler's house or job.

> Bank or loan company, you could just call 'em or
> stall 'em for a month. The bookmaker you can't

stall. He tells you you have to pay him Monday and
you don't, he will get on the phone and hound you
until he gets it. He comes down to your place of
business, he comes after you, and this harassment.

In the process of trying to get through to the person, either
the bookmaker or his customer may suggest a financial solution. There are three forms of bookmaker-induced solutions
that are generally practiced.[9] These include payment sched-
ules, settlements, and introductions to sources of money, in
decreasing order of frequency.

Most bookmakers are happy just so long as they know they
are going to get so much money a week. They will also shut
the client off until the bill is paid. If the bill is not large, then
the customer may be able to continue gambling at a reduced
level. His credit line is reduced until he has the bill paid.
After this, it is up to the discretion of the bookie as to
whether the old credit line will return.

The second-most-frequent means of resolving the problem
is settling the debt through partial payment. It is a variation
on the bankruptcy theme in legitimate enterprise. Originally it
may be a bookmaker who suggests settlement; but once this
mode is thought of, it can come into fairly regular use and be
exploited by the gambler for his own benefit.

> Ah, I made settlements with a couple of them. I
> owed them twelve thousand and paid 'em six. I
> owed one guy six and he took twenty-five hundred
> when I paid him. . . . [Another bookmaker] I
> think I owed him five grand and I said: "Hey, I
> have no way of paying you." He says, "I've got to
> have this money." I says, "The only thing I can do
> is if you want a settlement." It wasn't even a settle-
> ment. I said, "Maybe I can come up with a few
> bucks, but that's it." He took it. The guy, I think he
> took a thousand dollars.

> You'd give it to the bookmaker. Or you'd short 'em,
> even. You'd borrow, you owe him, you borrow five
> hundred, you tell him, "All I can give you is three

fifty." He'll call you even for it. And you'd bet with
him a month and he'd let you start again. You
know, he knew he had you.

The bookmaker would much prefer full payment and as a result is more likely to suggest a weekly payment schedule, but
if worse comes to worst will accept a settlement. Typically,
after a settlement the gambler is shut off but may resume betting at a later date on a reduced-credit or cash basis.

A final solution is the suggestion by the bookmaker that the
gambler get a loan. Some bookmakers have regular working
relationships with oxies, loan companies, and loan sharks and
steer their delinquent customers to them. The following is an
example of one such working relationship.

I owed the bookmaker money and I didn't have it. I
told him I didn't know where I was gonna get the
money, because I was startin' to get down to the
bottom of the barrel because I couldn't go to too
many more places to get the money. And he sent
me to the loan company, to see the manager of the
loan company. And I went in there and told him
who sent me down there. So I didn't have to say
what I needed the money for because he already
knew. I signed the papers and that was it.

Alternatively the bookmaker may offer to cosign a loan for
the gambler. This tactic, as well as the regular use of loan
companies, is not a regular practice with the majority of
bookmakers. While such arrangements do exist, none of the
bookmakers I interviewed admitted to this. They felt it to be
morally reprehensible.

Q. Did you suggest any ways of how he could get
money?
A. I never told a guy to go to a bank or nothin', because I don't know. I'm probably not cruel enough
to do that; I couldn't put a guy in that situation.

I never cared for Shylocks. Never want to bury

somebody with a Shylock. That's the worst thing you can do to a person.

For those who could not send a person to a bank or a Shylock, there was only one other alternative: hounding. Even this was given up after a week or two. After this period, the customer will be reminded every time they meet or will receive a phone call occasionally. If the bookmaker has a circle of bookmaking friends (which most do), he will pass the word that this gambler "stiffed" him and is a bad credit risk. If the gambler "stiffs" enough bookmakers, sooner or later he will have his credit reduced or be forced to bet on a cash basis only.

What happened, though, Henry, is that I became a bigger bettor than I was an office man. Well, this is when I started owing this bookmaker three thousand dollars, this bookmaker fifteen hundred dollars, this bookmaker a thousand dollars; and I couldn't cover them all. So my reputation was becoming really bad.

I had to gamble on strictly my check every week. I got a couple hundred bucks. I got cash and I owed so many people, bookmakers and everybody, that I was strictly on a cash basis with everybody. I certainly had to do everything on a very small scale.

I can remember bettors winning and I was in situations where I wasn't bettin', I was stuck so much. You know, I couldn't get down with a bookmaker any more, I owed the bookmakers so much money.

Bookmakers who wished to get their money, yet had a reluctant client, used threats of violence and actual violence. Most of the threats were empty and the gamblers knew it. The gamblers reacted to threats they perceived were empty in various fashions: reminded the bookmaker that they weren't going anywhere, or reacted with a counterthreat of going to the police or of doing the bookie himself bodily harm. In addition, bookies know they will not get any money if the gambler is dead, and the gamblers are all too willing to remind them of the fact.

Actual use of violence is rare. When a customer fails to pay, he has probably lost much money to the bookmaker in the past. Those customers who have lost much money over a long period and then fail to come up with an average week or two's worth of betting are commonly harassed but then written off.

> He's had to shrug off money. See, when a guy has to shrug off money, there was one guy in particular: "TV." He called up and said, "This is TV." I knew his voice, anyway. He owned a TV and appliance store. Now, TV was a big bettor. He would bet anywhere from one hundred fifty to four hundred in horse bets per day. Flat bets, not twenty here and twenty there. He would bet one hundred dollars parlay and one hundred to win on each. That was, like, his standard bet on two horses. But, so TV ended up out of business and owing him maybe for, like, two weeks of losing. Probably like, ah, a few thousand, OK? So, all he can do is shrug it off. Meanwhile, he's probably beat TV for about fifty thousand dollars in the last two years, so, really, how much can you go after the guy? What are you going to do? "Hey, TV, you owe me three thousand dollars." He was fair in all senses of the word. You know, whereas if, OK, say a guy hit him for five thousand last week on a couple a horse bets and now the guy bets fifteen hundred and he doesn't pay. Now he is going to go after the money.

Given the nature of the sample and the number of bookmakers hung up, it is surprising that more violence does not occur. The beatings that the gamblers receive are a product of a deliberate "screwing" perpetrated by the customer on the bookmaker. The customer may have won money from the book, but later, when he lost, failed to pay. Also, the bookmaker may feel that the guy is trying a deliberate setup—trying to "pull a fast one" on him.

The more organized the bookmaker and the more prone to the use of violence, the more screwings are going to be avenged. Even with all this, just the *show* of violence is adequate to get people moving.[10] Bookmakers and their collectors want to utilize just enough fear or violence to get the money up. Of those gamblers I interviewed, two had been slapped around and two felt sufficiently threatened by bookmakers or their collectors that they feared for their lives and those of members of their families. One of the bookmakers was beaten up by a layoff man's muscle after the layoff man suspected (justifiably) that the bookmaker was trying to take advantage of him by using inside information he was receiving. Of the runners (agents) interviewed, two worked for bookmakers who had used muscle in the past. Two of the bookmakers themselves admitted resorting to muscle: one used it himself only once and another occasionally hired muscle but only for substantial debts where he felt he had been screwed.

Screwing the customers

Bookmakers not only protect themselves against their customers; they may also take advantage of them by moving the line and failing to pay. This is more likely to happen with small bookmakers and compulsive gamblers turned bookmakers than with mob-oriented and larger bookmakers.

Moving the line is done by the bookmaker in order to balance his books. It is also done to try to "catch the middle" by taking advantage of customers who are "dumb shits." This type of client will say, "What's the point spread on the Team A game?" The bookmaker, knowing his client likes and will bet on Team A, will offer Team A at 8½ or 9 points instead of the 6 points he is offering the rest of his clients. (In other words, for this customer to collect on his bet, Team A must win by 8½ or 9 points instead of 6.) After this customer has bet Team A at 8½ or 9 points, he will call another bookmaker and put money on Team A at 6 points. He "catches the middle" if Team A wins by 7 or 8 points; otherwise, he just breaks even or, at worst, the customer loses and pays the vigorish. This is a true no-lose situation.

Although I ran into customers who intentionally "hung up" bookmakers, none of the bookmakers interviewed who failed to pay customers did so intentionally. In fact, three discussed loans they took out in order to be able to stay in business. Those who failed to pay customers were at the end of a long line of combined gambling and bookmaking. Their resources for cash were closed off (both legal and illegal in some cases), and they had no other alternative except to stall off their customers. They would turn to exactly the same tactics that their sports customers had used on them (if they were sports books). They would tell them stories, and fail to meet with them, and tell more stories.

The customer's main reaction to failure to pay usually depends on the amount owed. His first line of action will be to approach the bookmaker over the phone or the bookie's place of employment. He may even offer to "settle" or suggest a payment plan. He may threaten and otherwise harass him also. If his efforts are in vain and the person who "stiffed" him was a runner, he could yell to his boss and try to force payment in that fashion. The most common tactic, however, is to complain to his friends about what kind of a "piker" the bookmaker is in the hopes of getting them to stop placing their action with him (the bookmaker). This tactic is usually successful. This is because the bookmaker has broken rule number one of the relationship.

> Nobody would bet with me any more at the end. They knew I wouldn't pay 'em if they won.

THE BOOKMAKER'S SUPPORT

Only one bookmaker I knew claimed to have no business relationships with other bookmakers, higher-ups, employees, or partners. The entrepreneur (bookmaker) must protect his business and must *lay off* excess action (if he gets two hundred dollars on a horse that will pay twenty to one but he doesn't have four thousand dollars in case it wins, he needs to throw off [lay off] the action to another bookmaker). His business may get too big and he may have to hire agents (also called *runners*) to work for him. The police may be threatening him and he may need to hire someone (called a *writer*) to write the bets down somewhere else so he will not have betting slips in his possession. If he cannot collect on debts, the bookmaker might need *collectors* (alternatively called "bonebreakers"). Collectors are rarely used in the bookmaking business, because they charge a fee. The final actor in the bookmaking business is the *banker*. The banker may be a legitimate partner who is providing some working capital, but more likely the "banker" is a sucker who is being fleeced in a common con game.

Layoff

In order to protect his business, the bookmaker must be able to have a safety cushion. The layoff operation is that cushion. All the bookmakers but one stated that they used a layoff operation. How this works will vary with the type of gambling, the area of the country, and whether it is organized by the "wise guys" (called "the Office" in New England). For the most part, however, the bookie has two options: he can lay off with "wise guys," "big boys," "Mafiosi," "connected people," "dese, dems, and dose guys," or with "freelance books" like himself. Here I am assuming our "typical" bookmaker is free-lance, which most appear to be, since most are small-time operators in non-organized areas. Even in the organized areas covered by this research, most of the bookmakers are not organized. This is more so with sports than with other operations. Estimates range from 50 to 90 per cent unorganized, with consensus near 90 per cent. The numbers racket evidenced the highest degree of organization, with virtually all numbers books being hooked into "connected" books.

Several strategies are taken with respect to layoff operations. In sports operations, ideally, the bookmaker would like to have his bets balance. If Dallas is playing New York he would like to have an equal amount of money bet on each side. This way he would make an easy profit—the vig (vigorish) or interest he charges. Life is not so simple. He may get five thousand on New York but only two thousand on Dallas. If he keeps it all and New York bettors win, he will have to dig up three thousand (minus the vigorish on the two thousand dollars he collects—either two hundred dollars or four hundred dollars depending on whether he is charging a 10 or a 20 per cent handling fee). In this case he can get "destroyed" (alternatively called "buried" or put out of business). He has several options. First, he may try to get rid of three thousand dollars' worth of action on New York (or pick up three thousand on Dallas) by transacting with other bookmakers. He is balancing. Second, he feels that New York will not cover the point spread. Let us say, for simplicity, that New York is favored to win by six points. In this case he feels that Dallas will win or New York will win by less than six points—if New York wins by six on the nose there is no bet. Here he may decide to hold all the action (not use the layoff operation at all) and try to win three thousand plus the vigorish on five thousand. He is *taking a side*. The compulsive gambler is more likely to take a side. He may still lay off but lay off two thousand of the New York action instead of three thousand. Alternatively, he may decide to lay off all of the New York action if he feels they are going to cover the spread (win by more than six points).

In off-track betting, the bookmaker will lay off those bets that go over his "hazard." The hazard is the amount of money the bookmaker has set aside for paying off customers. He will use the layoff operation because if he refuses to take bets after a certain amount he may lose customers. Heavy action on a single horse will occur, for example, if someone in the factory or bar where he takes the horse action has a "hot tip" and spreads the word around. If he gets one hundred dollars' worth of action on a twenty-to-one-shot horse or dog, and has a one thousand dollar hazard, he may lay off fifty dollars' worth. Again, as in the sports-betting situation, he may think the horse is a "stiff" and might hold it himself.

In the numbers operation the need for layoff is greater, since numbers pay off at anywhere from 450–1 to 750–1 odds (the most common recounted was 600–1 odds). A group of bets adding up to even $10 on any one number means there is a potential payoff of $4,500 at 450–1 odds or $7,500 at

750–1 odds. As a result, there is a high degree of organization in the numbers racket, with smaller banks laying off to larger banks that lay off to even larger banks.

The layoff works on a *make-up* basis. Once a week, the bookmaker and the layoff man will straighten out (once a day for numbers action). If they made eleven hundred dollars' profit the first week, the bookmaker will make a certain percentage of that profit (anywhere from 25 to 50 per cent). If they lose one thousand dollars the next week, there is a one-thousand-dollar deficit that must be made up before the bookmaker can make any money. If they break even the third week, the one thousand dollars must still be made up the following week. If on the fourth week they make five thousand dollars, the one thousand dollars will be deducted (made up) and the bookmaker and the layoff man will split the remaining profit on the predefined commission basis. The following excerpt is from a man on a 50 per cent commission basis.

> I used to call bets in for other guys. They would say, "Put this in for me, put this in for me." You know. They thought that I was just being a nice guy puttin' the bets in for them. All the time I was getting 50 per cent of the action. Fifty per cent sounds good, right?
> Q. Right.
> A. It is only 50 per cent of the profit. If you go in the hole, you got to come out of the hole first.
> Q. You were on a 50 per cent make-up?
> A. Yeh.

The layoff operations are used by the bookmakers to protect themselves, but they are also utilized for personal betting. Since the bookies are making a percentage of the profits, they can use the layoff operations for cheaper betting. There is a catch, of course. They have cheaper betting for *net* losses. To help clarify this: The bookmaker bets $1,000 of his own money and loses to the layoff man. If he is on a 50 per cent make-up, he owes only $550 (assuming that 10 per cent is added on for vigorish). The second week, he may win $1,000 and he receives this from the layoff man. Until this $1,000 is made up, he must pay the layoff man *in full*. The third week, he loses $1,100 ($1,000 plus $100 vigorish). He must pay $1,000 and then one half of the remainder, which is $50, out of the $100 vigorish. The fourth week, he loses $2,200. He pays one half of this, or $1,100. The fifth week, he wins $500. He collects this, but now he must make up the money the layoff man has lost ($500). The sixth week, he loses $2,200. He pays $500 in order to catch up plus one half of the remainder, which is $850.

	Bookmaker bets	Bookmaker wins	Bookmaker loses	Pays layoff man	Receives from layoff man	Now needs to make up
Week #1	$1,000		$1,000 bet 100 vig —— $1,100	½ of $1,100		$000
Week #2	$1,000	$1,000			$1,000	$1,000
Week #3	$1,000		$1,000 bet 100 vig —— $1,100	$1,000 (to make up) ½ of $100 ($50) —— $1,050 total		$000
Week #4	$2,000		$2,000 bet 200 vig —— $2,200	½ of $2,200		$000
Week #5	$500	$500			$500	$500
Week #6	$2,000		$2,000 bet 200 vig —— $2,200	$500 (to make up) ½ of $1,700 ($850) —— $1,350 total		$000

Presumably his customers are paying him the bet plus vigorish when they lose.

Betting with the layoff man has other advantages as well. He will usually give the gambler an extra day or two to pay him, because he knows that the bookmaker must collect from his customers first. The gambling bookmaker can take advantage of this extra day or two. This period of time for some gamblers can be an "eternity." It is time to go to the track or a card game or dice game in order to get enough money to pay off the layoff man. It also will allow him time to get the money elsewhere if these sources fail.

Some layoff men will allow betting after the events start. This is most likely with sports. It is nonexistent with horse- and dog-race betting. The gambling bookmaker will utilize this edge to fullest advantage by gradually stringing the layoff men into later and later betting and in some cases using quarter- and half-time scores as hedges in personal betting. For some, even this doesn't help.

> **Q.** Could you lay off after the game started?
> **A.** Yeh. I did many times. I've bet games where I knew the half-time score and still lost.

Using the layoff man may have its disadvantages as well. Some of the layoff men are not nice people, especially when in the higher finance brackets. If the bookmaker lays off but the customer does not pay, the layoff man is still going to want his money. He will put pressure on the bookmaker, who will in turn feel he has to put pressure on his customers. At least one bookmaker took out a loan to pay the layoff man after several customers "stiffed" him.

An alternate way of making money from the layoff opera- tion is to create business and use the differences in the line between layoff men to win money. In this case, two or more layoff operations are used at the same time.

Due to the mood of the public, layoff men will change the line so they can receive balanced betting in each game. In baseball,[11] let us say Oakland plays the White Sox and Oakland is favored. The bettors are more likely to bet them if the line is 7–8 than if the line is 8–9. In the first instance the bettor will have to lay out (pay) $8 if Oakland loses, but they will have to pay $9 with the second line (8–9). If the layoff man has too much action on the White Sox and the line is 8–9, he may change it to 7½–8½ and then 7–8 in order to balance out the gross play. (One "connected" layoff operation, for example, moves the line ½ point for every $10,000 in excess on any one team over its opponent.) In baseball, betting is based on odds rather than point spreads. Odds of 7–8 means that if the gambler bets on the favorite he receives only $5 if it wins and must pay out $8 if it loses. On the other hand, if the gambler bets on the underdog he receives $7 if it wins and only pays out $5 if it loses.

Like the gambler looking for "middle shots" (catching the middle), the bookmaker also looks for discrepancies in the line between layoff men. These discrepancies exist because the public in one city may be betting differently from the public in another city.

Using this discrepancy, the bookmaker can hope to make commission off one layoff man at another's expense. In the Oakland–White Sox game, City A may have Oakland favored at 7–8, while City B has Oakland favored at 8–9. The bookmaker will bet on Oakland at 8 in City A (here he "bets the favorite"—bets the long odds in the 7–8 odds that City A offers—he pays $8 if Oakland loses and receives $5 if they win). *At the same time,* he bets on the underdog White Sox at 8 in City B (here he "bets short"—bets the short odds in the 8–9 odds that City B offers—he receives $8 if the White Sox lose and pays $5 if they win). In either case, he makes a commission at one layoff man's expense.

Oakland vs. White Sox

Results	City A line 7–8 bet favorite at 8	City B line 8–9 bet "short" at 8
Case A if White Sox win	the gambler loses $8 pays $4 (keeps $4 commission)	wins $8 collects $8
Case B if Oakland wins	the gambler wins $5 collects $5	loses $5 pays $2.50 (keeps $2.50 commission)

Over the season, one layoff man will lose more than the other and the bookmaker will make money from that layoff operation. This strategy was recounted by one of the bookmakers interviewed. An "outlaw" group (no connections to wider, organized-crime syndicates) figured out what he was doing, failed to pay him fourteen thousand dollars they owed him, and beat him up.

The runner (agent)

Any bookmaker who handles many customers will have a basic problem of maintaining contact with them every day. A simple way of solving the logistics problem is to hire agents who will work for a certain percentage of the profits or a set percentage of gross "play." If the runner is involved in horse action, he will pick up bets (usually in a factory or a bar) and "run" them to the bookie or phone them in prior to post time. In some cases the runner just collects the bets during the day and straightens them out later. The bookie puts full faith in him. But this kind of faith is rare. Here the bookie may ask the runner to perform layoff services for him at the race track in the hopes of changing the odds and thereby lowering the payoff should one of the horses he has a lot of action on win.[12] If the bookie wishes to lay off with another bookmaker, he will either do it himself or use another employee (writer) for this purpose (if he has one). The numbers activity is more complex. There are more agents working and (New York style) "runners" acting as individuals who collect ("run") slips from the agents and give them to a bookmaker who may have a large array of persons working for him in a "bank" (place where slips and money are collected and tabulated and money given out). The parlay-card business appears to be run like the numbers racket. For reasons to be discussed subsequently, sports action (that is, straight sports betting) has shown to be a dismal failure in the utilization of runners.

Runners are paid in several fashions. Those who just collect slips and run them to a central location are paid a salary. Other runners are semiautonomous employees. They develop their own customers and usually receive a certain percentage of profits on a make-up basis. What the percentage is on the make-up will depend on whether the bookmaker must lay off action. If he is getting 50 per cent on a make-up basis from the layoff man, he cannot very well give the runners 50 per cent. In this case he will give them anywhere from 15 to 35 per cent of the net profit. For that action he does not lay off, he would pay the runners 35 to 50 per cent of the profit after make-up. This commission pay is usually used in sports and horses. The numbers and parlay cards work differently. In these situations, runners will have runners working for them. The higher up the ladder the person goes, the more he is likely to work on a make-up (that is, receiving a certain percentage of net profit). The low-rung runners will get a certain flat percentage of whatever they turn in. This percentage varies from 15 to 25 per cent and may go as low as getting free parlay cards to play or a free number.

In addition to getting paid a flat amount of what he turns in, the low-rung runner usually "makes it both ways." His customers often pay him a certain amount (5 to 10 per cent) when they win. This is so common among numbers players as to be a firmly entrenched institution. Some runners automatically deduct it prior to paying the customer.

Whatever method is used to pay runners, involves risk. The runner may "hold back" action (that is, fail to turn it all in to the bookmaker). In fact, *all* the runners I knew held back action. All the runner has to see is that there are too few hits (a win is called a "hit") to really worry about paying off if they win. He does this, of course, knowing that there are certain risks involved if he fails to pay.

> If I didn't like what they were pickin' I used to keep the money. If they hit I would be in hot water. I'd cheat on them. Then if they hit I had to pay 'em off.

If the runner fails to pay, the customer has two choices, keep quiet or bitch and moan. If the people the runner is dealing with are harmless, he has nothing to fear, just a cutoff of his operation. If the people are the "wise guys" and the amount is substantial, the horror stories that are read about in newspapers become all too real. Several stories have been reported of people disappearing and being beaten up because the runner failed to pay off a customer.

Two of the bookmakers I interviewed have been put out of business for a short span of time because runners collected money from customers but failed to give the bookie the money. When some of the customers hit, the bookies felt obliged to pay them off. This was enough to put them out of action for a while.

While the bookmaker can hire runners to take horse, parlay-card, or numbers action, it is impossible to have runners who will give him any appreciable amount of sports action. It does not take long (the average length of time is two weeks!) for a runner (agent) to see that he can make money by holding back action. For example, if the Dallas Cowboys are playing the New York Giants and five hundred dollars is bet on Dallas and five hundred on New York, he realizes he is a fool if he gives the money to the bookmaker. A bookmaker put it this way:

> Agents you don't need in sports. You see, an agent on sports, he sees what you are handling, what you've got. You see, if his stuff starts coming in both ways, now I might as well become a bookmaker too. "Why should I call up [name] and give him five hundred on this side and five hundred on the other side? He's gonna end up makin' fifty dollars [the vigorish] for nothin'. I'll keep both those bets and keep the fifty dollars for myself."
>
> Q. Right.
> A. See? You don't need 'em.

The runner becomes *both* runner *and* book at the same time. He is a book for the action that he wants and a runner for the action he does not. In a sense, his bookmaker becomes his layoff man without knowing it.

The runner can take advantage of the situation in other ways as well. He can use the position to past-post the bookmaker. If the runner is a card or dice hustler, let the bookmaker beware.

Card and dice hustlers have various "scams" (schemes) for taking money from different people. They like to past-post, but their favorite is what they call "the locked-bag trick."

In this scheme a rookie bookmaker is approached and asked if he would like to have a runner working for him. Most new bookies are only too glad to get whatever action they can, so they agree. The "runner" (who is bringing bets from his "friends" at work or at a local bar) uses a bank bag with the zipper and locks and key. Prior to post time each day, the "runner" brings the bag with slips and the money to cover those slips inside. The "runner" keeps the key so the whole affair can be kept "honest" (that is, so the bookie can't slip in a few losing tickets in place of winning ones). After the races are run, the "runner" and the bookie go over the "bets" and straighten out on a daily basis. When the card hustler thinks the bookmaker is ripe he will add a few extra dollars into the bank bag prior to giving it to the bookmaker. There may be $1,000 worth of slips but $1,250 in the bag. That night, the "runner" opens the bag with the key; he has several winning tickets (betting slips) in his palm—card and dice hustlers are good at palming cards and dice, so this is no problem. The "runner" makes as if he is taking the tickets (which, all totaled, are valued at $250) out of the bag, but he is really only taking them out of his palm.

> You know, as you reach in the bag and pull them out, you got, like, five or six big-winning hits on there. You got, like, a one-hundred-dollar parlay with two limit horses (the horses will win with a maximum payoff) and it comes to, like, four thousand. You got one hundred fifty to win on a twenty-dollar horse, there is another fifteen hundred. Bang, you got the guy for like seven or eight thousand dollars. Just out of the bag. And he has got to pay you, because you got to take all this money and pay all these guys supposedly that you are running the action for. Usually puts him out of business.

THE WRITER (OFFICE MAN)

The writer (alternatively called an office man) exists solely to protect the bookmaker against arrest by the police. The writer takes telephone calls from the bookmaker and records the bets so the bookmaker will not have betting slips in his possession. In larger offices (usually organized-crime-connected), the writer acts as a clerk. He takes phone calls from customers and records the bets. In this case he may work on a salary basis. In smaller operations, the bookmaker either hires him or brings him in as a partner. In any case, he will receive a percentage of the profits. If he is an employee, he may also receive a salary, but most partnerships are on a 50–50 split.

The division of labor usual in such a setup is that the book-maker takes the bets from the customers and telephones them to the writer. The bookmaker usually is calling from a bar, a newsstand, work, or a club. The writer's functions include taking down the bets over the phone and figuring out the win-nings. Since figuring results can be quite complex, especially in "junk" action (the added goodies that bookmakers use to attract customers), a major qualification to be a writer is to be a "good figurer" (have a good head for figures). The writer also takes care of layoff action. If he gets too much ac-tion on one horse, dog, team, or number, the writer will auto-matically call up another bookmaker to see if he can take the action. In addition to these functions, the writer may act as a collector. This occurs only when action is taken on credit (usually sports action—track animals are not usually taken on credit). He will go out on "straightening-out day"—any designated day of the week for collection or payoff. A final task the writer may perform is treasurer. In fulfilling this function the bookmaker is most vulnerable. Several compul-sive gamblers who were writers played with the money that was used to pay off the customers. Here the situation is quite analogous to embezzlement.

Q. You quit makin' book. How did that happen?
A. Well, because we were supposed to have some-thing like five thousand dollars; I was the treasurer and I had something like five dollars. My partner always thought I had the money and I got kinda scared, 'cause if I got hit I knew I was in big trou-ble. And, ah, we had a system where he would take all the calls. They knew he was bookin' but nobody knew I was, so I was the writer and he would call me and he was the only one that had my number

and I used to do all the wiring (calling the layoff man) and the figuring and all that. In desperation one day, ah, of course all the bets were supposed to come through him and I told him well, here I am with my *partner* now, right? Here's my partner now, now I'm in debt and I want to get out of debt, so, ah, I would have the paper here while he was booking and I would be puttin' in bets. I would tell him: "My brother-in-law called me and he wants to put this in and that." You know? And then, finally, one day what happened I had put in a good bet one day and, ah, said: "Maybe we ought to give this off [to the layoff man]." He thought we had five thousand dollars and we only had you know. Well, ah, I remember this first horse won and it was a tremendous bet and he needed to win. I can remember that night I had to wait till seven o'clock to get a Buffalo station to get that result. And I stood here in this house walking and praying. I would walk in the pantry and say, "God, give me this one, that's it, no more." And finally, when seven o'clock come and I went into the room and I had the radio; I had my ear; it was a faint station, and, ah, sure enough the other horse had won.

Q. You won the five thousand dollars, or . . . ?"

A. Yeh.

Q. You were clear again.

A. I was clear.

Several of the bookmakers who had writers mentioned problems they had with them. Those who collected and acted as their own treasurers had no such problems.

Partnerships

Partnerships in the gambling entrepreneurial business are quite common and develop in several ways. A bookmaker may run into trouble with the law and decide that he should not have betting slips in his possession. As a result, he decides that he can use a writer to take bets over the phone. Another bookmaker wants to take horse action but can do it only five days a week, so he gets another guy to take bets on the sixth day. A card hustler is asked if he wants in on a chopped game so they can fleece two ways instead of one. A person wants to run two tables in his card game and needs a second guy to help cut the pot. A kid who is running numbers or selling parlay cards decides to cut a friend in on it. However partnerships arise, there is always the potential for conflict.

The type of conflict that can arise in partnerships will depend on the type of gambling involved. The partner may "subway" the profits. He may decide to put the profits in his pocket. The extent to which this occurs can be planned, as when hustlers go in partners with a sucker, or it can be the unplanned act of a guy just "borrowing" from joint funds, much as an employee or legitimate-business partner would embezzle from the business. Alternatively, a partner in a chopped game can "subway" some of the cash he has chopped from the game. None of those who were partners as youths mentioned screwing their friends. As in all partnerships and business relationships, the degree of trust that one person has in another will determine the extent to which trust can be violated. Since the writer is in the most trusted position, it is here that the bookmaker is most vulnerable in partnerships.

The final route to partnerships is for suckers. Several gamblers get together and suggest to a sucker that they all go in partnership in a bookmaking venture. Each will put up an equal proportion of the money (or some variant thereof). In the process of the bookmaking activities, one of two things happens. The business venture "fails" miserably and they lose "their" money, or one of the "partners" (usually a hustler from out of town) has absconded with "their" money. I have interviewed two gamblers who were conned out of money and at least four who conned others.

"BOOKMAKERS ARE THEIR OWN BEST CUSTOMERS"

Both compulsive and non-gambling bookmakers know that bookmaking and gambling do not mix. Gamblers who bet take sides.

Q. If you had to instruct me how to make book, what would you tell me?

A. First of all, don't be a gambler. That would be the first thing. You got to know how much you can handle. In other words, you are not going to take more than you can chew. Once you start handicapping them, either you are going to go one way or the other.

The bookmaker who is strictly a businessman does not gamble. He feels all the other guys out there think they are the smartest handicappers in the world. When they bet there is no doubt in their minds as to who will win. He knows that if he starts thinking this way, he will take unnecessary chances. The business is risky enough (the failure rate is incredibly large) without adding additional problems.

For those who combine gambling and bookmaking, the mixture adds to the possibilities for more gambling and more risk-taking as well. New avenues for betting are opened. The gambler knows he can bet with the customers and "take shots" that he wouldn't normally have taken. While he may be a twenty-dollars-an-event bettor, some of his customers will be fifty-dollars- or a hundred-dollars-per-event bettors. (This is most likely with, but not restricted to, sports bettors.) If the person bets on a team (or a horse) he thinks will lose, he may back all of the action rather than tell his customer that he cannot handle it.

Q. If you were to tell me how to make book, what would you tell me?

A. The most important thing is not to bet yourself. It has cost me thousands.

Q. How did your personal gambling and bookmaking conflict?

A. That was my only problem. I combined them. If I really like the team they were playing against, then I could make one hundred twenty, I could only lose a hundred. . . . I've gotten beat; many times I've gotten beat. But I've got a big mouth, and I have a tendency to swallow it. Some days you got a feeling, gees if anybody bets like, for example, Chicago Bears today, these bastards don't have a chance. The first three guys call you up and bet a hundred on the Bears. Oh, gees a chance to make three hundred sixty dollars. You know they can't win; there's no way they can beat it. So you put it in your pocket. By some miracle, a guy kicks a field goal, or hits the goal post, or something, and they win. Bang, you've ruined three hundred dollars.

Alternatively, his customers may bet on more teams and/or more races than he would have bet. If he feels the horses are "stiffs" or the teams bet are "going sour," he will hold the action. He feels he has "easy money." As a result of either of these two actions, the bookie has a greater stake in the results. He will begin to listen to more and more events on the radio or TV with greater excitement and intensity. Once he is a thousand-dollar bettor, two-dollar bets lose meaning. His own action, with his bookmakers and at the track, will be affected as a result. A frequent comment of the compulsive gambler-entrepreneur was that bookmaking (or other related activities) intensified the financial problems he had. The money made by booking was used to support the added gambling.

These two friends of mine asked me to come and book horses. So I was bookin' horses in the tavern. That lasted for about a year. That helped put me in debt, and all the money that I had won in the accident case, all that money had to pay for what I went in debt. The only reason I went in debt was because I was gambling much more than I was makin'. I wasn't satisfied with this.

Not only will bookmaking increase involvement because of the increased stake in the outcome, it can also change the outlook toward certain forms of gambling. Several of those who bet only sports became horse bettors as well, and at least one who was a dice and card player became involved in horses and then became involved in sports. Several persons were introduced to numbers betting through bookmaking and eventually were betting thirty–forty dollars per day in numbers action alone.

## CHAPTER VI

Getting Money from Lending Institutions

A compulsive gambler must get money to finance his gambling. So he borrows from banks, loan companies, credit unions, oxies, and Shylocks, and makes use of credit cards (BankAmericard, Master Charge, and American Express being the most common) and overextended checking accounts.[1] Let's take a look at how he gets this money.

LEGITIMATE LENDING INSTITUTIONS

Most compulsive gamblers get money from lending institutions. Some finagle more than others, as shown below.

Number of Simultaneous Loans Held
by Compulsive Gamblers

Number of Loans	Gamblers[2]
0	6
1–4	22
5–8	15
9–12	5
13–16	0
17+	2
Total number of compulsive gamblers	50

Now, many people in the general population could conceivably hold one to four loans at the same time. But few would hold five loans and more concurrently. Over a twenty-year period, if a gambler takes out five loans and holds them concurrently, he will visit banks and loan companies one hundred or more times for taking out and refinancing loans.[3] Gamblers use lies and deception as well as criminal fraud in order to get these loans. Also, most rely on defects in lending-institution policy.

Gamblers rely on role-playing in the borrowing setting: putting themselves in the position of the person they are asking for money and searching for acceptable rationales for needing it.

> You'd have to look at yourself in the eyes of a bank and see if you were a banker if you would lend me money if I said certain things. You just have to find your ideas on, ah, I always looked at things from another person's point of view. If I was a banker and a guy came up to me with a story to borrow money, what would I accept. There are certain things I would accept as a legitimate reason.

And, of course, there are certain reasons that are not acceptable; gambling is one of them.

When the gambler engages in role-playing, he sees that certain stories will be acceptable to some people but not to others. Whether or not they are in fact does not matter. It is only the gambler's perception of the situation that counts. One bank, for example, accepted a gambling problem as an excuse but required an extra cosigner.

The stories used to get loans (from friends and relatives, as well as banks and loan companies) ranged from playing the nice guy—

> I remember saying it was for my nephew's tuition. Goodhearted, nice guy. My nephew's tuition, you know, he was in a poor family and he was studying hard and I wanted to help him out. . . . They thought I was a wonderful fella.

—to vacations, "personal" loans, buying stocks, anniversary presents, hospital bills, emergency situations, car repairs, household appliances and furniture, and consolidation of other bills at the small-loan level to home improvement and business improvement or expansion at the larger-loan level.

While stories are necessary, the gambler may also put on various fronts to enhance the possibility of being given a loan. One perceptive gambler talked of getting $7.50 haircuts and wearing three-piece suits on "tough" loans and using righteous indignation whenever necessary to achieve desired results. Alternatively, some of the gamblers put extra acting ability into their stories to gain their loans.

> One time, I told them that my brother had an awful car accident. It didn't look like he was going to live and my mother and father desperately wanted to go up there to see him but I needed seven hundred dollars more to send them up there. I was laughing to myself at the time, because I caught a guy that was really, the poor guy, I could actually see tears coming down his cheeks.

As the gambler gets more and more loans, he will gradually realize that if he puts down all the loans he has, the bank, loan company, or credit union may turn him down for a loan. The steps he takes at this stage will depend on other factors of experience that will help determine his access to credit.

Determinants of credit

Age, background and reputation, occupation, marital status, awareness of lender operations, help of gambling friends, degree of complicity on the part of the lending institution (*victim-precipitated fraud*),[4] and past credit of the gambler all affect credit.

The most important of these is *age*. Banks and loan companies will not give loans to people under eighteen years of age unless they have an older person as a cosigner. Failure to obtain legal resources when young may mean the juvenile will turn to alternative avenues for funding (to friends or to illegal means).

After age, *background* and *reputation* are important to lending institutions. Gamblers who have relatives who are well known in the community are more likely to get larger loans just on their signature than are other gamblers.[5] And, of course, they could fall back on these relatives to cosign loans for them. Along the same lines, those in business can use the company name as a resource for loans. All the gamblers I knew with loans totaling fifty thousand dollars or more had a business they could use for collateral. Several used phony financial statements to get loans to "beef up inventory" or "improve the business." At least one gambler mentioned using the financial statement of a business that had folded several years previously. Businessmen also used suppliers to get loans for them for improvements that were never made.

While business ownership helps at one end of the scale for getting loans, the non-owner must hold down a *job*. If he doesn't have one, he may have to enlist the aid of a friend in creating one. The following gambler tells how he asked a fellow gambler who owned a barroom to state that he was employed there tending bar, so he could get a loan.[6]

> I told him I was going up to borrow some money and would it be all right if I gave him as a reference to say I was working there the last few years for one hundred fifty dollars a week plus tips. And he said sure.

Marital status and *domicile* also affect credit. If a gambler is single and living alone, he has fewer problems than if he is married or living with his parents. The presence of a wife or parents in front of whom he wants to maintain respectability means that the gambler has to apply for confidential loans or forge his wife's signature if that is necessary; he also has to have the loan payment book mailed elsewhere (get a post-office box or meet the mailman as a move designed to prevent discovery). However, marriage increases the chances of home ownership and hence ability to get loans on that basis.

Of equal importance is the gambler's *awareness of lending-institution operations*. Two gamblers I knew used to work in loan companies, and three worked as new- and used-car salesmen. A product of these connections was an insider's knowledge of how credit bureaus work. They become aware of the holes in credit operations, knew what things credit bureaus can and cannot check, and as a result, knew what they could lie about on credit applications. Later in their career, when loans started piling up, they utilized this information for maximum effectiveness. An ex-loan-company official who had nine loans for "good chunks of dough, anywhere from fifteen hundred to twenty-eight hundred apiece," had the following to say:

> **Q.** What types of things would they check and wouldn't they check?
> **A.** Ah, they were sloppy about checking income, very sloppy. Ah, I always gave them only my best loans, the ones that I was super de luxe on. Ah, the ones that I would be reluctant to pay would be the ones that I didn't feel they would check; for example, small loan companies. At that time, credit bureaus would not supply that information. Now they do, but at that time they didn't.

These gamblers also took out ninety-day notes at banks, which are also not part of credit-bureau information.

Gamblers also receive inside information of the above sort from other gamblers, occasionally at GA meetings. The more common method of communicating this is in the subculture of losers, where tips are shared for mutual benefit. For example, when Master Charge and other credit-card operations first started, the fact that you could have more than one Master Charge card (and hence more than one loan) was widespread knowledge among certain gambling groups.

Victim-precipitated fraud

In the course of his borrowing efforts, the gambler will soon find out that the banks, credit unions, and loan companies he deals with are quite sloppy in checking out certain things. They are free with their money and are frequently all too happy to lend out cash. Of course, for a gambler in trouble this is great. All of this leads to exploitation of the situation by the gambler. The "victim"—in this case a lending institution that may wind up with a bankruptcy or an amortized

loan—precipitates the fraud through the following eight practices: confidential loans; refinancing policies; failure to check
basic facts on loan applications; failure to have the cosigner
appear (or in some cases even the signer himself); overea-
gerness to get loan customers, which leads to various types of
advertisement and suggestions of tactics not previously
thought of; desire to help others in need; involvement in the
fraud itself; and finally complicity with bookmakers. For the
most part, loan companies are more hasty than credit unions,
which in turn are more hasty than banks.

What gamblers—especially the married ones—like best
about lending policies is the *confidential loan*. Under the conditions of this type of loan (about which finance companies
appear to be freer than credit unions or banks), the lending
institution official stamps NO CORRESPONDENCE on the loan
application. In this case, no mail and no phone calls are allowed for routine matters. It is also possible to keep the book
at the institution itself so all records are kept there. Of course,
confidentiality is kept only if loan payments are made within
a reasonable (the definition of reasonable varies with the institution) period. Otherwise letters are sent and phone calls
are made. The gambler uses various lies in order to obtain
these confidential loans, such as "buying a surprise gift for
my wife" or "doing something to help someone out, but my
wife would be against it."

Compulsive gamblers also like *refinancing policies*. The
gambler's career bobs up and down with winning and losing
streaks. His losing may be extended over a long period of
time and he may need more money several months after he
took out a loan. In order to refinance, many of the finance
companies and credit unions would invent or go along with
any excuse just to protect themselves.

> Well, they'd check your book, and see this guy pays
> regular. And has been in debt to us for the last
> twenty years. "Give him six hundred dollars," and
> they'd say, "Well, we have got to put something
> down for a reason." "OK, repair my car." "You
> can't put that down." "Why not?" "Well, we put
> that down the last six times."

Q. They were complicit in your loans?
A. Yeh, then they didn't know [or care to know] what it was for, if they knew they'd get their money back. "Well, we can't put down repairing the car." "I'm buying furniture." "Furniture!" They'd put that down. They would do this; they didn't care.

Comments such as "With all the furniture I should have my own furniture company," "I must have bought the same refrigerator eighty times," and "I could have staffed an office-equipment company" are exceedingly common. Many gamblers are strung along continually for long periods of time, by the same loan companies, with constant refinancing.

Just as the banks are less likely to refinance, they are also more likely to check basic information. The furniture-company or used-car salesman may be called to verify a sale, the employer will be called to check out employment, and a credit check will be made that will be more thorough than that done by the finance company or the credit union.

At the time this failure to check things out occurs, the gamblers feel they are receiving "manna from heaven," a "godsend." "It was just great." However, for some of those who join Gamblers Anonymous and resolve to pay back their debts, there is intense bitterness about these particular failures in policy.

I mean, if they had checked my credit in the first place I wouldn't have got these loans. I wasn't even working at the time. They should leave me alone. So they're part wrong just as I was for taking it. You know.

Another common failure on the part of the lending institution is the practice of giving the gambler the loan contract and having the cosigner (usually the wife) sign without the signature being notarized. With this opening came the most frequent avenue for criminal fraud. All but a few of the married gamblers signed the wife's name, and several forged the names of friends.

It is in connection with failure to check information and signatures that the most systematic fraud occurs. Two gamblers I knew had siding put on their houses: one did not own a house, and the other had siding put on "five or six times." They got the loans through a siding salesman who obtained them for many gamblers. Another gambler used to help others get loans on insurance policies without the insured party knowing what was going on.

Two of the used-car salesmen told me about getting loans for "customers" who were "buying cars." They created loans out of thin air, using fictitious auto serial numbers and stating they were going to take care of everything for a customer—including bringing the payments to the loan company. This fraud was possible only because of the incredible trust that bankers and loan-company officials have in home-improvement, insurance, and auto salesmen.

Loan companies, in their efforts to increase business, often advertise and suggest tactics not previously thought of by the gambler. Also, in their desire to help others in need, bankers and loan-company officials may become unwitting precipitants of fraud. The gamblers receive ads in the mail about loans, immediate credit, raises in credit limits, and new schemes such as credit-card loans and loans by mail. These efforts to add business—especially from new bank branches, finance companies, and credit unions—give the gamblers new ideas. Some of these efforts are quite overt. Those who have filed bankruptcy, for example, are the most prone to these advertising techniques. After the bankruptcy becomes final, the loan companies know that the debtor cannot file again for seven years.

While advertisement opens routes for new money, some of these routes are suggested in the bank and loan-company offices. One gambler I knew who had been caught "kiting" checks (a system of using one bad check to cover another bad check) had ninety-day notes suggested to him. Several of the gamblers have consolidation of debts mentioned to them by banks when they haven't previously thought of it. This is thought to be "just great," because it raises the limit of the loan to include consolidation plus the amount originally asked for.

Some of the desire to help others in need goes so far as to be potentially troublesome for the banker. One gambler told me he convinced a bank president to take a loan out in *his* (the president's) name in order to help him (the gambler) pay "hospital bills." Others convinced lending-institution officials that theirs was such an emergency that raising credit limits in this exceptional case was OK.

Some of the help given to debtors approaches fraud itself. Employees help friends out by giving them loans in more than one name (for example, Joe and Joseph) or using aliases. I knew one person with five different loans at the same bank under five names; several had two loans; and two had three loans. Alternatively, others used friends who would get loans for them in the friends' names while the lender knew what was happening.

The final form of victim precipitation is the regular connection between a bank, loan-company, or credit-union official and bookmakers,[7] either with or without higher bank officers' knowledge. Certain finance companies in the major cities have systematic connections with bookmakers, especially of the "connected" variety.[8]

The gambler's past credit

While the gambler will utilize as many of the defects in loan-company policy as possible, if he obtains a bad credit rating somewhere along the line this will often have an effect on future credit. This, of course, will depend on whether the companies he is dealing with are tied into the credit-bureau network, and if he is aware of the tie-in if they are not. The institution will engage in a credit check, investigate employment, and request a financial statement, which is checked with greater or lesser intensity depending on the institution. Several gamblers are denied loans because of their position as poor credit risks, as in the following example.

> One time, I borrowed five hundred dollars from Bankers Trust, a long time ago. That's when I started to work for my cousin. He OKed the fuckin' loan. I didn't pay 'em back in full till about two

years later. I paid 'em back the whole fuckin' five
hundred dollars but I didn't make a payment. I
made one payment and I stopped. I gave 'em the
whole five hundred dollars probably two years
later. . . . [Later on, he tried to get money from
another lending institution.] I couldn't get any
money. My credit rating was pretty bad 'cause of
that Bankers Trust job.

Despite the credit check, however, this gambler resolved that
problem.

I had other people get fuckin' loans for me. They
would go out and get a loan for me and I would
pay it off.

Not all gamblers have friends they can rely on when banks
refuse credit. So some try another bank, others rely on other
means of getting money, and others are unable to get a loan
anywhere.

The attempts made by banks to uncover those people who
would not be able to pay back loans have certain defects, as
noted above. In order not to be one-sided about the activities
of loan companies, credit unions, and banks, I must state that
they do have credit checks; they do ask for the wife's signature; and they do check employment.[9] While these moves are
all aimed at protection against fraud, only some are geared
toward uncovering potential fraud.

ACTIONS AFTER DEFAULT

The actions that occur after the gambler has defaulted on
the loan prove threatening to him. Institutions mail out no-
tices and make telephone calls when the gambler is late, despite the confidential feature of many of the loans. In addition
to this, they may attempt to contact cosigners and employers.
The following gambler was a finance-company official at one
point in his career:

I thought that anybody that didn't pay in time was

an absolute rotten scum who was to be trampled. I collected loans that way. I was vicious about the way I collected. No compassion with anybody for not making a loan payment on time.

Q. What would you do to collect?

A. Hound, harass, cause them to be fired from their jobs, sue 'em. . . . Oh, I was, and on the phone. I remember one woman I had fired from job after job after job. I trailed her right around. Harassing her on the job. Sending a sheriff out to her. Every time I finally got a wage attachment on her, of course, she blew her job, and I'd viciously track her down week after week after week.

For those who pay on time there are no problems; others are called at work and at home—"getting caught" attests to that. The wonder is that most of the companies put up with the phone calls and the mail at work.[10] Rarely does a person leave his job as a result of loan-company harassment.

Pay-garnishment proceedings are also possible. By law the loan company can take everything but a certain amount for living expenses (this law is not the same in every state). A modified attachment takes less than is allowed. With this attachment, no other creditors can attach (garnish) the paycheck.

I got a modified attachment. It was the best thing that happened to me, because, ah, nobody could attach me while this was on. They could get in line and wait, but nobody could attach me, so all that come off my pay was ten dollars a week.

Q. For how long was that?

A. Ah, for four years. I'm still paying on it.

Lending institutions also may try to make cosigners (if there are any) pay the loan. But while threats are made, they are often not executed, because of the gambler's pleadings for amortized loans, which are eventually granted. An amortized loan is a renewal of the old loan for a longer period of time. The loans remain the same, but the payments are reduced. In most cases no new interest was added on.[11] Gamblers Anonymous clues new members in to this procedure. For those with payments higher than their paycheck, this is a godsend. However, if the cosigner's signature has been forged, criminal proceedings are possible.[12]

Banks and other institutions have the full force of the law to collect within the means of the lender to pay. They can use the courts, and in some jurisdictions sheriffs are hired to act as collection agents, legally or illegally (if illegal, the sheriffs are "enforcers" in the true sense of the word). While their protections are strong, their uncovering moves are weak, as shown in the following comments by a used-car dealer who had forged the names of "used-car buyers" to at least seven loans.

> They never did uncover the evidence that I had fraudulently gotten the loan, believe it or not, just that I hadn't paid; so they got the sheriff after me.
> **Q.** The sheriff was just acting as a collecting agency?
> **A.** Right.

THE SHYLOCK

Loan-sharking is the lending of money at usurious interest rates. The definition of "usurious" is established by each state. For our purposes, I will use "any person or institution that charges more than the legal rate of interest per year." The most common form of Shylocking is the six-for-five loan. In this case, the individual borrows five dollars (or multiples) and pays back six dollars (or multiples) at the end of a set period, anywhere from a week to ten weeks. If the note is not paid, then the vig (interest) must be paid and the loan is compounded (interest is charged again on everything, including the "vig" if that is not paid). The payments can get out of hand with a ruthless Shylock. In addition to the usurious interest, a second feature of loan-sharking is the use of various pressure tactics to collect on unpaid notes. For the first sergeant in the military who loans out money at 50 or 100 per cent interest (from the time of obtaining money to payday, be it twenty days or one day), the pressure may be in the form of refusal to give weekend passes and giving harassing work details. For the "Shylock," the pressure brought to bear can be threats or actual use of violence to collect.

Shylocks come in many varieties, depending on where the money is borrowed and the amount of interest the Shylock charges. If the gambler is in the military, he may borrow from a first sergeant. Most gamblers make their introduction through a bookmaker or an organized card or crap game. The bookmaker himself may be a loan shark and "make it both ways": when the gambler loses and when he must borrow to pay the bookmaker off. When borrowing through a bookmaker, it is usually to pay gambling debts. At an organized crap or card game, the object may be to reverse a streak and/or stay in the game—debt and vig payable that night if the streak turns then. For others, the introduction is through gamblers they hang around with/ a club, a bowling alley, or a golf course. The introductions are gambling-related except for those in the military and three who knew the loan shark in the neighborhood apart from gambling.[13]

Most gamblers go to the loan shark as a last-ditch effort to get funding. Even illegal activity (such as passing bad checks and stealing at work) may be preferable to borrowing from the Shylock.

> I knew him [the Shylock] from working in the crap games. And I knew they were always there. And I knew I could borrow money from them anytime I wanted. But I was afraid, because I knew if I wasn't in a position to pay him I would get myself in trouble. But when I had the checks out and had reached the point of no return and couldn't get money anywhere else—banks, loan companies, or anything like that—these people were my last resort. And at that time I didn't care who I went to.

Failure to go to the Shylock is caused by lack of opportunity (which is more likely with loners and middle-class gamblers) or the fear of possible consequences. Some gamblers absolutely refuse to go to the Shylock when a bookmaker suggests it. Even those who go show great reluctance.

> The very word [Shylock] struck terror in my heart. And bad as I— dream as I would about how I was going to get it [the money] back anyway . . . [by gambling], now they are talking about physically damaging me [laughter]; that is getting serious.

Most of the gamblers who borrow from the Shylock borrow only from one or two at one time and in small amounts. If the gambler has a reputation as a "producer," however, his chances of getting more money from more loan sharks increase. In addition, he may receive favorable interest status with the Shylock. A "producer" is anyone who "hustles" in some fashion to make money. He may be a bookmaker, card cheat, systematic check forger, pimp, or fence, or have some other illegal source of income.[14]

CHECK FORGERY

Of the gamblers I interviewed, twenty of the compulsive gamblers and one of the borderline compulsive gamblers forged checks in various ways. Two out of the twenty-one were engaged in "systematic check forgery in that they thought of themselves as check men; had worked out or regularly employed a special technique of passing checks; and had more or less organized their lives around the exigencies or imperatives of living by means of fraudulent checks." (Lemert, 1967b: 109)

While the check men passed fraudulent checks *without* the intention of redeeming them, the other gamblers who passed checks were basically "honest"; they had in mind using the money for a short period of time and eventually "covering" the check(s) or returning the money to the rightful owner. There was one exception to this rule: a college student who stole and cashed a lottery check from the mailbox of a student who had moved. Four of the eighteen "honest" check passers had stolen the checks from work.

Getting into checks

Check forgery is a step that occurs when the gambler can find no other avenues of funding for gambling, when all others have dried up. There is no alternative that is subjectively available other than passing bad checks. The gambler has borrowed from every gambling friend he can think of and has gotten loans where he thought he could.

> All I remember is that I had lost more than I could. . . . And I couldn't come up with loans, banks. I had so many loans that I couldn't get any more. Everybody that I knew had seemed to have lost the same week. You know, it was incredible. It was just a week that I couldn't believe. I had nowhere else to get money, so I started using checks.[15]

The initial stimulus that entices the gambler to seek a source of money is not the only precondition to actually doing so. The gambler must also see that cashing checks is a viable option. Three of the seventeen who passed personal or business checks stated that they had heard about this activity from friends who were doing it. Most of the others stated that they thought of it on a very situationally oriented basis. Those with check-passing friends, however, had more sophisticated procedures for covering checks.

Gamblers make a clear distinction between passing or kiting a worthless business or personal check and cashing a stolen check. One is easily rationalized; the other is not. Passing stolen checks is a last resort that is often preceded by other illegal activities.[16] The difference in rationalization is depicted in the following quotes by a person who did both.

Personal checks:

> It didn't even occur to me that there was anything wrong with it, because I was certain that on Monday I would straighten it out, and I always did. So, whenever I wrote a check it was always with the 100 per cent conviction that I would pay. Other

times, I wrote just to get out of a situation, and I would worry about how I would pay it later.

Checks stolen from work:

I knew that was heinous. That was an indescribable crime at the time. That was a time when consequences certainly entered my mind. If I had had any, any possible remote outside alternative to that, I *would* have exercised it, I knew all the possibles, they were creeping in my mind, all the things that could happen.

Despite the "heinous" nature of the theft of company checks (which by its very nature is a middle-class offense), it is justified by the thought that the money will be returned.[17]

Whatever the preconditions to check passing, getting into checks is conceived of as *borrowing* or a way to *buy time.*

Why not pass checks? Those who never pass checks have quite simplistic rationales for not doing so. Most do not have checking accounts. Of those who have accounts, there are two reasons why they do not pass checks: they have a joint checking account and fear their wife will find out, or they just never think of it.

Checks as borrowing

Checks are often thought of as a harmless way of getting money to gamble with. Using a check is conceived of as a way to borrow money for a certain period of time. Since no other avenues for getting funds are available, the gamblers use money intended for the checking account or just write a bad check for the money with the conviction that they will cover it later. This money can then be used to go to the race track or a card or dice game.

Checks as buying time

The gambler may be in a card game and has lost but does not want to leave, his business may be going under financially, or he may be in any other situation in which he is

"barreled" under temporarily. To get out of this stress-evok-
ing state, the gambler may decide to use a check. In addition
to cashing a check, he can postdate it and buy even more
time. Whatever tactic is used, he may do this despite the fact
that he knows there is no way he can think of at the moment
by which he will be able to cover the check. In this case, he
feels that he is *buying time* with the "rubber" check, and besides this the check may not clear for three or four days—an
eternity. This span of time is such that he knows he may be
rich through gambling or, if not, he will have devised some
other scheme to come up with the money.

Checks as routine

Once "into" checks, there no longer need be any strain-
provoking situations or closed-off opportunities for funding,
for the gambler to resort to checks as a means of "borrowing" or buying time. Checks become like any other avenue
for financing activities. It is now seen as a matter of convenience, even if other avenues open up later.

> It was either that or borrowing it from friends. And
> if there were no friends available, I'd simply write a
> check. It was the quickest and immediate way for
> money. If I wanted to go to a card party and I
> needed three hundred dollars, I'd write out a check
> for three hundred dollars. I didn't have to go all
> through that trouble of borrowing. Just write the
> check.

Covering the check

The activity of passing bad checks to store owners, banks,
fellow gamblers, and others is not the only pursuit engaged in
when the gambler passes checks. He must also *cover* them in
some fashion. Several schemes for doing so were utilized: he
could attempt to get money by gambling, borrow from another source, or do something illegal, to cover.

The most common scheme utilized by the gambler in an attempt to put the money in the bank to cover the checks he
has out, is to proceed to the race track or a crap or card game,

or bet sports. This activity has the effect of heightening the intensity of the chase the gambler is in.

> I didn't worry about it, because I thought I would make a hit and probably cover it up.

> It was only a few hundred dollars that I cashed in checks. Again, I cashed them at a bank and a clothing store, as I remember. I used that as my kitty to take off with. I proceeded to go to the track, and I had the idea that I would get the money back to cover the checks. But I proceeded to lose when I got to the track, so I really wasn't able to cover the checks that I cashed.

While gamblers try to use their gambling to cover outstanding checks, if they lose they have to find other sources for funding. In this case, they may be willing to go to another financial avenue that now becomes less threatening than it was previously. It is in these circumstances that "Uncle Joe" may be hit up for the money. Surprisingly, however, the checks gave most of the gamblers the time they needed. In several instances, sources of money opened up to relieve closure, or else their luck changed and they were able to cover the check with winnings.

An alternative means of "borrowing" to cover checks is to use other checks to do so. Bankers call one such procedure "kiting" checks. This involves the use of more than one checking account. Borrowers cash a bum check (a "bouncer" or "rubber check") with one account and use an equally worthless check from another account to cover the first. One person told me he used a bum check from a nongambling friend's dormant checking account to cover his own. Every Friday afternoon, this friend would give him a blank check from an account with no funds in it. While one of the accounts was not his, it served the same purpose—bought him time until he could cover the checks in a legitimate fashion. The kiting procedure involves knowing how long it takes for a check to clear and using that knowledge for personal advantage.

If I cash five hundred dollars worth of checks on bank one, now I don't have any money in the checking account anyway. Now I use bank two to cover the checks for bank one, before they bounce. And then, again, I use bank one to cover bank two.

Q. You always had two checking accounts?

A. I always had three so I could just keeping going in a circle and I never run out of days where I couldn't cash a check without it bouncing. I used to have it timed so good I never lose.

This same tactic is also called juggling accounts, moving money, and buying time. Another way of doing this is to cash more checks and then use the money from the second spree to cover the checks from the first. Only one gambler mentioned this tactic, but he stated it was common among his gambling friends. This procedure involves much more work than a kite.

I would go to three Stop & Shops and cash checks for two hundred dollars, two hundred dollars, two hundred dollars; or three First Nationals and do the same. Then I'd go cash a check at Sears, Roebuck for maybe three hundred dollars, which totals fifteen hundred dollars. I would take this fifteen hundred dollars in cash, go put one thousand dollars in the account because this is for the old checks I had written to cover the old checks. Keep the five hundred dollars in change and go gamble with it. Or if I won money, on occasion I won money, and I used to go put it in the account.

Those tactics are the most common procedure for covering checks. But some gamblers engage in systematic illegal activity at the same time they pass checks, and these activities (bookmaking, fencing, and swindling) are used to cover checks at various times.

FAILURE TO COVER

Failure to cover a check may occur in three fashions: deliberately, inadvertently, and involuntarily.

Deliberate failure to cover checks is practiced by those who "bounce" checks. They make out the check and worry about the consequences later. In these cases, the gambler goes to the person who has the check (typically a businessman or a fellow gambler) and gives him a story such as "There must be some kind of a mistake" or "I deposited the money yesterday." After the story, he rushes to the bank and covers the check. Alternatively, he buys the check from the complainer to forestall any legal problems. In some cases bank officials intervene to warn or help the gambler (in one case by suggesting a loan). If too many checks bounce, the gambler's account is closed by the bank. For some, this stops their check writing, while others simply move to other banks.

Inadvertent failure to cover checks is more common among "check kites," although it happens to "bouncers" also. The book work gets all fouled up.[18] This happens to the "kite" more frequently because he has more checking accounts to keep balanced. For the gambler who has such other things on his mind as point spreads, handicapping systems, or where he is going to get the money to pay for a gambling loss, checks "start bouncing all over the place" because of book-work failure.

> When you start bettin' heavy, you aren't thinking right. You forget which check is supposed to cover which check. You don't write 'em in the book half of the time. You are too anxious to go to the track or something. So you get to the point where I forgot which check was supposed to cover check one. Was it check two or check three? And I'd get them all confused and they'd all start bouncin' all over the place and that's when you get in trouble. That happened a couple a times, and that ended the check situation.

In the case of the inadvertent failure, the banks are approached more often in order to placate them. Here the stories are told to the bank clerks, who swallow them readily. The blame may be foisted on a "friend" who was supposed to deposit the money to cover the check, faulty bookkeeping, or some circumstance beyond the person's control.

In some cases, try as he might, the gambler cannot cover the check. As a result, the checks bounce *involuntarily*. When this happens, the circumstances are of the type that may induce threats of arrest and actual arrest. In these circumstances, the gambler may blurt out a partial truth or fabricate a story to a store owner or banker in the hope that the case will not be turned over to the police. Alternatively, the gambler could resort to relatives (two cases) or run away from the impending doom (three cases). Out of eighteen check passers, three were turned over to authorities and an additional four just missed getting caught (three of these were aided by relatives, two at the wife's request).

## CHAPTER VII

Getting Money Through the Gambling Setting

Gamblers get money from the gambling setting in various ways. Some use the setting to get money from gambling, others borrow money, and still others use the setting to get help from friends, fence stolen goods, hustle, cheat, swindle, or steal. Some gamblers act alone, others in groups.

Gambling alone or with the help of others

	Gamblers
Loners	11
Loners but gambled with others	13
Group-oriented	18
Part of "action system"	8
Total number of compulsive gamblers	50

These gamblers differed tremendously in the degree to which they consulted, cried on the shoulders of, schemed with, lied with, and engaged in fraud and crime with, other gamblers.

The *loners* were middle-class people. They held white-collar jobs such as schoolteacher, owner of a business, public-relations man, real-estate broker, sales clerk, and draftsman. They did the bulk of their gambling alone at the race track or with a bookie, and consulted no one when they had problems. As a result, all their efforts to get even, gain money, and hide losses were solitary adventures.

What are the rationales for gambling alone? Most important is the embarrassment gamblers feel over losing. Another reason, more popular with those who gambled predominantly with others at one point and alone later, involves handicapping ability. In this case, the belief that others cause one's own personal failure (usually at the track) induces gambling alone to avoid contact with others. Still another justification is the gambler's sense of bitterness when borrowed money was never returned to them. This prompts the desire to stay away from others, especially when winning.

Some gamblers are loners for, say, calling the bookie or going to the track, but gamble with others on a frequent basis at pool, bowling, golf, cards, or dice games. Yet they still hide most of their problems from the other gamblers. They have the feeling they are worse off than their friends. *Loners who*

How to Get Money
in the Gambling Setting

Type of Action	Number of Gamblers	
	Alone	*With Others Helping*
Gambling-setting-produced options[a]		
Borrowing from gamblers	–	39
Help with loans	–	at least 22
"Illegal shit"	–	9
Fencing ("moving" goods)	11 (8 through gambling circle)	4
Gambling-setting usage[b]		
Hustling suckers	11	–
team hustles	–	10
"bag" matches	–	at least 2
Cheating suckers	–	6
Swindling suckers	–	5
touting	5	–

a) Gambling-setting-produced options are those ways of getting money that originate in the gambling setting but do not involve gambling itself.
b) Gambling-setting usage is the use of gambling itself as a way of getting money other than by "legitimate" gambling.

gamble with others use personal resources most of the time but are able to borrow from other gamblers and overhear conversations that could prove useful.

The compulsive gamblers who are *group-oriented* consult friends and cry on their shoulders when they lose. Since everyone knows when a gambler loses, help is quickly forthcoming. Some also engage in illegal activity together.

The eight gamblers who are part of an *"action system,"* which includes many compulsive gamblers, are almost certain to help and be helped by others and engage in questionable and illegal activities with them.

The more gamblers are involved in patterns of collective action the more likely they are to use the gambling setting and the help of others in the gambling setting as an option to get money. Those gamblers with gambling friends become more deeply involved in debt and illegal actions than those who are loners. Gambling in a group, then, is a career contingency of major importance for the compulsive gambler. It opens the way for several options that otherwise would not be available.

GAMBLING-SETTING-PRODUCED OPTIONS

Borrowing from Gamblers

Gamblers who gamble with others also borrow from them. This happens before, during, and after gambling. Before going, the gambler may take advantage of the fact that a friend asked him to come along and may mention that he is kind of broke but would go if the friend gave him a loan.

At the bowling alley, poolroom, poker game, race track, or wherever the action is, other gamblers will lend out money to those in need. There is an "unwritten code" (this term was repeated by several of those interviewed) that winners will let losers borrow money so they can "finish the night" or "get even."[1]

> If you are a horseplayer, you are usually around horseplayers. So you usually know who is winning and who is losing and so forth. So if you are in the track, say, and a guy wins and you lose, you are always good for fifty to one hundred dollars. It is like an unwritten code, 'cause you know, you would do the same for him.
> Q. You have let other people borrow money?
> A. Oh, yeh.

While other gamblers are borrowed from, this can be a source of friction among friends. People who borrow but don't pay back (for example at the track) induce dishonesty about winnings. Gamblers often reduce accounts of how much money they are winning so they do not have to lend much out. They also go to the two-dollar window rather than the ten-dollar or fifty-dollar window. A "trip to the bathroom" or to "buy a beer" is later used as an excuse to leave while they go to the ten-dollar or fifty-dollar window. If they subsequently win, "winnings" are reduced so they can "save money" (for future races or to pay bills). Finally, they lend out money but at a reduced rate, knowing that they may need to borrow from the lendee at a later date.

Gamblers also borrow from hangers-on, bartenders, and club owners (especially if any is a bookmaker). The gambler may be a good patron and a good friend, so there are no qualms about borrowing and lending. In addition, the in-house loan shark or credit may be used to continue gambling.[2]

After the day is over, winners again will let losers borrow money, possibly to live on until payday. All borrowing from friends, whether before, during, or after, is of short duration (until the next time they gamble together) and for small amounts of money (five dollars to two or three hundred dollars may be considered "small," depending on the setting).

While borrowing in one form or another is quite frequent, the gambler may gain a bad reputation for borrowing and not paying, and as a result may lose credit with his friends. Most of the gamblers, however, tried to pay their close friends off as soon as possible in order to keep this line of ready cash open for future difficulties.

Help with Loans

Some gamblers, even those who are fringe members of groups, will overhear conversations. Some concern ninety-day notes, defects in loan-company tactics, borrowing from the checking account, and other schemes for getting money. All these ideas are put in the memory bank for future reference if needed. This was primarily the case with loners who gambled with others.

Those who gamble mainly in groups will probably be happy when each wins and cry together when they lose. They may agree on a mutual rationalization ("If we'd a . . .") and also search for a way to get money. Gambling in groups not only brings about solace but also exposes the gambler to more solutions to financial misfortune.

Most of the solutions to money problems are legal. Friends will suggest loans or an advance in pay, or the exploitation of flaws in loan-company policies may be noted. They may direct the gambler to "easy banks," loan companies, and Shylocks. One gambler will say that he had a similar problem and went to Household Finance or some other institution and got a loan, so it is possible.

> Well, a friend of mine, you know, he is all right, he went to a finance company, he said why don't you try it and I did and got the money.
> Q. Was he a gambler?
> A. Yeh.

> Amongst gamblers it is like a big joke. Borrow money from here and there in different ways.
> Q. Like how?
> A. You know, like, if they knew there was a place where they were loaning money out easy, like, you know. A certain spot, a loan company or something, you know. You borrow money, you know. A certain incidence happened in a bank or anything like that, you know.

Those who hang around together at the corner, poolroom, bowling alley, or gin mill will consult one another about strategies to use and will take an active part in getting loans. There may be introductions to the loan shark, cosigning of loans, and reference to loan-company officials.

For eight of the interviewed gamblers, this helping with getting loans achieved dramatic proportions. Several stated that the ability to do so was a source of status within the group. The individual who could con and manipulate people

and money was revered as a good "mover" or "manipulator."
The following quotes are illustrative:

> **Q.** Did they ever talk about it [loans] amongst your
> friends?
> **A.** Yeh, they were always saying, "Hey, I just
> rehashed again." They were proud of it. They
> conned the guy into giving them more money.
> Every day, someone was refinancing or opening up
> new loans, you know. That was a proud thing. You
> were proud of them things. You know, you pulled
> something over on somebody again.

> They used to brag all the time over a sucker. In this
> circle that these people was in, anything they did to
> obtain money, right away they would pass it on to
> another gambler so they, he could do it. It was
> something that he didn't think about.

The interviewees who were embroiled in this type of action
system were totally immersed in gambling. They were part of
the gambling elite—the twenty-four-hours-a-day, seven-days-
a-week action-seeking crowd.

Friends also plan fraud together involving banks, credit unions, and loan companies. Gamblers receive loans on insurance policies in which the policyholders have no knowledge
their policy is being used for this purpose; they have inside
connections with loan-company officials who get paid for giving a loan; they get Master Charges from several different
banks; and in some cases gamblers get lawyers to give loans
on the potential accident-claim settlement (the accident may
be created with a sledgehammer) or forge statements to use
in getting loans.

"ILLEGAL SHIT"

Certain gamblers talk about doing "big jobs": burglary or
robbery. Often this is said in jest or as an offhand comment
along the lines of "Wouldn't it be nice to hit him over the
head, grab that money, and run." "Him" in this case may be

a loan shark, bookmaker, or someone at the track. For the most part, these comments are stored away for future use or flaws are discovered in the scheme.

> Like, ah, puttin' a guy in a bag match or, ah, or, or how they were goin' to— oh, there were so many things. Get in a card game and put a guy in the middle. You know, or rob a gas station, and some other things. But I never talked it over with them. I just listened. Never said nothin', but I was scheming all the time, at the time thinking that maybe I could do this, or I would find flaws with it and I would forget about it.

While many gamblers reject the opportunity to steal, others allow the small talk to mushroom into action.

Of the gamblers I knew, three committed burglary with other gamblers. The burglaries occurred after discussions of where to get funds to pay the bookmaker. Two gamblers jointly burglarized a drugstore. The gamblers used to consult one another constantly about sports betting, agreed on the same teams, and were happy when they won and sick when they lost. In the losing situation they regularly pooled ideas to get money for each other. There were mutual visits to the credit union, where each cosigned for the other, and one introduced the other to the local loan shark.

At one point they both owed money and a plan was "cooked up" by one of them, who "knew" there was a lot of money in a drugstore safe. (One of the two said he thought there would be eight thousand dollars in the safe. The other spoke in terms of getting possibly seven or eight hundred dollars apiece.) In the process of thinking about the drugstore, both mentioned that the insurance company would pay for the loss and one talked of the Robin Hood theory of justice: steal from the rich and give to the poor. The burglary itself was supposed to be an "easy job," but this was based on faulty information, which they used to plan the operation. When it came time to execute the plan, however, each in turn backed out, only to be "faked out" by the other, who said he would get all the money. During the burglary itself one stayed in the car while the other broke into the store. As it happened, the safe that was supposed to be free was bolted to the floor and they were caught ten minutes after they left the place. In the end they spent time in jail for their offense. When they were in jail, they experienced what one of them called "shock therapy."

> Ah, I think the next day it was like a shock therapy. "What the hell did we do?" I remember saying to [name] the first night in jail, I said to [name], "Do you think this will make the newspaper?" I couldn't *believe* what came of it. It was really bad. It was really bad. You didn't have, there was no ramifications of what could happen. What could happen? What were you doing wrong? You didn't think of that at the time, you know.

Not all crimes that are committed by gamblers together are long, planned-out ventures in which each person is "faked out." Some get involved in such impulsive gestures as skipping out on (not paying for) meals together and stealing minor items rather than buying them, in order to "save money" to spend at the track.

Others plan crimes carefully and coolly. Of the gamblers I knew, one was involved in an armored-car heist, another in the systematic theft of meat from a race-track restaurant, a third committed a series of burglaries, and a fourth engaged in systematic check forgery.

In the armored-car heist a fellow gambler had devised a plan to steal money from a parked armored car and had sounded out the gambler I interviewed. It was a "foolproof plan" that went without a hitch except for one minor item: a key that was to be used didn't fit the truck. The theft of meat was a plan elaborated by two cooks at a race-track restaurant as a result of their discovery of someone who would buy beef. They continued to do it until they were fired. The burglaries were a result of suggestions by a fellow pool hustler. The interviewee's financial situation as well as gambling losses provided sufficient push toward the activity. The systematic check forgery was introduced to a gambler as he was reading the *Morning Telegraph*. The check man asked if he was broke and was interested in earning "easy money." In this way he was introduced to an apprenticeship in crime. All these people were given and accepted an opportunity to engage in "illegal shit" as a result of their gambling.

"MOVING" GOODS

Many gamblers are in a bowling alley, a poolroom, or a card or dice game when someone asks them if they want to buy hot goods. Boosters (professional shoplifters) know where to go when trying to unload the items they want to sell. Stolen items are readily peddled in gambling circles, as the simplistic logic of the following quotation reveals.

> Sometimes they would bring hot stuff in when I was gambling. When you buy hot stuff it costs less, right? You needed the money to gamble, and so you would buy the stuff.

The prospect of getting needed items cheaply appeals to many of the gamblers who are in gambling circles.[3] For some, the boosters (or whoever have the goods, be they burglars, truck drivers with overstock, or someone who has stolen from work) provide an opportunity to get money that may be needed to pay the bookie or go to the track.

Gamblers will start "moving," "hiking," "manipulating," or "middling swag" (buying and selling stolen goods) when they see an opportunity to obtain the goods, sell them, and make a profit.

> I just heard that a guy had some TVs one time. He had these TVs and another guy happened to mention that he was looking for a colored TV. I said, "Hey, I can buy it here for a hundred." This guy wants to go to the store and pay four hundred dollars. I'd tell him I can give it to him for two hundred dollars, he can't say no. He didn't. I just took a chance, I gambled. I gambled that if I bought it, he'd buy it, and he did.

In this instance, as in many others, the person to whom the goods were sold was a fellow gambler on a winning streak or a fellow pool or bowling hustler.

After the gambler first sells the goods, it gradually becomes known that he may be the one to go to if you want to buy or sell something at a low price. For a few gamblers, there is a steady clientele, but because of financial problems most of the would-be fences develop only a small, sporadic business. If the TV above was for sale at one hundred dollars, the gambler had to have the hundred dollars before he could make the one-hundred-dollar profit. In some cases, gamblers get cash payment in advance from customers in order to be able to buy the items that are being sold. In other cases, they get money from other sources in order to finance the operation. For most, whenever they can they will use ready cash or borrow from some source in order to finance the middleman operation.

Gamblers also develop partnerships with other gamblers to fence loads of goods. Each puts up one half of the price, and then both will engage in efforts to sell the goods. In some cases, a gambler will have a buyer but need financial backing. He has the choice of going to the Shylock or some other lending institution for the money or going to a fellow gambler. The gamblers are quicker and are often turned to despite their desire for a larger cut of the take. Occasionally a gambler will use a social club and his gambling buddies there in this fashion:

> We had a club where we used to keep a few suits, furs, jackets, stuff like that. . . .
> Q. Who's we?
> A. Oh, me and ah, maybe you'd be my partner on one load. The corner's full of guys that are trying to make a buck, so if I need an extra thousand and you're around and you want to invest it to make maybe five hundred on your money or double your money, you'd be my partner. I know you from the corner, so it's not like you're a total stranger.

Gamblers also steal items from work and have to be involved in an analysis of the selling market for this reason as well.[4]

One person I knew fenced in a different way. He would go to stores and put down payments on items and say he was going to take them home "so my wife can try it out." He knew (from discussions with other gamblers who were partners with him at times) that if he did not sign a contract he was not criminally liable for the goods that he took. After he took the TV, appliance, or whatever, he would look for a buyer. He would sell the item for as much as he could get. For this gambler, this was a form of borrowing, however, because he would attempt to pay for the item in thirty, sixty, or ninety days if at all possible. In a sense, he was borrowing at usurious interest rates without the business knowing about it. In several instances he failed to pay for the items and finally bankrupted to relieve the financial pressure.

GAMBLING-SETTING USAGE

While gamblers get together to help each other out, the gambling setting itself is also a means of financial support. There are many suckers waiting to be fleeced. Gamblers fleece suckers in three different ways: hustling, cheating, and swindling.

Hustling Suckers

The pool hustler deceives the mark by failing to show his "speed" (which means never revealing how good he really is).[5] The mark (alternatively called a "sucker" or a "fish" —the latter term being reserved for those who can be reeled in for repeat performances) is exploited through the use of various tactics that center on putting on a false front. One gambler put all of this in the following apt statement:

> I considered myself a good gambler. Good hustler.
> I considered myself a hustler of people.

Hustling occurs in many sports, not just pool. Gamblers hustle others at cards, dice, pool, bowling, golf, tennis, ping pong, shuffleboard, throwing grapes in the air and catching them in the mouth, one-on-one basketball, and many, many other games. In all these games, the object is to hide personal skill from your opponent. In certain other ventures—touting horses or sports events, for example—the object is to get the sucker (in this case the person who will buy the betting services) thinking you are *better* than you are. I will stick to those hustlers who underemphasize their skills, e.g. those in pool, bowling, and golf. This is done by various tactics, most of which rely on a false front. The hustler becomes a fast talker and conniver.

Pool:

> You just play easy and you talk a lot. A lot of guys that I knew used to tell me that if I ever had to shut up I couldn't play. You talk to people, you tell them, "Yeh, nice shot you made," and I would miss a ball and call myself stupid and stuff like that, you know. It is just hustling.

Golf:

> A lot of it is in negotiation in the first tee. A lot of the wins, whoever can outfox the other one. That's part of it, and we all enjoy it and I think we all know it.
> Q. What kind of attitude do you take into that negotiation? How do the negotiations work, first of all?
> A. I'm a conniver (heh, heh, heh). I'll try and finagle a good match. I'll tell you how bad I am. I love to tell people that. I'm bad, you're good. That's all. . . . Play guys that are terrible and give them shots and don't give them enough.

Bowling:

> I might lose to a point where I was bowling a guy and I knew I could beat him five straight; I may win two, lose one, win two, lose one, that kind of situation.

Q. In other words, lose one purposely?

A. Yeh, so that if you beat him five straight he may not come back; if you win two, lose one, win two, lose one, and grind it out of him easy, he'll come back for more again.

Q. Were there any other tactics you used?

A. Ah, basically, I believed in letting the other person bury himself. I never tried to convince anyone of how poor I was so that he would play me. I usually let them talk me into the match; or I might antagonize them a bit, you know.

The tactics used will, of course, depend on the sport involved. A golfer, for example, may use the vanity of his opponent with a handicap that is too low. Similar things occur with bowling-league averages.

Hustlers also restrain themselves from making extremely difficult shots, win by as small a margin as possible, and let the mark win occasionally.

A person who hustles mainly by bowling may also hustle others at gin games in cars in the parking lot and then play pool the following day. The most common "follow-ups" occur with golf and gin rummy at the club house, pool and bowling at a bowling alley-poolroom complex, and pool or bowling followed by cards (usually gin rummy).

There were certain people that I'd bowl. I'd gamble on anything. There was one kid that I used to shoot a lot of pool with and I would play cards with him. If he wanted to bowl, I would bowl him. I could hustle him into giving me fifteen pins. I could hustle him into giving me fifteen pins. I could beat him by fifteen pins any day of the week, but I always hustled him into giving me fifteen pins. You know, he always felt good, and then, when I won a game, I would tell him, "OK, take five pins back." If he beats me a game, you know, "You got to give me the five pins back." It was just a big con with this kid. . . . I used to get him over here to play gin rummy. He could play but I was just luckier than he was in anything we did. He was a stupid gambler.

Most of these hustling activities are accomplished alone. Sometimes the gambler has backers (financial assistance) or engages in team hustles. Team hustling is more common in bowling and golf than pool. Here two hustlers team up in order to hustle two suckers.

Team hustling can occur in two fashions. The most common occurs when the gamblers are engaged in a two-on-two situation. In this case one team is hustling another team. The second form of team hustling occurs in a "bag match." In this situation two people are playing against each other, yet there is an attempt to defraud spectators who have side bets with the players.

Like, I call a guy up in New York that is making ten pins better than me. I says I need a thousand dollars, I beat you the first three games. We split it. OK, when he shows up everybody bets on him, I win the first three, and then they start betting on me, and he wins the next three, you know. And we end up with all the money and we meet a couple a hours later at a bar or sumpin' and we split it.

In this case, and in the other "bag matches" discussed, the interviewee was a compulsive gambler. Hustling may be going on at the bowling alley, but losing is occurring at the track or with the bookie. Further analysis of the relationship between compulsive gambling and hustling appears to be necessary, especially with respect to "dumping" and "moonlighting" (other illegal behavior engaged in by hustlers, some of which is undoubtedly used by gamblers to support their habit).

Cheating Suckers

Card and dice hustlers call themselves hustlers; others call them cheats. They are different from most pool, bowling, and golf hustlers in that their major activity centers around manipulating the objects of play. A comparison one could make would be for a pool hustler to put a magnet in the cue ball, which he could direct at will when his opponent shot. In this case the pool hustler would become a cheat.[6]

Card and dice hustlers work best in teams. In this case, one person is called the "mover," "manipulator," or "mechanic," while the other is usually called a "shill." The mechanic is the person who can manipulate the cards or dice. He can deal whatever he wishes to whomever he wishes. If he is good he is called a "super mechanic" or a "magician," and extra status goes to this position. The shill is the person who ropes in customers and gets winning hands dealt to him by the mechanic.[7]

The shill acts as a roper for the mechanic in the card or dice game. He convinces "marks" that the game is easy money. He is hustling up business. The shill also may play an active role in the game itself. If the game is poker, he will get dealt to and may "make moves" while the mechanic is slipping in a "cold deck" (a deck that is marked or stacked in a certain fashion—it is "cold" because it has not been handled by warm, sweaty hands in the course of the evening). He can distract attention by playing with chips, knocking over a pile of chips, asking for a light, or slurping on a straw. He can make false cuts for the mechanic, who has just crimped a card at the spot he wants the cut made.

If the game is two-handed, such as gin rummy, the shill can play either the role of card player or that of reader. In this case, the card cheats give each other "the office." "The office" is a series of verbal and non-verbal signals that are used to communicate among thieves. It is used in gin rummy to maximum effect. For example:

> The system we have for gin rummy is unbelievable. You could spot God fifty in a game of one hundred and He would never win. . . . Like, . . . you are in a position to see an opponent's hand in gin and I'm playing and they say something insignificant . . . "That's a hell of a nice-looking girl over there." Hell of a nice means that I am going to discard the nine of hearts. If my opponent needs the

nine of hearts my partner will tip me off in an incon-
spicuous way . . . like . . . taking a drink out of a
glass.

Gamblers also like "putting a sucker in the middle." This is
an amateur operation in which several gamblers get together
beforehand and work up a system of signals. They play cards
with the sucker and tip each other off as to what they have
in their hands, pass off the correct cards, and make the
proper cuts in the deck whenever necessary. While these activities occur among the amateurs, they are engaged in only
sporadically; whereas, among the shills and mechanics, this
cheating is a regular activity.

Swindling Suckers

Gamblers hustle suckers in ways other than by cheating at
cards and dice or by hustling at pool, bowling, and golf. In
the chapter on bookmaking, for example, hanging up the
bookmaker, past-posting, the "banker" swindle, and the
locked bank-bag trick were discussed.

Gamblers who get together and realize that they share a
common problem can engage in hundreds of different
hustles.[8] Most of these hustles involve taking advantage of
suckers.

Some tout information to other gamblers at the race track.
They sell "inside information" on horses or dogs (without a
license) to race-track attendees. A gambler might tell nine
different people about the inside information on nine different
horses. In this way he would have at least one, and possibly
two or three people come to him the next time he touted. He
would have more than one person because the people who received the second and third horse that came in would think
that the tout was close and "if only" they had put the money
to place or show it would have paid off.

Some gamblers sell stag-party tickets solely as money-mak-
ing operations. A stag party might be the effort of a shill to
get naïve gamblers to come so they can be fleeced by card
and dice mechanics.

One gambler I knew had tickets made up to raffle off a television set that would then be won by an associate. Ten times

more tickets were printed than the television set was worth.

Other swindles run from the bizarre (convincing a sucker that there is a "hit man" out to get him and that it would take five thousand dollars to get another hit man to take care of the first one) to the simple (betting a "fish" one hundred dollars that he cannot come up with one thousand dollars and then proceeding to hustle the money away from him). Yet a gambler who needs money can always come up with a new way to swindle a sucker.

Most of the schemes discussed above were used by those who were enmeshed in gambling groups. These swindles (except for touting, which was more common alone) were conjured up among losers in an attempt to hustle suckers out of yet more money. As such, they were typically a product of those who were involved in action systems that included hustlers and cheats.

Subculture of the Compulsive Gamblers

Acting in concert *makes use of* and *produces* various cultural features of the gambling setting. Fencing, touting, hustling, and cheating are ordinary (institutionalized) parts of the gambling setting. Other actions are *produced* to resolve financial difficulties. Compulsive gamblers in groups have institutionalized borrowing and help with loans to such an extent that we can describe this as a "cultural form" in a "subculture of losers."

In an article entitled "Secrecy in Job Seeking Among Government Attorneys: Two Contingencies in the Theory of Subcultures" Malcolm Spector discusses the rise of cultural forms as building blocks of subculture. He defines cultural forms as:

> a widely consensual solution to a problem including attitudes toward it and strategies for solving it. We document its existence through observations of members of the group implementing the strategy, socializing new members into the perspective, and collectively ratifying, re-affirming, and recreating or modifying the form, especially in the face of chang-

ing conditions or circumstances. To say that a cultural form is absent is to say that the subculture does
not include it. Thus cultural forms are the building
blocks, or major constituents, of subcultures. (1973:
218)

Cultural forms arise, says Spector, when people have similar problems, are involved in affective interaction, identify
their problems as similar, and focus collective attention on
solving the problems. The more compulsive gamblers are embroiled in action systems the more they exhibit these traits
and engage in cultural activity. Examples of cultural forms
in the world of compulsive gambling include jokes about
losses and losing, borrowing from other gamblers, help in getting loans, and in being introduced to bookmakers and Shylocks.

With respect to systematic fraud, "illegal shit," and swindles, we may speak in terms of *situationally constructed* activity. They are responses to situations shared by two to four or
five people. In this sense we are speaking in terms of *collective action* and not a cultural form. For example, the "hit
man" incident occurred when an absolute stranger bumped
into a wealthy sucker in a bar. The stranger and the sucker
had a few words and the stranger abruptly walked out. After
a short consultation, one of the groups of compulsive gamblers that was with the sucker came up with the "hit man"
idea in order to get money from the sucker, and the other
agreed. It is both cultural form and collective action that go
together to create the subculture of compulsive gamblers.

## CHAPTER VIII

Crime, Options, and Concerns

The gambler has five considerations before turning to crime: opportunity, external agents of social control (police, family), beliefs and justifications, closing of available options, and threat (to self-esteem, of a financial nature and of bodily harm).

OPPORTUNITY STRUCTURES

Before the gambler engages in any illegal activity, he must have the opportunity. This opportunity is gambling-related for hustling, cheating, and swindling suckers as well as bookmaking; whereas, for checking accounts and loans, it is related to one's credibility with banks and loan companies. For example, seventeen- and eighteen-year-olds are cut off from legitimate borrowing structures and therefore from the fraud that is possible. While age and credibility may be a hindrance, banks, loan companies, and credit unions themselves may open the avenues for fraud that gamblers make use of. The degree of supervision and the availability of something to steal that is negotiable or salable are the most crucial factors in determining whether a person will steal at work.

There are basically two remaining openings used by gamblers to solve their problems illegally: professional criminal opportunities and opportunity due to situational circumstances.

Opportunities on the borderland of crime

Most of the relationships that gamblers have with professional hustlers and thieves are made through gambling circles. We discussed the connection between boosters and gamblers earlier. While some gamblers also have connections with burglars, it usually involves only small-time fencing.

I knew only six gamblers who achieved anything similar to an apprenticeship type of training with professional thieves.[1] All but one of these occurred outside the gambling context. One of the gamblers was introduced to boosting by his brother-in-law. He did this for about three weeks and then quit, not for moral reasons but because "It just didn't ring a bell with me. . . . I didn't enjoy it." He had also been involved in many burglaries as a youth and had fenced (and continued to fence) for the boosters. The second gambler became involved in hijacking and burglaries after what he perceived to be serious pressures for him to pay bills. He had known the thieves "on the street" and contended that he always had the opportunity but only used it when the pressure became too great. He was eventually jailed for selling cocaine, which abruptly ended his career. A third gambler met boosters and burglars at a "fast-living" woman's house. The woman had parties, and many of her guests were professional thieves. He became a fence and tipster (telling burglars where to go for good scores) and eventually went on a job with the burglars, acting as a lookout. One of the burglars was caught the first night; the other took off for another state. That abruptly ended his apprenticeship. The fourth gambler was introduced to a burglar at an all-night diner near where he worked.

> I used to see him at three o'clock in the morning and he used to tell me that he had a few jobs lined up. If I was interested, he needed a car. You know, when you are down and out and weak, that's when you turn to that shit. There was nowhere else to turn to. . . . There's more pressure on you for that than anything else.

This career, too, ended on the first night.

> We had one of the hinges off [the safe]. We were going for the other hinge and the hammer

broke. . . . I must have been a fuckin' jinx for him.

While the careers of these four gamblers ended very early, the two systematic check forgers I interviewed engaged in check passing as an occupation. One of the check men grew up as a "cowboy" (in criminal argot, this is someone who acts with a gun rather than his brain). He used to do small-time stick-ups in his teens and twenties with other cowboys. These actions were, as he said, to "get ahead, get ahead." He spent most of his adult life in prison, starting in reform school and then state prisons, where he was in and out on parole violations (fifteen years in all). In prison he developed many contacts with other thieves and eventually met up with a check man at a thief's house while out on parole. They stole business checks by taking jobs as security guards for a night and then proceeded to cash them with phony IDs. Their actions were very professional, taking care of fingerprints with the use of spray-on surgical gloves that covered the prints, using phony IDs from other thieves, using a graphite-and-cold-cream mixture that creates a glow on any photo taken in a bank, and obtaining autos by renting cars with other phony IDs. They also had an intense knowledge of the banking business.

This gambler was attracted to the check man both because of the check scheme and because the other thief, like himself, was a track nut. Presently (he is now in federal prison on check charges) he would like to quit gambling so he can "really make money" with checks.

The second check man was introduced to checks indirectly because of gambling. He was in debt to loan sharks when he was approached by a stranger. The stranger (an old-time check man) saw that he was reading the *Telegraph* and introduced himself. He asked the gambler if he ever got in the hole, and the gambler replied that he did and was. The check man approached him with the check scheme, tested him out, and eventually sold him checks that he made on a "pay-order machine." In time the gambler had his own U.S. postal money order machine and was cashing checks in drugstores, liquor stores, bar rooms, and other businesses. He was in and out of jail on a variety of check charges. Unlike the first check man, this one professes to want to quit gambling and checks.

Situational opportunity

The illegal and unethical actions that gamblers engage in are linked to opportunities with loans, checks, and employment or arise from gambling interests and relationships. Opportunities result from accidents. Examples of this type of activity include theft from girl friends, parents, and other relatives; blackmail; "finding" property and keeping it. One gambler stole a large pile of money and ran. He took advantage of an open opportunity. He was tight-lipped about details, as the statute of limitations had not run out and the FBI was involved at one point. The most common accidental opportunity occurs in auto accidents. Accident cases are expanded to get as much as possible from insurance companies.

> Not getting hurt or anything, putting a claim out and getting a five-hundred-dollar settlement. You know, before they had the no-fault. Ah, I'd claim a back injury and get three hundred bucks or eight hundred bucks or something like that.

> If I got into an accident I used to get the guy for all the insurance was worth, you know, bad back and all that shit.

Some gamblers do more of this type of action than others, but there is no pattern linking them together.[2]

While opportunity may knock in several ways, much of it depends on *practical contingencies*. For example, how available is the money needed to finance illegal actions? Will the crime be rewarding enough to get the person out of debt? In the first instance, to forge checks the gambler has to have a checking account; to embezzle or steal items from work he has to work where this can be done; to fence stolen goods he must know someone who has stolen; to get a fraudulent siding, insurance, or used-car loan it helps to know a siding, insurance, or used-car salesman. Many of those who failed to engage in illegal actions simply did not have the opportunity. In the second instance, the most important practical consideration is how much money is involved in a certain line of activity. Many small-time plans were rejected out of hand for that reason. As one gambler said, "Here they're talking peanuts and I need thousands."

EXTERNAL SOCIAL CONTROL

A second consideration for the gambler is external social control: the risk of getting caught, attachment to relatives and friends, and the immediate harness of those with whom he lives.

The aspect of social control most feared is the idea of getting caught. As a result, those actions with *lower risks* are more likely to be considered. The possible gains, along with the possible consequences, are weighed. Therefore, those who do steal are more likely to burglarize empty buildings and use stealth or take advantage of rare opportunities in their acts of larceny. Robbery is a last resort for this reason as well as for its potential for violence.

Some gamblers fear jail, others the embarrassment and loss of respectability that might occur if they are caught. Fear of potential public reaction deters many from engaging in acts of theft.

On top of the concern over the reaction of the general public and friends, there is a fear of letting down one's parents, children, or wife.[3] Gamblers do not want to let down their parents and others in the event they are caught. You only let down other people if they find out about the illegal behavior you are engaged in. With many things—loans, fraud, checks, and embezzlement, for example—no one need know or find out about the activity.

While gamblers are attached to their relatives, they are also constrained by the people they are living with (usually their wives). The moral stands that their wives take are important in restricting the types of activities the gamblers engage in. For example, a few gamblers told me that they never fenced stolen goods, because their wives would "throw me and what-

ever I brought in outa the house." One gambler experienced
something similar: his wife threw a stolen TV he had bought
into the garbage. Needless to say, he retrieved it and resold it.
Still other gamblers did not make book at home, because "It
wasn't convenient at home without causing a gigantic up-
roar." While the wives objected to certain lines of activity,
this closed off only one avenue among many possible ones.
There were checks, embezzlement, and more sophisticated
loan fraud to fall back on.

BELIEFS

Each gambler has different internal constraints, or beliefs.
Most are a product of early childhood training and contacts.

> I was brought up and my father was a school-
> teacher. I was brought up pretty strait-laced. The
> people that I hung around with, not the people of
> the street.

> What my parents told me when I was a kid proba-
> bly stuck with me.

Moral beliefs differ drastically. The "strait-laced" life mentioned above is one extreme. The other extreme is illustrated by those gamblers who see the hustle and achievement
of status through the hustle as being a part of their local
(lower-class) life. These gamblers often remember their juvenile street hustling days as periods filled with B and E's
(breaking and entering—burglary), fencing stolen goods,
and other searches for status as the best hustler. Gambling is
part of what one of these gamblers calls "booze, broads,
bangtails [horses], brawls, and butts."

To portray the lower-class youths in this fashion is not to
say that children of middle- and working-class parents do not
engage in juvenile delinquency. Two middle-class gamblers I
knew were involved in shoplifting rings (one to finance card
playing), and others committed theft for the thrill of it all.

Most juvenile hustling is related to gambling. Pool, bowling, and card hustlers have their start early in their teens.

Through their friends they are introduced to the values and beliefs of the hustle, which include rationalizing fencing and condemning suckers. Some gamblers also become numbers runners (lower- and working-class pattern) or parlay-card sellers (middle-class pattern). For the most part, these gamblers spurn theft. However, they justify hustles such as pool, golf, bowling, card, and dice hustling, bookmaking and other entrepreneurial activity, fencing, "selling pot," and pimping.[4] The bases for these justifications were ideological beliefs.

Pool, golf, bowling, card, and dice hustlers have strong justifications supporting their activity. They impute no immorality to the action itself. The hustlers hustle suckers. They are taking advantage of situations in which they can make money from the sucker, who is conceived of as a "stupid gambler," "a dummie," and is continually laughed at behind his back. There is an extreme amount of ideological support for letting "fish" be reeled in for replays and allowing them to "bury themselves." It is an attribute of the sucker to be taken advantage of in these situations. Anyone would be a fool to do otherwise.

The bookmaker and other gambling entrepreneurs also have ideological beliefs that gain support among other gamblers. Bookmakers have great status among their friends; they are "big shots."

> When I became a bookmaker I thought I was a big shot. Ah, I felt like, ah, I didn't feel like I was doing anything wrong. I felt like, ah, like a guy who owns a fleet of horses. I felt I knew all about 'em, what they are all about, and it made me feel like a real big shot.

No rationalizations are needed to engage in such positively valued behavior. Only when gamblers are questioned do they evoke ideological beliefs. "Just because somebody in Washington says it is a crime, that don't make it a crime" and "I knew it was against the law, but I did not consider it a crime." Bookmakers say they were "doing somebody a favor," and "If I didn't do it, someone else would, so why not me?" The activity is of such a nature that it would go on whether they personally were involved or not.

Some of the bookmakers who go to Gamblers Anonymous change their opinions after being in the organization. At the meetings I attended, I noticed that a few ex-bookmakers were the most vociferous opponents of "profiting off the misery of others." One person said that he would book again only if he could be sure he was making money off non-compulsive-gambling doctors and lawyers. Others said they would not book at all (mainly for fear that they would start gambling compulsively again), and still others remained silent when these statements were made.

The fence also has a vast array of justifications for his behavior. The first and foremost is "It's not a crime"; "I ain't hurtin' nobody." In this case, the fence compares himself with the booster and the comparison comes out favorably. "I am not a thief" is a common statement made by the fences. In addition to nothing being wrong with fencing, gamblers think they are "doing somebody a favor," much like the bookmakers who think they are helping gamblers "get down." The people who buy the goods are thought to be only too glad to buy them at a cheaper price.[5] The gambler's explanations of why his fencing is not immoral have some degree of ideological support in the community he comes from and from other gamblers.

Like hustling, making book, and fencing, the two gamblers who "sold pot," one person who ran a whorehouse in the Navy, and a gambler who "took money from women" (he avoided, condemned, and reserved the term "pimp" to "low-life scum that treats their old lady like shit") praised their activity in terms of providing a desired service. Again, the same beliefs were evoked as in fencing and making book. The activity is illegal only because someone else says it is. One used the term "victimless crime" to describe selling pot. The only qualms they had about their behavior was the fear of getting caught. On this score, the Navy cook who ran the whorehouse didn't have this problem. The shore patrol was taken care of: "I paid them off with ass . . . ; it didn't cost me a dime." The two who sold pot quit because of this fear; the "procurer of women" was imprisoned under the Mann Act, which prohibits transporting women over state lines for immoral purposes.

For those who "sold pot," the activity was intertwined with their involvement in the community of marijuana smokers. The two who received money from prostitutes had started as lovers of the first women who gave them money. In all four cases the desire to have money to feed their gambling habit served as an impetus to begin "dope dealing" and "selling pussy."

Not all of the behavior gamblers engage in has ideological support. Despite this fact, the gamblers who take out fraudulent loans, write bad checks, embezzle, steal from work, fail to pay income taxes, and engage in larceny and burglary *justify* their behavior.[6] They believe there is nothing wrong with their actions. These gamblers act in "good faith."

The loans, though gotten fraudulently, are signed with every intention that they will be paid. Besides this, the gamblers are due to "turn the corner" on a losing streak and will be able to repay the loan with the winnings. If anyone is to be blamed for the fraud, it is banks and especially loan companies and credit unions, for failure to adequately check credit. Each loan, like the losses that the gambler incurs, is conceived of as a mistake that won't be repeated.

Personal checks are written with the intention of covering them as soon as possible. If the money is not available, it will be by the time the check has to be covered. Again, there is no doubt, because the three or four days it takes the checks to clear are an eternity. Those who steal company checks rationalize by telling themselves that they will return the money, they hope, without anyone ever knowing about it.

Those who embezzle say they are "borrowing."[7] Sometimes they take money and return it on a periodic basis, often between audits. A bowling-alley manager, for example, used to use the weekly receipts to pay debts and then juggle from another source to return the money prior to the time the alley owner came in, on a weekly basis. Another gambler used trophy and prize money every year when he was the treasurer for a bowling league, only to return it prior to the banquet. In juggling the accounts, these men had every intention of returning the money. Others held *different* rationalizations, in some cases similar to those who engaged in employee theft (theft of items). An electrician who stole wire, a Navy cook who stole meat, and a public-relations man who "scalped" on his expense account said that everybody did it. Additional rationales included inadequate pay, the boss was a crook, and "It was no big crime; they could afford it" (a comment on the theft of meat).

The "borrowing" rationales of the gamblers are what Sykes and Matza (1970) called *denial of injury*. In this case there is no crime in the mind of the actor, because no injury occurs. The other rationales fall into what Sykes and Matza call *denial of victim*. In this case, there is no crime because the victim is somehow unworthy, too large to be hurt in any fashion, or "deserved" what he got. (In a sense, then, hustlers deny the victim also but with ideological, i.e., group, support.) In addition to these rationalizations, there is further protection provided for those who see that everybody does it. If everybody does it, there can't be too much wrong with the behavior. This justification (common also with professional thieves who say that "everybody has his racket") could be called a *strength-in-numbers* justification.

Four of the gamblers who stole items or money from work stated that they did not rationalize the activity to themselves. One (who stole boots from where he worked in order to resell them) said, "I was a crook." Another (who stole unemployment checks from the state) talked in terms of not thinking he would get caught. A third (who stole a vault bag of money and then ran away) said that he thought what he did was just great at the time. The only thing he thought about was going to the track. The fourth had a ship condenser "retooled" that was never done. He spoke in terms of a "caper." "I thought it was a brilliant piece of work."

Much like the use of personal checks and embezzlement, the non-payment of income taxes is a way of using someone else's money for a short period of time. Two of the gamblers mentioned deliberate failure to file. One withheld employee taxes without forwarding the money to the federal government; the other just failed to file on his quarterly returns, since he was a self-employed nightclub singer. In addition to these two, none of the gambling entrepreneurs paid income taxes on their business. Two of the interviewed bookmakers were incarcerated for income-tax violations. In their cases, they weren't "borrowing"; the tax evasion was necessitated by the illegal nature of the business.

In one case of larceny, the gambler told me he "borrowed" ten dollars from a friend without his knowing it. This was the only case of larceny in which this rationale was used.

> I once took ten dollars from a roommate I had a couple a years ago. . . . Well, he wasn't around and I knew where he had his money. And, ah, I knew he was very lax as to how much he had. I mean, he wouldn't a missed ten dollars, I don't think. He had, like, a couple a hundred. I borrowed ten dollars to get by for a while. I know I eventually paid him back and I told him I had taken ten dollars. I suppose if I wasn't able to pay him for a while I would have forgotten about it, but I was able to pay him back.

For those who "borrow," either from the banks, checks, friends, work, or the state, there is little, if any, moral dilemma about the activities they engage in. This is true also for those who do things that "everybody else is doing." The only fear, it appears, is that of getting caught.

Just as some forms of employee theft are rationalized by denying the victim, so smaller-scale larceny and some burglaries are justified. Two burglars told me that the insurance companies would pay rather than the owners of places burglarized (in this instance the victim is too large to be hurt). In one burglary, the victim had just recently died. For another, the gambler burglarized his relatives' residence and said that at the time he thought they were "too greedy."

Those who engage in larceny also have a tendency to deny the victim by either attributing unworthiness (for example, one gambler shortchanged a drunk on a sale), perceiving the victim to be too large to be hurt by it all (as in the theft from a large department store or the case of insured victims), and otherwise demeaning the victim. The most common term they use is "sucker."

"Suckers" come in many varieties. They may be called "stupid" people. One gambler, recalling his theft of a lottery check, rationalized it on two bases: it was a lottery check and not some other check, and "the kid was stupid enough to have the check sent here [a fraternity]." Another gambler stole from a store owner who "ran his store ass backwards." Still a third stole from a "dink."

CLOSURE AND THREAT

Most gamblers experience little or no moral dilemma regarding the illegal activity they engage in. They justify these crimes. Yet, for other kinds of crime strict moral barriers exist. This is most likely in those cases in which there is potential for violence and injury and these kinds of crime are considered but rejected. Crap games, card games, bookmakers, Shylocks, and race-track attendees are not relieved of their money, because the potential for violence is too great. Many of those who fence, write bad checks, make book, and hustle in other ways cannot use violence, as the following rather common statement from a person who did all these things demonstrates:

> Oh, I thought of robbing a crap game. That was the only other thing I ever thought of. Maybe I could put a stocking over my head and hold them up, but I didn't. I never did that, because what if I did and another guy made a move for me? These guys are all nuts. Then I would have to shoot 'im and I never could do that.

Those people who cannot justify the acts they commit, yet eventually do commit them, excuse these crimes by saying they were necessitated by pressures that were pushing them to "do what I had to do."

Closure

The gambler will try to manipulate money for as long as possible. He will try to hold the lines of funding open by buy-

ing time and otherwise handling the situation as well as possible. At many times throughout the gambler's career, however, various routes for getting money become closed off.[8]

Things start tightening up.

There was no other avenue to go to.

I'd reach my, ah, saturation points as far as loans were concerned.

This closure state occurs prior to using *any* avenue of funding that is subjectively closed—be it Aunt Mary or armed robbery. This restriction of behavioral alternatives is of a dual nature: *closure of options already tried and closure of options yet to be attempted.*

Some routes are impossible because *they have been tried.* Friends are asked and they refuse, usually because the size of the request is larger than they can handle; they feel that letting the gambler borrow the money would only be a disservice to him, which it is in reality; or the gambler has defaulted on previous loans. A loan company turns down a request or a bank closes a checking account.

Other moves *appear unfeasible.* After the loan company turns him down, the gambler thinks that the bank will do likewise, despite the fact that he has gotten a loan there in the past. This is based on ignorance of reality and is common among loners.

Other *options not yet attempted* are subjectively closed off because of personal belief, practical considerations, or attachment. Unwillingness to engage in actions that are perceived to be immoral or impractical, or that will go against the desires of someone to whom one is attached, also occurs constantly. This unwillingness, however, may be altered by pressures or threat.

Threat

The gambler is subjected to several varieties of threat and pressure in his gambling career. The most common are threats to self-esteem and financial pressures. The threats to self-esteem foster a *non-sharable problem*. Few compulsive gamblers disclose the full extent of their debts, losses, or illegal activities to anyone while they are gambling.[9] Some reasons are given below.

> Everybody gambles, and that is socially acceptable. People don't get twelve grand in the hole. That ain't socially acceptable.

> If I told the story that I just told you to certain people that I know, they'd just, they'd want me in the nuthouse. They'd really think I'm crazy; maybe I am, but they couldn't appreciate the fact that you cannot, under any conditions, stop. They can't appreciate that.

> I would never admit to anybody that I was a failure. Ego. The image.

The fear of embarrassment and loss of respectability that result from disclosure is enough for gamblers to lie on loan applications and to friends and relatives. The problem then reduces the number of people who can be approached. After all, if the problem has to be hidden from the wife and parents, more lies are needed to cover this up. In addition, people who would normally help are not asked, because of fear of disclosure to the wife and parents. These threats reduce the available options. The larger the debts and more questionable or illegal the activities he engages in, the more unsharable the problem becomes. The gamblers who have not resolved a state of closure and who experience this type of threat go to employee theft, embezzlement, check forgery, and other justifiable illegal activities before exposing themselves. No gamblers engage in activities they cannot justify morally with only this form of pressure in evidence.

Regarding financial threat, several cross pressures work at exactly the same time: The bookmaker wants his money—threat of cut-off may be sufficient inducement toward illegal behavior for some gamblers. The lending institution wants its money—fear of loss of credit provides impetus for "borrowing" from other sources, be it legal or not. The gambler fears that if he fails to pay the lending institution, his wife will find out through a phone call; his quest to maintain respectability in his wife's eyes induces him to engage in embezzlement, employee theft, or check forgery.

Most of the pressures the gambler has are of the above kinds. The pressure, however, is not uniform. Bookmakers, banks, credit unions, loan companies, and loan sharks use different collection procedures, which range from an overdue notice in the mail to threats of bodily harm. The more the gambler personally fears these threats, the more likely he is to engage in questionable activity to relieve the pressure. If he has a wife who "bitches and moans" loudly and in a very harassing manner, he will fear her harassment more than the possibility of getting caught with a bad check out. In turn, ignorance of the relatively harmless status of most bookmakers will naturally be more of an inducement to crime than will knowledge about how to "screw the bookmaker."

Threats, justifications, and excuses

Since threat increases as the gambler's career becomes more intense, the changes in support system take place in a *sequential* fashion. There are three stages of moral change in the gambler's career regarding the activity used to finance gambling. Typically, the gamblers start out by using those options which are perceived as moral. This includes behaviors which are ideologically or situationally justifiable. Most responses to threat are legal. When pressure is applied, usually other avenues of funding are opened up and credit unions (or some other resource) are turned to when the crunch comes. If these choices have been used up, the gambler reverts to justifiable illegal activity.

After those actions which are totally justified have been used up, the gamblers revert to *partially justified* behavior. In this case, while actions are justified, they are also *excused* at the same time. Some activities could not be *totally justified* personally. Theft of company checks is partially justified by the fact that the money is being "borrowed."

However, the gambler also realizes that the activity is still wrong, despite that fact. In this case, the action is also *excused* at the same time. *Whatever justification is chosen is coupled with an excuse.* The excuse takes the form of blaming pressure or threat for the activity. If the Shylock or bookmaker wasn't after him, the gambler would never do such a thing. The present instance is looked upon as an exceptional case, with mitigating circumstances. Seventeen of the fifty compulsive gamblers moved on to engage in *partially justified* behavior.

A similar combination of excuse and justification is evident in almost every case of burglary. In these cases of combined excuse and justification the act cannot be totally justified but, given the pressure that exists, it can possibly be excused. One series of burglaries, for example, involved a tipster who told professional burglars where to go to steal money. These burglars split the take with him. Later on, he acted as a wheelman. All this time he told himself *he* was not a thief. They were. In addition, he said he thought of unpaid rent and other pressures when he helped the men out.

Last in the chain of events during the gambler's career come those crimes that are *not* justified. According to the gambler's value system, these activities are immoral. They are engaged in only because they can be excused, given the circumstances. The gamblers who use excuses for these behaviors qualify the crimes by thinking of the present situations as unusual and abnormal. This is more likely the more serious the activities are that they feel they have to turn to. They divorce themselves from the activities. While the actions are crimes, *they* are not criminals.[10] For example, a gambler said this about his situation at the time of an armored-car heist.

> My financial situation was getting extremely bad. It was, this is something I would say, through my financial situation I was driven towards. I would never have considered doing it under normal situations, as I do not believe I am a criminal.

Gamblers who are involved in such "big jobs" as hijacking, muggings, and burglary say "the opportunity was there, but it wasn't until the last few years that I did that stuff." For example, a gambler who was involved in muggings, hijackings, burglaries, and selling cocaine had this to say:

> It's wrong, you know, I *could* have gotten into a lot of things, because it's around you every day. It's around me, I guess it's around most people in here [prison]. As far as I am concerned, it is around you no matter where you go. You could avoid it. I did, but eventually it caught up to me.

Activity that is perceived as morally unacceptable is turned to only when the pressure gets too great to bear. The morally acceptable options are closed off, while at the same time the gamblers are under pressure. For example, one person had borrowed from every friend and relative he could, had at least eight loans, had exhausted his checking account, and had gotten beaten up the previous day by a loan shark, when he contemplated robbing a bank.[11] Either way, he lost out; so he took what he felt to be the only way out. After a full day of agonizing decision making that included going to church, he robbed the bank. His appeared to be the most severe moral dilemma discussed. He could not think of any way of committing suicide in which his wife and children would collect on his insurance policy. The dilemma was resolved by robbing a bank with a toy gun. Threat *excuses* the crime. It is this excuse which allows the final movement toward the activity. Only five out of fifty compulsive gamblers eventually went on to unjustifiable behavior.

## CHAPTER IX

Abstinence-and-Relapse Cycles Among Compulsive Gamblers

Throughout their careers, compulsive gamblers go through periods of abstinence and relapse. These periods become cyclical as similar things happen over and over again and both reverberate in and are reflective of the spiral of options and involvement. Abstinence is either enforced or voluntary. The enforced periods of abstinence are caused by the insistence of wives, parents, or parole officers that the gambler quit gambling. Voluntary abstinence, however, comes from disgust or a state of closure.

While an individual may abstain, his thought processes are the same as when he was gambling. He is still obsessed by loans he has to pay and people he owes and how he could pay them if he made a hit. There are loans that his wife knows nothing about and people who have not been told the truth. While loans and problems of option use bother the gambler, lack of action bothers him as well. The result is that periods of abstinence are boring and full of nervous tension.

The sequential patterns of abstinence and relapse as well as the form these sequences take change as the gambler moves up the spiral.

ABSTINENCE

Enforced abstinence

Gamblers usually are constrained by external forces. Their gambling has repercussions for their family and anyone else they exploit in the process of attempting to continue gambling or pay for past debts incurred by it. This exploitation, if secretive and unexposed, does not have any feedback for the gambler's career. Periodically, however, these factors act as precipitants to abstinence. This happens in three different ways. Either the gambler "gets caught" by agents of social control (parents, wife, employer, banks, or police), or he feels he must "face the music" (that is, turn himself in to agents of social control for a violation he feels will surface in the near future), or he *feels* "jammed up" (avenues for getting money are closed off) and goes to someone like his wife or parents for money. After each of these three possible occurrences, the promise that he will quit gambling is usually a condition of forgiveness.

The family setting will include all three of the above springboards for abstinence. In reality, the gambler is promising not to exploit the family again by being foolish, dumb, stupid, idiotic, and any other negative adjective the wife can think of. These instances are more common with married gamblers but occur among *all* gamblers. At the very least, the gamblers go through these periods at earlier points, when they have to deal with their parents. After the repentance, gambling becomes synonymous with exploitation itself and is frowned upon. As a result, many of the gamblers quit gambling after each discovery episode. This process is more likely to be at the wife's urgings than voluntary.

"Getting caught" means being apprehended for a deviant act and being labeled a thief.[1] In contrast to this, "facing the music" is a self-labeling process. The gambler turns himself in because he thinks that the inevitable will happen. He perceives that the truth will surface sooner or later and is tired of trying to hide. The following quotation illustrates well the pattern of "facing the music":

> At first I called my father-in-law. I had been living for months figuring that the minute I stepped into [state] they would be there with handcuffs. I called the lieutenant at [town] station because I knew him. I told him that I had a problem that I thought that he knew about and I would be in to see him that afternoon. He says, "Well, just come in tomorrow morning." My father-in-law came and

got me and I stayed with him and I turned myself
in. I find out that there wasn't any warrant ever issued. So then they call up the bank and decide to
issue 'em then. This is four months after the fact.
They turned around the same day and issued out a
warrant. Bang, I was off to court.

While the individual will possibly have the strategic advantage if he gives himself up to the police or employer (by
exhorting them not to prosecute), he is put in the same circumstances as those who "get caught," once he is in the arms
of the law. Both situations lead to enforced abstinence if the
gambling problem becomes known. He may blurt out his
troubles to the detectives, prosecutor, or probation officer and
receive probation rather than prison or receive a lesser sentence. If this fails he can go to court and give the judge a
"sad tale."[2] At present, most judges fail to place compulsive
gambling on the same plane as drug addiction or alcoholism.

I told the judge that before I went to jail; he asked
me why did I do it, and I told him that I have an
uncontrollable urge to gamble. And he said, "Ah, I
don't believe that." That's really a sickening thing.
If you're a junkie with needle marks you'll get away
with it, or an alcoholic staggering in front of him.
They don't treat this like any kind of sickness or
anything. I don't think they ever will.

Two possibilities exist for those found guilty: imprisonment
and then parole, or probation instead of imprisonment.
Whether out on parole or given probation, the possibilities for
enforced abstinence are the same. This is providing, of
course, that the defendant mentions the gambling during the
prosecution or in prison. Their gambling usually remains hidden from the administrators of criminal justice.

If the gambling surfaces at some point in the criminal proceedings, the probability that not gambling will be a condition
of parole or probation increases.[3] It will also increase the realization by the gambler that gambling has a new meaning:
incarceration.

Q. Did you gamble when you were working cutting meat?
A. I didn't do anything then. You know, I was, I was parolee. God forbid. Or whatever word it was. I wouldn't do anything then. I wouldn't gamble. I was really down at the lowest, lowest end of the totem pole. Of course, who would lend a prospective jailee money in case I lost? And I probably started at [company name] gamblin', I don't know when. Um, I, ah, I would certainly preach against it, that's for sure. It's as bad as dope. I've seen enough addicts to know.

While abstinence or attendance at GA meetings can be a condition of probation or parole, it will depend on the probation or parole officer whether the pressure to remain abstinent is maintained.[4] Gamblers often feel their only period of abstinence is a direct product of the fear of loss of freedom. This tactic works, but it does nothing about the justifications and other supports the gambler has for continued gambling.

Voluntary abstinence

Voluntary abstinence occurs in two different ways: becoming disgusted and feeling "jammed up."

When the gambler is betting at full speed and losing consistently, the possibility arises that he will get "fed up" or "disgusted" with constantly losing. Most of this disgust is a passing thing that occurs after a heavy loss, a bad day at the track, or a losing week of sports. The despair lasts only until he starts over again or recoups his losses with a loan. Yesterday is rationalized as part of a losing streak or bad luck. Now he can look forward to tomorrow. While, normally, the gambler looks toward tomorrow, when he will get even, at times he may reflect back on his life.[5] He looks at the shambles he has created of his life, home, or work. Rather than being engrossed in the gambling setting, he experiences disgust with himself for being a fool, idiot, asshole. The obsession he had come to experience as normal is suspended. Now, rather than reflecting on and rationalizing the last race, the day or week's events, he looks back at the total scene, where he has been and where he is going.

> For some reason or other, I always wanted to take the track home with me. I wanted to break everybody. I got greedy, I started bettin' more and more. My bets went up from a ten-dollar bet to fifty and one hundred. The next thing I know I was in the hole. Losing money like crazy, borrowing off my cousin, getting off my salary, you know, in advance [he worked for his cousin]. I think I got in the hole with him for ten thousand dollars. Borrowed money on paper, and I knew I had to pay it back. So I finally decided I better quit this job, 'cause I'm gonna end up owing my life to him, 'cause I wasn't getting nowhere. I was losin', livin' on nothing, just a skimpy sandwich in the afternoon, a peanut-butter sandwich, whatever. All I was doin' was going to the race track and working, going to the race track and workin'. I never saw a dollar. Whenever I made a score I'd blow it back the next day or I'd give most of it to my cousin, you know. Gambling got me sucked in pretty bad. And at the age of eighteen, or nineteen, I quit my cousin's job, paid him back everything I owed him.

> I've quit more than twice, you know, but the time before was the longest time. It was four or five years. And I just got disgusted with it, you know, I, ah, I was making good money and what did I have? Nothing. You know, I said: "You are going nowhere fast." It took me a long time to realize.

For some it takes a long time to realize they are "going nowhere fast," for others there is a periodic seasonal progression. They ponder their past gambling enough to quit until next year, or they feel they should "skip a session" until their luck changes. Only one person mentioned skipping a season, and two gamblers quit every year at the end of football season only to start again the next year.

For still others there is one point at which they reflect on the seriousness of what they have done. They have done something they would not have contemplated "normally." The action they have engaged in is no longer justifiable; they are disgusted with themselves. The precipitating event is one that brings on "closure," or being "jammed up," and is of such a magnitude subjectively that quitting (in this case via GA) appears to be a viable answer.

> God, let me tell you, the day I blew the forty-six hundred plus the check, I had never been that. I had never been in a mental state such as that, because when you are gambling you always think of tomorrow. Even then I knew there was no place I was going to find five grand in a hurry. When I thought of how much, *how* much money—five hundred you could handle, even fifteen hundred, but five thousand. How do you justify five, how do you justify a roll so big you can't get in your pocket at four in the afternoon and at two in the morning with *lint* and a bad check out. Not for that amount of money. There was no way.

After disgust, being "jammed up" is the most common initiator of voluntary abstinence. In this case there is no money to continue gambling, or at least the individual *perceives* that there is no morally acceptable avenue for getting money. It may occur at *any stage* in the gambler's career: when he thinks no other people will give him money, when he feels he just cannot go to a certain person or do something he feels is not morally justifiable. Subjectively, there is no way of getting money.

> Lost about three thousand dollars between mid-September and, ah, December. I was out borrowing, ah, there was one banker who would give loans just on my signature, but I didn't want to go to him any more. I didn't want to go to finance companies. I went to another bank and he approved a loan. I think I needed about two thousand, and he would

not give it to me without my wife's signature. That was a crisis for me. I could have forged her signature and got the loan, but I couldn't do that. That's when I came clean to her and that's when there was a crisis in our marital situation and, ah, that's what I, since then I've been, the longest stretch in my life and, ah, it's been, ah, a year and a half.

This is an example of a gambler who never engaged in crime. Still others can't stretch their checkbook any farther; can't get some "swag" to "move" (stolen goods to sell); or can no longer juggle, manipulate, or move money in any fashion, legally or illegally. It stops them from gambling. Similar things happen at all stages of the career, whether the involvement now includes justifiable activity (stage 1 of the gambler's criminal involvement) or actions that are partially justifiable and excused (stage 2).

Person who had stolen from work:

Then we had a couple a winners and a couple a losers and then one night got hit for a little bit and then we had a real bad week. I mean a real bad week. We lost a little over five thousand apiece roughly. I couldn't go any more. I mean, I was down as far as I could go. I had to borrow the money to pay it off and everything. While I was trying to find the money, that was when [name] from GA called me and that is how I got into GA. Someone contacted him. I don't know who. He just called me up one night on the phone. I wasn't above listening to the guy and I listened to him and I said: "What the hell! Instead of hiding all this from my wife and making life miserable for her, it is time to cut all this bullshit out." And I did.

Person who had swindled, fenced, and written bad checks:

I was just so barreled in I never had a dollar on me. Couldn't even borrow from gambling friends any more. Couldn't move money, couldn't get it, couldn't get it, couldn't do anything.

Here the desire to gamble is stifled only by lack of money. In a sense, then, this type of abstinence is partially voluntary and partially enforced—voluntary because the gambler is not willing, at this point, to engage in behavior (e.g. bank robbery) that would allow him to gamble. Systematic check forgers never have this problem. The others think, "If only I could get another loan, if only I could find some money somewhere." For some, Gamblers Anonymous appears to be the answer.

When I think back now, at the time I was really hopin' that Gamblers Anonymous would show me a place to get money. That's what I really went there for. I figured they would show me where to get money, how to pay these bills, and I'll be back in gamblin' again. Just keep it down this time where I don't get hurt, you know. So I went home, you know; Gamblers Anonymous, they don't tell you where to get money.

Gamblers often experience disgust after they "get caught" or in some other fashion have to quit gambling involuntarily. In these circumstances, an original "God damn it, if I could only gamble without her finding out . . ." turns into "Well, maybe she's right; I probably should try to quit. All I've got is headaches."

Running struggles during abstinence

Once in abstinence, the gambler will be involved in several running struggles with himself, his wife (or parents), gambling friends, and others. During these periods of abstinence all is serene in the household; the family is happy; there are no arguments and confrontations due to gambling. The husband doesn't dare gamble again, because the wife has tightened up the reins of accountability on his time and money. In addition, he wants to convince her he is not gambling. His

wife is watching every move he makes and there may be spies
in the area (the wife's immediate relatives) who are also on
the lookout. His *time* is now accountable as well as money.

On top of all of this, his debts are still in existence. The
principal does not go up but remains the same. He thinks of
how long it will take for it to be paid. Unpaid bills are a reminder of the self he does not want to be. This is often quite
perilous, because he may have more debts than his wife or
parents know about. The gambler rarely admits he has more
loans than they have found out about or more than he needs
their help with. He has two logical reasons for concealment:
he is too ashamed to tell them more than he has to; and he
feels he can take care of it himself. They don't need to be
bothered with his misery. Loans of the second sort are from
gambling sources or those from loan companies that are almost paid off. Again, like the periods of abstinence, this occurs at *all* stages of the spiral, whether relatively early in the
career or later. The second quote illustrates the periodicity of
this concealment procedure. The time he discusses includes
intervals *prior to* and *after* having embezzled and engaged in
systematic loan fraud. The "end" he speaks about is the
financial bankruptcy of his business coinciding with FBI curiosity over a fraudulent loan.

> Then came D day. The big loss, the first time
> [wife's name] knew about it, fourteen hundred
> dollars. OK, I told her. What I didn't tell her was
> that the other loans I was trying to scalp on my ex-
> pense account.

> Every so often, I can't remember exactly, maybe
> every three years, she'd find out somehow that I
> gambled and I'd have to explain to her what hap-
> pened or how. Like, one time she found a post-
> office box off a box-number receipt. I had to tell her
> what I had there and things like that.
> Q. Did you ever tell her the whole thing?
> A. Well, I always seemed to hold out something.
> Hold out one or two; in other words, never tell her
> the whole story, until the end. She knew the whole

story then. But never did she ever the other times know everything. I always seemed to hold out one or two different loans, figuring, well, you could straighten it out yourself, but you never could.

This situation of untold loans is most perilous where the wife demands to know where all the money is going. The pressure to pay the loans by creating a hidden resource is tremendous.

While he struggles with his wife (or probation officer), he must also deal with himself, especially if abstinence is of the disgust variety. Despite abstinence, old habits hang on. He may want to read the sports page or look at sports events or the race of the week on TV, and in fact will tell himself that his interest is for the sports value alone. He makes "mind bets" to himself. He thinks of which team or horse he would have bet and condemns himself for not betting it when the team or horse he had a "mind bet" on wins. He may go to the local card game "just to watch" or "for something to do," and he will end up playing the hands that others get in his head and will condemn the player (mentally) for making the "wrong" moves he wouldn't have made.

In addition to the sports page, the gambler must deal with gambling friends who come around taunting him (in some cases with short-term loans) and the fact that he has free time on his hands. Instead of action he has boredom.

RELAPSE

Relapse occurs after periods of involuntary abstinence; because of commitments produced by the continuation of the spiral; due to the influence of gambling friends and acquaintances; as a result of the resolution of closure; because of a desire to gamble "normally"; and as a result of financial crises.

In those periods of involuntary abstinence, the gambler's only reason for not gambling is to keep his wife, parents, or others quiet so he will avoid the inevitable "bitching and moaning." Fear also prevents him from gambling on probation or parole. The only thing the gambler waits for is release from social control. He waits until the questions about where he has been subside, whereupon he sneaks out of the house or else resorts to sneaking phone calls to the bookie.

The other routes back to gambling are slightly more complex, since they follow periods of semivoluntary or voluntary abstinence. The second route is by far the most common. In this case, despite the gambler's attempts to quit, the spiral's momentum grows. The options the gambler has used come to feed back into his career. The gambler feels he *must* become involved again in action and the chase.

Gambling becomes a self-enclosed system in which losses occur, yet there is an expectation (due to *past* successes) that the gambler will be able to win the money back in the same way he lost it: gambling. With this thought in mind, he comes to feel there is a way to relieve the anguish that was created by gambling. That relief is gambling. He forgets the anguish of the past and again focuses on the future. He tells himself that this time things will be different; he will be more careful this time. He will not make the same mistakes he did before (that is, he will not move up the spiral).

> And then I would say, "That's it; I quit." And maybe I would for a week or two, maybe three, but then I would pick up the paper some night, turn to the sports page, and start to look for something. You know, the debts, the debts that you had to pay become a factor. "Oh, I owe this one a hundred this time, another fifty here, eighty there per month," you know; and how do you pay this? You know; and then you would start to look through the sports page again and look for, really be careful how you pick one out. Then you would keep on going and you'd—the idea of getting even. You couldn't wait around till there was, there was a maybe a good game the following, you know, next week. You would go for the damn hockey game that night or something. You know, just take a shot, a wild shot at something. Just to get even. Getting even seemed to be a goal, an objective that almost forced you to

want to find the easiest way of making that money, which is the same way in which you lost it.

This same process occurs in an alternative fashion because of some debts about which he had failed to tell his wife. He will attempt to hide these debts. All too frequently they creep up on him or he attempts to solve the problem by gambling. The cycle starts all over. In the following excerpt a compulsive-gambling hustler reverts to "sensible" gambling but eventually gets roped in himself.

> I told her about everything but one loan. This was my mistake. I told her about everything but one loan I had that I was paying sixty-five dollars a month on. It wasn't too far from being paid off. The other loans were paid off, and we bought a house out there [he and his wife sold their house to pay gambling debts and moved to Colorado for a geographical cure], and when I first started I was making enough money to pay the loan. I put the money aside and paid it, right? But then they took out the overtime. I wasn't making enough to cover it. I had to do something to cover it. [He took advantage of an opportunity to play a "sucker" at gin rummy. The sucker introduced him to the local dog track. The end result of the dog-track excursions was a three-hundred-dollar debt.] . . . I got to make up three hundred bucks or she is going to find out that I lost it. She would be furious. So I said, "Oh, Jesus." So I went to a bank in Colorado. I got five hundred dollars. That started me on the thing again. So now I got two things to pay.

In most cases the thought process of relapse involves reverting to the most successful mode of gambling, being careful not to make the same mistakes, or revising systems. The gambler is caught in the full-fledged chase, in which the prime desire is paying debts or winning back losses. Inevitably, however, in the effort to redeem himself socially or financially, the debts mount and the spiral continues.

The third precipitant of relapse is another external force: the fact that others are gambling around him. Gambling buddies come around and taunt the gambler. They tell him he is leading a boring, unexciting life, and he knows it. They constantly bring sports, horses, or other gambling-related interests into conversations. Constantly eating away at the reasons for disgust is the reminder that he should become involved once again in action. In addition, they offer him money or make suggestions as to how being "jammed up" can be resolved ("misery loves company"). If he has lost credit with the bookie, the friends offer to be the middleman for betting purposes. This influence of friends is more likely to occur right after he quits, and as a result most periods of abstinence are of short duration. The following is an example of disgust followed by relapse after a few weeks of not gambling. The friend facilitated involvement by opening up an option that in turn drove the spiral upward.

> And he pulled out this roll, you know, he had been winning a lot of money. So he said, "All right, I'll cover you. You want to win that three thirty back tonight, don't ya?" And I said, "I don't know if I really want to bother with this; I'm getting sick of losing, you know." He said, "No, really, just try it, you know." I said, "All right." And we won all five games; we won one thousand dollars for a night's work. I gave him his three thirty back and kept the rest [$170]. And, ah, a few weeks after that I lost more, just lose games, heh, heh, you know.

Even among those with few or no friends, an incident with an acquaintance who does gamble sparks off the gambling binge. People at work join office pools, or a guy he meets at a bar asks him if he is "down." (The more common situations are work-related.) A casual bet serves as an impetus to reinvolvement. As the Gamblers Anonymous pamphlet urges:

> Don't tempt or test yourself. Don't associate with acquaintances who gamble. Don't go in or near gambling establishments. Don't gamble for anything

—this means buying a raffle ticket, flipping a coin, or entering the office sports pool. If you don't make the first "tiny" bet, you can't make any big ones.

This admonition is based on years of experience with relapse. The reason for it is simple and clear. In periods of abstinence, the gambler can easily start thinking that small bets will not hurt. Reinvolvement occurs because the gambler does this seemingly minor thing and starts thinking of the action he is missing or the debts that could be paid if he is careful.

The fourth route back to gambling is the resolution of closure. During the closure state, unpredictable things happen that resolve the dilemma and increase involvement at the same time. Gambling friends are a common source of the closure resolution. Equally as important are chance occurrences, meeting an "old buddy" on the street who can, for example, be hit up for needed money, or having someone suggest seeing a certain banker who is "giving money away." Alternatively, the gambler justifies something that was not previously justifiable. The money is employed to gamble with or pay the overdue debts. After closure is relieved, the spiral moves up a level because of new option use.

The fifth route back to gambling occurs through a desire to be "normal." He wishes to think of himself as similar to the other gamblers out there, who can bet ten dollars on one race and leave the race track after that race. The Hyde portion of his Jekyll and Hyde personality is something he would like to deny. As a result, he goes to the track or "lets" himself be taken by a friend with the intention of betting just one race. Alternatively, he takes someone's hand at a poker game or places a small bet with the bookmaker. These efforts are designed to "test" whether he is really "normal" rather than a person who has lost control over gambling or is "sick," as the GA model would label him. Only one person I have interviewed succeeded in this type of experiment; all the others went back to gambling as heavily as before, even if for only a period of several days.[6]

The sixth route back to gambling is the financial crisis. At least two of the gamblers I interviewed relapsed after the first interview because of financial problems. One had not gambled in over five years, when his business burnt down. He spent three months at local race tracks trying to redeem the business. The other had not gambled for at least eighteen months, when a "connected" gambler to whom he owed several thousand dollars bumped into him one day and threatened his life. He went on a gambling spree until he spilled out his problem to his wife.

For two of the gamblers the financial crises came in the form of badgering by the wife over why there was not enough money coming into the house. Both stated they went to the race track to try to relieve this pressure.

Similar forms of financial "mini crisis" are possible, especially where the gambler is not totally honest with his spouse. The gambler when trying to quit will frequently tell himself that he can handle his problems and will hide loans as a result, or he may actually forget them because he has so many. Because these loans, no matter how small, can cause friction later on, Gamblers Anonymous has "pressure group" meetings in which the gambler tells the spouse about *all* the loans he has from *all* sources. In this way, old loans do not creep up to breach trust that has been breached all too often.

INVOLVEMENT AND ABSTINENCE: CYCLES

Abstinence and relapse are intertwined with the spiral of options and involvement the gambler is in. The *shape* of the cycles of abstinence and relapse change in a sequential fashion as the gambler becomes more involved in compulsive gambling. In this chapter I have looked at abstinence as a period of *uninvolvement* in gambling. The nature and shape of uninvolvement change as the gambler goes up the spiral. Since the careers of the gambler change so much from person to person, we can speak only in terms of early, middle, and late stages.

The first stage of the career occurs prior to any great debts. *Early* in their careers many gamblers get "sick of losing" and try to "tone down" the gambling in order to cut heavy losses —all in an effort gradually to win back what they have lost. "Toning down" occurs in two fashions: lowering the amounts wagered, and quitting the one or two forms of gambling they were losing at and still gambling at the "sure thing." The lessening of the action, excitement, and tension produced by less betting makes toning down of short duration (average time appears to be one week). Getting involved again at this stage is almost always a result of the influence of gambling friends.

The second, *middle stage* of the career depends on option use. After the gambler has used up several options, stopping gambling is likely to be a result of closure. This quitting is temporary, however, as closure is resolved in the majority of cases. During this span of time, toning down may be attempted but occurs more often at the beginning of relapse than during periods of gambling. Toning down, if it does occur, is involuntary. The pressures that work during periods of abstinence start to take on real significance. The gambler misses the action and makes "mind bets," and his old habits begin to creep up on him.

In the *late stage* of his career, as periods of more intense disgust and closure occur, there is more to be upset about. However, since past efforts to quit have been tried and all were unsuccessful, the gambler starts to think that quitting is not possible and gives up on trying. It takes a *greater* loss to bring on abstinence. When and if he does quit gambling, all five pressures to return from voluntary and semivoluntary abstinence are working. The irony has run its course: the more outward signs of problems appear, the less likely it is the gambler will quit gambling.

The periods of *involuntary abstinence* also occur in three stages. These occur in a slightly lagged fashion behind the stages of voluntary abstinence, but with a tremendous amount of overlap.

Involuntary abstinence is most frequently a product of the parents' or wife's admonitions. *Early* in his career the gambler will be discovered and repent for his sins of exploitation. The prime "penance" as the gambler sees it is abstinence from an activity he thoroughly enjoys and "knows" will recoup his past losses. The first few times, the gambler will have guilt feelings and be *truly* remorseful. As a result, while the abstinence is involuntary, it is partially a product of "maybe she's right." Almost invariably he will get over the guilt feelings and start gambling "sensibly." Here the quitting is partially voluntary. But gambling friends haunt him and minor pressures of the spiral rear their head; for example, gamblers ask him for money he owes them and the bookmaker will want to know when he is getting paid and why the gambler isn't "putting in any action."

After the first few times the husband has gone through this process, involuntary abstinence and relapse reach a *middle* stage. During this period the gambler will quit gambling merely to pacify his wife. He waits for the opportunity to return to gambling. During this time, abstinence lasts at most a week. By this time, the spiral is in full gear, the gambler is enmeshed in a fully self-enclosed system, and he feels he has "got to go" to the track, card game, or phone. All the running struggles during abstinence are working. As soon as his wife reduces social control, he is back in action. He gives her con stories; and while she wants to believe her husband, she becomes accusatory and may actually accuse him of gambling when he is not. The accusations provide an "excuse" for relapse. Of course, other gamblers and the continued spiral also exert pressure for relapse.

In the *late stage*, the wife comes to think she can no longer handle the problems herself. It is at this point that she can no longer stand the exploitation and decides to resort to outside assistance or threaten a "trial" separation or a divorce. This shock may be enough for the husband to make an honest effort to appease his wife again until something like gambling friends or the financial difficulties that have mounted interfere. It is during the last stage of his career of abstinence and relapse that confrontations with police, employers, and other agents of social control are likely to happen, when he "gets caught" or has to "face the music" with them. By this time all six forces are working to make relapse a greater probability.

## CHAPTER X

The Spiral of Options and Involvement

We have seen that compulsive gamblers are engaged in a spiral of options and involvement. The *options* include all those avenues the gambler uses to obtain money to continue his habit: family resources, occupational resources, bookmaking, lending institutions, fellow gamblers and suckers, and finally crime. Each of these is related to an increased *involvement* in compulsive gambling. This involvement consists of the chase, action, and increased troubles, financial worries, personal trauma, and above all an increase in *simultaneous use of many options*. While the options are used simultaneously, they are also *used up*. Therefore as the spiral moves upward, with increasing involvement, it gets smaller and smaller, as fewer options remain available. It is to the increasing troubles of involvement and the constriction of options that this chapter is devoted.

The cyclical movement of the gambler's spiral occurs in three repeated steps: (1) the attainment of money; (2) "moving," "manipulating," or "juggling" the money; and (3) a tightening of resources, called the closure state.

INVOLVEMENT AND OPTIONS

Each of the options is related to involvement in compulsive gambling in that the involvement in gambling necessitates the use of options that in turn produce more intense involvement and so on *ad infinitum*. The gambler becomes enmeshed in a *self-enclosed system* with its own force. Chasing and action as features of involvement produce losses by the sheer nature of the gambling system. The odds run against the gambler, and an additional vigorish is taken out that eventually creates losses. In order to redeem himself, the gambler resorts to the six option groupings, each of which has a force of its own. This produces the upward spiraling movement into deeper and deeper compulsive gambling.

The family acts as an agent in three fashions: First, getting married puts added pressure on income that is already typically strained to pay debts or gamble. Second, the family illustrates the nature of gambling as a *non-sharable problem*. Losses and loans prove to be ugly evidence of exploitation, and the gambler resorts to further gambling in order to preserve his *respectability* in the eyes of parents, wife, and others. The gambler is constantly hiding at least some of the loans he has out. Inevitably, these loans creep up to haunt him later. Because he has hidden them, however, he must resort to further gambling to resolve these problems. The result is always further debt through gambling. As a desire to hide *exploitation*, the gambler lies and signs his wife's signature to get loans. If he later defaults on the loans, the loan company, bank, or credit union will attempt to contact the "cosigner" (his wife). Fear of her finding out produces a drive to gamble and win to pay the loans.

Third, the use of family resources as an option generates pressure to hide that use by putting back "borrowed" resources. After these resources are used up, the gambler must look beyond the paycheck and family savings as a way out or as a way to recover the "borrowed" family money.

The occupational situation does not in and of itself produce strains to increase involvement. Free time at work through a less supervised occupation or self-employment, however, does provide an opportunity for intensified gambling and efforts to get even. There are now extra card games to go to or more afternoons at the track. With more chances to gamble come greater possibilities to lose money. The free time is, in a sense, a blessing in disguise. As for those who "borrowed" from work, the tension produced accelerated the gambling spiral. Again, with more gambling comes a greater chance that losing streaks will extend beyond the budget and force the gambler to use up another option, thus constricting future choice.

Bookmaking has an influence for those who bet with the bookie and for the bookies themselves. Betting with book-makers generates two factors that tend to increase involve-ment: credit, and fear of bookmaker response. The *credit* na-ture of sports betting allows the gambler to bet with money he does not have in order to "get even." After the bet is over, however, he has to pay. The result is greater option use and more gambling to win back losses. *Fear of bookmakers* takes two forms: fear of being cut off and fear of violence. The first is very real and served as an impetus for borrowing to pay, and in a few cases the pressure induced petty crime. The second fear—violence—was evidenced in only a few cases, but this, too, served as a force toward more gambling and in some cases crime.

In the career of the gamblers turned bookmakers, book-making, with the opportunity for "cheaper betting" with the layoff man and the example of customers' wagering, increases involvement by raising the probability that the gambler will raise his stakes and bet on more events.

Problems with customers and support-group members such as various schemes to "screw the book," partners who embez-zle, and pressure from "connected" layoff men to pay off when customers fail to pay take their toll. Each of these ac-tions feeds into the spiral in a self-producing fashion to in-crease involvement in compulsive gambling.

The use of lending institutions as a way to get money for gambling heightens the spiral by the added problem of paying off the debts along with interest without anyone's finding out. In the case of Shylock loans this debt is of sufficient magni-tude to be threatening in itself. In addition there is the threat of disclosure and the threats of harassment from finance com-panies and of physical violence from loan sharks. Check for-gery poses pressures all its own in that it includes fear of con-viction for crime as well as the loss of respectability that discovery would entail.

Gambling friends are perhaps the major medium to other options. Just by sheer association, involvement becomes more intense as friends provide rationales for gambling as well as certain illegal actions. Those who were members of gambling groups were more likely than loners to have loans with a loan shark, hustle, make book, cheat, swindle suckers, and fence. Being part of an action system almost assured involvement in at least two or more of these activities. You can borrow only so much from loan sharks and other resources within the gambling world; the pool, golf, and bowling hustler may become "burned out" as others find out about his playing abilities and he begins to take bad matches. There are only so many suckers to swindle, given the coming ability most of the gamblers possessed.[1] Once these resources become constricted, others must be relied upon.

The constriction of options and the pressures and threat were seen to be major incentives to illegal activity engaged in by the gambler. As noted in Chapter VIII, there are three stages of involvement in illegal activities, each of which is preceded by a constriction of previously available resources: (1) ideologically and/or situationally justifiable actions; (2) partially justifiable actions that are also excused; and, finally, (3) unjustifiable actions that are excused based on threat. Only those actions that are conceived of as "borrowing" feed back into the gambling spiral. This is because "borrowed" money must be returned. The illegal nature of the "borrowing" provides more pressure.

The cycles of abstinence and relapse also feed into the spiral. According to at least three of the gamblers, the probability that bets would increase is higher after a short span of abstinence. As the following gambler attests:

> It seemed that, I guess that I got discouraged and, ah, would stop it for a while and then after get the itch to, ah, start goin' on it again and, ah, it seemed that when I would go back the stakes would increase each time. They would either be the same or go up. I figured it out that I would be able to make more money by betting more, so it, it would be increased when I would go back.

This is also a popular theme in Gamblers Anonymous.

The interaction of all these features produces an upward spiral in which the gambler gradually uses up resources for funding. This spiral occurs in a *cyclical* fashion. The cycles have three steps.

Step One: getting money to gamble or pay debts

The various options the gambler uses to finance his gambling occur in a roughly *sequential* fashion. The decisions to order the options in this manner are rational choices involving the pros and cons of each line of activity, such as cost in respectability, ease of access, the degree to which the lender understands the problem, as well as the degree of a gambler's support system for illegal behavior. There is a natural *progression* that is followed.

All gamblers start by using personal spending money (including hustled money for those who hustled and stolen money for those who were juvenile delinquents) as well as winnings to finance their gambling. Interspersed with this are the very common short-term loans from gambling friends. These are the most commonly used resources before marriage. For some of the gamblers there are mistakes and disaster prior to marriage, subsequent loans, and "facing the music." For the bulk, however, loans come after marriage. The married gamblers get their gambling money by gradually expanding the domain of "spending money." Simultaneous with this, if away from home and out of money or if personal resources have run low, they first borrow from gambling buddies. Gambling friends are chosen first because they understand the problems the gambler has and usually will attach no conditions to the loan.

> These people can identify with your problems. If I lost all my money at the track, it's easier to borrow from a gambling friend, because he understands gambling. He knows why you lost all your money at the track. You can't go up to your father-in-law, who's never placed a bet in his life, and say lend me one hundred dollars because I just blew all my money in a card game. He'll take a more severe attitude; he'll say, "Well, I'm not going to lend it to

you; that'll teach you a lesson." You see, you'd
never get that from a gambler.

If gambling buddies do not have the money, a gambler will
borrow from household resources (bankbook being the most
common). Loan companies come later because of the desire to
maintain respectability.

Loan companies first [after gambling friends and
household resources], because I didn't want the [non-
gambling] friends or family or anybody to know
what I was doing or how involved I really was.

Following loan companies come the parents or the wife. This
is avoided at first because of the conditions the gambler
knows will be attached.

If I couldn't get it from the loan companies, then
I'd go to my mother and say, "I need the money
but I'm not gonna gamble no more. This is it."

After the parents or wife are approached, other (old or
new) sources open up and the gambler pursues them until
closure occurs, whereupon he may pass bad checks, fence
stolen goods, or engage in other illegal activities. One gambler
talked of this constriction of available options in the following, sequential terms:

Credit union, finance company, and then banks.
And then, when they were all dried up, then you go
to your parents and then your—stuff like that. Parents and friends. And then, when that's dried up,
you start stealing.

Once the gambler is taking out loans, the sequential pattern
of behavior begins to break down. In order to investigate the
pattern that exists after loans were taken out, activities that
were on career sheets (see Appendix A) were listed in rank
order of their use by the gamblers to finance gambling. These
activities are listed in the table on pages 224–25.

The table uses chronologically ranked order. A rank of 1 means that this activity was engaged in first, a rank of 10 (only one person did ten different things) means that activity occurred tenth. For nineteen gamblers, there was either a point at which they started many things at approximately the same time or they had problems remembering exactly what came before what. In these cases ties resulted. For example, one gambler began hustling suckers and juvenile delinquency at approximately the same time. I scored both at 1.5 rather than giving one an arbitrary rank of 1 and the other a rank of 2, and scored all ties in this fashion. The early patterns of hustling, juvenile delinquency, and running parlay cards, numbers, and betting slips were noted above. These were essentially adventurous activities that were geared toward excitement and status within the community.

The four persons (28.5 per cent of larcenies) who stole early in their careers were all college students at the time. The actions are explainable in terms of early closure, which was a product of an inability to obtain credit in a legal fashion. Two cases in which drugs (marijuana in both instances) were sold to finance gambling were also of this fashion. Each of these persons had depleted their bank accounts and saw these activities as an easy and ideologically or situationally justifiable way of getting money. The following was a rather typical comment when I asked one gambler about the circumstances surrounding selling dope:

> When I was really down and I owed money, I had wasted all my money that I needed to survive on in the week. Lunch money, carfare, and shit like that. I blew it all playing poker. . . . There was nothing left in the bank account.
> Q. OK, did you ever think of taking a loan out?
> A. Yeh, but I was too young, first of all. I couldn't think of what to say. You had to be at least eighteen. I thought about that. I hate borrowing and I hate loaning. There was nothing really substantial. I wouldn't have lied to take out a loan. Selling dope isn't that bad, you know.

Options (percentaged in Chronological Order) Used by Gamblers

Options

Chronologically Ranked Order	Hustling Suckers	Juvenile Delinquency (a)	Loans	Making Book	Shylock Loan	Larceny	Pimping (a)	Employee Theft + Embezzlement
1–1.5	90.9	(4)	60.0	16.7	11.5	21.4		4.5
2–2.5	9.1	(1)	20.0	33.3	42.3	7.1		18.2
3–3.5			4.4	29.2	19.2	21.4	(1)	31.8
4–4.5			8.9	12.5	7.7	28.6	(1)	27.3
5–5.5			6.7		11.5	14.3		9.1
6–6.5					3.8			4.5
7–7.5				4.2	3.8	7.1		4.5
8–10				4.2				
Total (b)	100	–	100	100.1	99.8	99.9	–	99.9
N	11	5	45	24	26(c)	14	2	22(d)
Mean rank for the option	1.14	1.2	1.82	2.97	3.0	3.46	3.5	3.59

In addition we have seen that behavior is ordered in terms of the support system used. The moral stands a gambler takes and the system of rationalizations he can use are most important for his life and sanity. This support system, combined with varying degrees of threat, changes throughout the gambler's career. The following shows the progression in the support needed as threat increases. There is a clear preference

	Act accomplished perceived as	Stages of support system usage
increasing threat ↓	totally moral	1. ideological or situational justification ·
	partially moral partially immoral	2. partial justification along with excuses
	immoral	3. excused only—not justified

for *legal options* in the order discussed above. Following these legal options are *illegal options*. However, certain illegal options have *ideological support* and are therefore very likely to occur *prior* to any *legal* option. If they are used after, it is not because of a perceived immorality but, rather, as a result of restricted opportunity, agents of social control, and percep-

Income Tax Evasion (a)	Cheating Suckers (a)	Checks	Systematic Fraud	Selling Drugs (a)	Burglary (a)	Fencing	Swindling Suckers (a)	Armed Robbery (a)
			7.1					
(1)	(1)	35.0		(1)			(1)	
	(2)	10.1	28.6	(1)	(2)	18.2		
	(1)	10.0	14.3		(2)	18.2	(2)	
		20.0	21.4		(2)		(1)	(1)
(1)	(1)	10.0	14.3		(1)	27.3	(2)	
	(1)	5.0	14.3		(1)	36.4		
		10.0		(1)			(2)	(2)
–	–	100.1	100	–	–	100.1	–	–
2(e)	6	20	14	3	8	11	8	3
4.0	4.33	4.33	4.5	4.5	4.81	5.68	5.75	7.0

(a) percentages not calculated for those options with fewer than ten engaging in the activity; number in parentheses
(b) total percentages do not add up to 100 per cent because of rounding error
(c) one case with missing data (true N = 27)
(d) two cases, engaged in theft of both items and money, are counted twice (true N = 20)
(e) total on income tax evasion includes only non-bookmaking-related actions

tion of risk. This was the case with those who made book only after having loans out.

Even *after* illegal options are commenced, legal avenues frequently open and are made available at a later date. When this occurs, the gambler will use the most immediate means of financing that is within the justifiable range.

The ordering of the other activities fits into the framework discussed in previous chapters. The gamblers borrow before stealing. That there is a *relatively* sequential ordering of activities is evident by looking at the average rank for each option. For *absolute* ordering, however, knowledge of situational opportunity is necessary. What is surprising is that, given their ideological base, fencing and swindling suckers did not occur earlier. One would hypothesize that the deterrent effect of punishment is strong for fencing (the fences mentioned being careful to whom they sold the hot goods) and that certain types of swindles are in reality perceived to be stealing. As a result, the sequential ordering of support could explain the later occurrence of these activities. They are seen to be only *partially justifiable* and follow totally justified actions the individuals engage in. It is possible that what I perceived to be an ideological support was an account to me for the behavior despite my attempts to separate accounts and ideology. An alternative that should be explored in future research is that the ideological support is accepted only later in the career.[2]

Following the partially justified options are the *unjustifiable* acts. The last place of robbery in the rank ordering provides some support for this. In addition, if we divide column 6 (larceny) into grand larceny and petty larceny, the three cases of grand larceny account for the three highest-ranked cases. They have a mean rank of 5.66, higher than burglary. These three cases, along with the two robberies with a rank of seven, were the only unjustifiable acts committed by the gamblers.

Step Two: moving money

After the gambler has gotten money at each stage of the spiral, he will manipulate money so that he can maintain credit and continue gambling at the same time. In addition to manipulating money, the gambler manipulates sources of funding in order to "keep lines open." He will try to "buy time" and use other ways of stalling creditors so he can keep on manipulating and gambling. This manipulation is yet another feature of involvement. As the gambler is gambling more compulsively, he will also move money in more complex ways.

When the gambler first starts borrowing money, he will not have to juggle his funds too much. As he progresses, however, the juggling takes on massive proportions as the number of options used simultaneously increases. When this occurs, the gambler appears to feel more and more that his life is organized around wheeling and dealing in various ways to get money to feed his habit.

Several ways of moving money are possible. Each of them, in turn, is more complex and serious (financially or legally) than the previous methods. The gambler can borrow from one person to pay another, borrow from one institution to

cover another, get consolidation loans, delay paying people
while using that money to gamble or to pay others, juggle
with bookmakers, use "bouncing" checks (without sufficient
funds to cover them) to pay loans, and possibly use other
checks to cover the first, resort to embezzlement to pay loans
or cover checks, fence, swindle, burglarize, or in some other
fashion try to pay bills by hustling or theft.

The most common form of moving money is to borrow
from one source in order to pay another. It can be rather simple, as in the consolidation of debts by taking out a loan to
pay other bills or the use of borrowed money to make a loan
payment. The following types of comments are exceedingly
common:

> I just managed to borrow from Peter to pay Paul.

> I used to play one of them type of cons. . . . Bor-
> row from one Shylock to pay back the other one.
> You know what I mean?

Many did not just stop at "borrowing from Peter to pay
Paul." They also borrowed from Paul to pay Peter and vice
versa in a cyclical fashion. This is true with individual loans.

> Even at work you tell the guy, "Give me twenty
> dollars till payday." So payday comes, you ain't got
> the money. 'Cause you need it for gamblin'. You
> borrow from another guy to pay that guy. You pay
> him next week. It sure is easy to get money. I used
> to have ten guys at work I would borrow from
> every week. Five one week, five the next week. I
> used the present week to pay the other five from the
> past week. Now, I never used to have to use my
> money to pay back money. It is very easy to do.

It is also true with consolidations. Several gamblers use
banks to consolidate loan-company loans and use loan companies (or credit unions) to consolidate bank loans despite
the seeming illogical nature of the move because of the higher
rate of interest at loan companies.

Any activity that gives the gambler recourse to funds for a certain period of time, be it one to four days with a check or possibly months or years with embezzlement and some varieties of swindles, will allow him to use this money to pay pressing bills at the moment they are due and thereby maintain credit. "Borrowing," hustling, or theft are capable of fulfilling these functions. Illegal activities are ways out of problems created by loans.

If after a gambler has "borrowed" from his checking account or work, new avenues for funds become open, the legal avenues can be used as a resource to solve problems as they arise from illegal resources. In a sense, *money can be moved in both directions.* Once more "serious" forms of activity are engaged in, the gambler can resort to old avenues of funds in order to recover. Of course, this is feasible only if these old avenues become "open" again for some reason. For example, he may have paid three payments on one of his finance-company loans and as a result can "rewrite" the loan to cover outstanding checks.

While the gambler juggles funds, he does so with the intention of "keeping lines open" and relieving pressure from creditors. In the case of consolidation, when a new loan is taken out to consolidate old debts, the previous debtors now become free and credit is maintained.

> You borrow (these are all numbers, of course) one hundred dollars, one hundred dollars, one hundred dollars. Well, you consolidate it. You go to another place and borrow three hundred dollars. You pay off these three places. Now you owe three hundred dollars to this one place. Right? But now, what you've done is you've opened up the other three places all over again. They're avenues all over again; you can go back and borrow from them again. Because you made a loan from them and paid them off. They're happy and your credit is good.

These two functions (keeping lines open and relieving pressure) are exceedingly important for the gambler, because he knows that without credit he cannot gamble. As a result, the gambler will pay his gambling friends and the bookmaker *first* because of their proximity to the gambling situation. With these lines open, the gambler is assured of staying in action for the day.

> If there were two guys that I knew I could always borrow two fifty to five hundred off, I would always keep them paid. If I had to, I would go anywhere to get the money to pay *them*. This way I know if I come up the corner and say, ah, I need five hundred, I would get it right away. Always juggle other money to keep them happy. So, whenever I needed it I would get it from them.

As another gambler put it, he was "buying insurance for future credit." The idea here is to maintain some "operating money." If he could not get it from the loan company or bank right away, at least he knew where he could get it if he needed it. A similar thing is done with regard to lending institutions. They are paid off at first because bills are owed. Later on, they are paid in order to insure future credit. While manipulating money occurs in credit situations in which friends and institutions are borrowed from, it also occurs in the relations with the bookmaker. Again the emphasis here is on maintaining credit and "keeping the lines open." This form of moving money was discussed under the backdrop of bookie-customer relations.

A major move to "keep lines open" is the attempt to stall creditors by using various tactics to "buy time." Manipulating creditors to extend credit or grant a reprieve of some sort from payments or disaster was employed to forestall closure.

Gamblers pay their debts on time and rarely stall, especially in earlier phases of their career. With increasing debt, however, came increasing problems with paying creditors. The gamblers would have trouble manipulating money and subsequently have to deceive creditors in an effort to continue with their activity.

The tactics used to "buy time" vary depending on the amount of control gamblers have over the flow of information to their wives or parents. If the gambler is not that afraid his wife or parents will find out, he will fail to show up at the loan company, bank, or credit union. If he is afraid, he will show up. In either case, there are several stories the gambler can use when the institution inquires about failure to pay. The most commonly used lines take the form of: "I am out of work." "I was sick." "I didn't get paid—the accounting system. . . ." "Business is unusually slow." In these cases the blame is foisted on someone else—a common pattern that flows through much of the gamblers' lies and other deceptions.

Following this, the gamblers rely on promises about future payment: "It's in the mail" or "I will be down to see you." These tactics are relied upon whether or not the money really is in the mail and even if in fact he intends to see the officials just in order to "buy time." In the meantime, the gambler may win at the track or move some money from somewhere (legally or illegally) in order to satisfy this commitment.

If worse comes to worst, the gambler can attempt to bargain with the creditors about paying them. One person mentioned settling with the loan companies he owed money to by paying off only the principal in a more rapid period of time. What is more common was an amortized loan—typically suggested by Gamblers Anonymous—whereby the gambler paid the present debt but at a reduced rate per month. The gamblers had to bargain as to whether the interest would also accrue. The typical response is to pay only the original note at a reduced payment per month with no new interest being added. A final alternative is bankruptcy.[3]

With heightened difficulties and more loans and other manipulative avenues of funding being used *at the same time,* more moving or wheeling and dealing occurs. The gamblers talk about life as a "big round robin" or "cycles" in which manipulating money becomes extremely important, for without it the gambler cannot gamble.

> Well, when you gamble, Henry, it's always to move money. You always owe, but you never, ah, you get it from one place to pay another. It's a big round robin. Consequently, you get in deeper and deeper

until you just can't catch up. If you borrow one
hundred dollars, then you have to pay it back. You
might borrow one hundred ten dollars to pay back
the one hundred dollars and have ten dollars to
gamble with. If you're gambling, you don't pay the
one hundred dollars; you save that, and you just
keep moving money all over the place. But you always seem to be able to move money. Then there's a
thing you borrow (these are all numbers, of course)
one hundred dollars, one hundred dollars, one hundred dollars. Well, you consolidate it.

When the gambler reaches a stage where his bills become
greater than his paycheck can handle, his gambling becomes
further intensified, and he will get loans to pay old loans, as
in the above quotation. With more avenues used, there is
more "finagling" going on. It may increase with such complexity that the gambler actually forgets whom he owes what
to. It is not uncommon for a new GA member to fail to list
all his creditors in a pressure-group meeting, a session designed to reveal to the non-gambling spouse all the money
that is owed. In some cases this occurs because he actually
had forgotten to whom he owed money. The following quote
is one among many.

I don't even know today how many people I borrowed from or how many people I still owe. I don't
even remember how much money I borrowed from
my brothers, my mother, my father. I just know
that when I needed money they had it. I got it. If
you ask me how much I repaid 'em, I don't know. I
forget. I'm all absorbed. What do I care how much?
The only thing that I was interested in was that I
got what I was after. I needed a loan of one hundred dollars that day, I got it, I was gone. I went
saw them two months later, got another one hundred, two hundred; it never made any difference
to me. I got my money, I was gone. I used to keep
telling myself that I am going to repay 'em, but I
never give a damn. You have one obsession: get

the money. Once you get the money you don't care.
You are off and running.

Not only do the gamblers forget whom they owe money to
and exactly how much they owe, but they do not want to face
this ugly reality.

You get into such a financial situation that you really have no idea of exactly how much you owe.
You really never know; you don't want to. You
don't want to sit down and list it. It scares you.

Not only borrowed but also stolen money feeds into the
process. Although stolen and hustled money relieves some
pressures created by gambling and debts, for all but three of
the gamblers, the amount of money stolen was not enough
to totally eliminate pressures. These three were thieves by occupation: two systematic check forgers and one card and dice
hustler and pimp. They were under pressure for two reasons:
they were chasing their losses and they were frequently in
debt to Shylocks. Two of the three had continual loans that
they manipulated. However both eventually produced enough
to get out of debt. The third was making $100,000 passing
bad checks and went through $90,000 of it at the race track.
He wished to quit gambling so he could really "make money"
passing checks instead of blowing it at the track.

Step Three: the closure state

The gambler can move only so much money among so
many people. Gradually and periodically "things start tightening up." There is no place to go to get money, or at least the
gambler *thinks* there is nowhere to go. Closure sets in. Closure is a state of mind as well as a perception that there is no
money. Since it is a subjective state, the number of times it is
experienced varies among the gamblers.[4]

Resolution of the closure problem depends on the situation.
In the gambling situation, closure is resolved by gambling
madly in an attempt to recoup losses, borrowing or using
other legal means of getting money, using illegal sources of

funding, escaping (physically or into nervous breakdown or suicide), or by quitting gambling.

If money cannot be moved—"no way, no how"—the gambler attempts to gamble madly in the hopes that he will bail out and be able to relieve the pressure. For some this works; for others it does not. Gambling madly as an option may be closed, as the gambler may have no money to go to the track or casino with and the bookmakers can have him "shut off" until he pays what he owes.

Several options are still available to the gambler after he has gone to all the people he felt he could approach who he felt had the money and would let him borrow it and has "gambled madly." He can run away from his problems (four ran away from bookmakers, the law, and loan sharks; two others took off for Las Vegas in the hopes that their problems would be solved there); or he can commit suicide. Running away solves the problem only temporarily. Sooner or later he must return if he has any commitments at home, such as a wife and children. In addition, running away may jeopardize his job.

Some gamblers all but give up hope of getting money, lose sleep, and have anxiety attacks, when something like the following happens:

> Lo and behold, a letter came in my mailbox at school. "The credit union has just upped the, ah, you know, the signature loan from fifteen hundred to two thousand." Here it is, beautiful. I mean, it is amazing how it is that things would just sometimes happen, or you would think of something.

"Think of something" is what most gamblers did. This was made easier if the gambler was tapped into a group of manipulators who knew of the defects in the structure of lending institutions. He may overhear a conversation among other gamblers about Master Charge, ninety-day notes, or some other scheme about which he was unaware. For some gamblers it is bankers or non-gambling friends or relatives who make the suggestions. For most there is a combination of gambling and non-gambling sources of resolution suggestions.

If there is no outside help or suggestions, the gambler will think up schemes to resolve his closure. Most frequently the gamblers resign themselves to the inevitability of asking someone they did not want to ask for money, going to another bank or loan company, or thinking of some other scheme to get money in whatever fashion. For some gamblers, there are periodic bail-outs from parents, wives, relatives, or friends to whom they go for help. Bail-outs as such are more common among middle-class than working- and lower-class gamblers.

If bail-outs are not possible either because the last bail-out was a month ago or because of a promise that bail-outs had ceased, and threat is intense enough, the gambler goes to those avenues he had subjectively blocked out as feasible. Loan fraud, bad checks, embezzlement, fencing, etc., are used at this point for some, yet not for others. Many gamblers think up solutions while in bed, after which they can go to sleep. Insomnia is reported by 60 per cent of compulsive gamblers.[5]

> I remember laying in bed and I just couldn't fall asleep. I can remember on Sunday, Monday was always the worse day, 'cause that's the day you had to pay the bookie. I used to stay and watch television until it was time to go to bed, and then I'd lay there and think about where I was gonna get money the next day. I think the only time I'd fall asleep was when I'd think of somebody who would lend me the money. Then I'd fall asleep. Waking up in the morning was cruel. Because now it's no longer night; now you're facing the world. You know, you've got to go out and face it, whoever it is you want to borrow the money from. It was a cruel thing.

This worrying and tension brought on various types and degrees of physical ailments. High blood pressure and ulcers were the most common, as well as jitters and nervous tension.

Three of the four who had nervous breakdowns went for regular, systematic psychiatric treatment; the fourth received medicine from a doctor to calm him down (his heart was beating so fast he thought he was going to die). The three who saw psychiatrists were committed to mental hospitals for varying periods of time. Several other GA members have gone to counselors and priests about their problem. The remark common to all was that these people failed to understand the gambling problem.[6]

The state of depression can be such that *suicide* is considered. There are stories at GA meetings of friends who have shot themselves, died in auto accidents, or killed themselves by carbon-monoxide poisoning. One Mafia-style killing was thought to have been planned that way. Half of the compulsive gamblers I interviewed seriously contemplated suicide. The methods thought of varied: "tying a few bowling balls to my wrists and going," to cutting oneself with knives, using a gun, carbon monoxide, and automobile crashes. The last was most preferred; 50 per cent of those who stated methods gave this one. Death in an automobile is thought to be relatively fast (especially driving off a cliff) and had the added incentive of being insurable.

> I had a tank of gas one night, riding around one night trying to get enough nerve; I drove around the reservoir. And I even thought about committing suicide with the car. The sad part about that is my friend who was a compulsive gambler did just that last summer, thirty-nine years old, carbon-monoxide poisoning. When I read about it in the papers, it gave me the shivers. At the time, if I did it my wife wouldn't get any insurance money. I figured, jees, if I'm gonna commit suicide I want to fix it so it looked like an accident because of the insurance policy states that my wife wouldn't collect for a suicide. After all the misery I caused I could at least leave her with the bills paid, anyway.

Contemplating suicide is more likely for married than nonmarried gamblers. Only one of the single gamblers seriously thought of or planned suicide; he was one of the three gamblers who had been hospitalized. Several married gamblers took out extra insurance policies and hoped they would get a blowout in their car or prayed their plane would crash. In a *sense* they deliberately gambled with death, hoping it would come without overt action on their part. Unsuccessful attempts are also discussed: driving one hundred miles an hour on canvas tires (here hoping for a blowout that never came) and hitting telephone poles (one person hit a telephone pole at seventy miles an hour and came out without a scratch). Most, however, "didn't have the guts" to kill themselves. For those who seriously considered it, there were thoughts of the shambles they would leave behind in unpaid bills and an insurance policy that would not pay if suicide was found to be the cause of death.

It is obvious that the solutions that would work to get the gambler out of the spiral are not used. People do not run away because they have commitments at home, they do not become professional thieves because of moral belief structures and they do not commit suicide because they "didn't have the guts" and because it is not insurable.

CONTINGENCIES IN THE SPIRAL OF OPTIONS AND INVOLVEMENT

There are seven contingencies of great importance in determining the *shape* of the spiral in the career of the compulsive gambler. Five of these have already been discussed: marital status, degree of supervision in occupation, extent of involvement in gambling circles (from loner to subculturally oriented), credit and its determinants, and social class.[7] The other two factors are personal values and the ability to move money.

Some of the effects of value structure on the career have been previously discussed. At one end of the value-structure continuum are those gamblers who saw theft as a way of life. Coinciding with this way of life is a conception of stolen money as *"free money."* There were two systematic check forgers who made one hundred thousand dollars a year passing checks and a gambler who "took money from women" and acted as a shill in large-stakes poker and dice games who earned forty to fifty thousand dollars a year doing these things. They all saw this illegally obtained money as free to spend and use to "live it up."[8] The paradox of the compulsive

gambler with "free money" is that his use of the money is se-
verely constrained. These three gamblers conceived of themselves as being "sucked in bad" by the urge to *get even*—the
desire to win back all that was lost. Since the amount lost is
greater than that lost by the "working stiff," getting even is a
much more remote reality. Two of the three borrowed heavily
from loan sharks in addition to the crimes they used as a
source of "free money." They "produced" however and eventually paid their debts.

The ability to "move money" is also a major contingency.
All the subculturally oriented gamblers were good at manipulation. It brought status within the group, and hints about
whom to hit up and how to wheel and deal were commonplace forms of discussion. The ability to juggle present funds
and open up new opportunities without resorting to actions
that are not fully justifiable can conceivably stretch out the
period of time it takes to reach later stages in the career. In
the subculture, however, introductions to the "wrong kind of
people" (that is, "connected" bookmakers and Shylocks) in-
tensifies other threat.

Two out of the three "movers" who extended their careers
in the longest fashion were *not* group-oriented. These were
the two gamblers with seventeen and twenty-two simultaneous
loans. The first, with seventeen loans, borrowed on non-existent used cars. The second, with twenty-two loans, asked
friends to take out loans for him. Both these gamblers came
to think that they could borrow their way out of debt. Their
last loans were made just to pay loans. Both put most of their
effort toward manipulating these loans and thinking of how
they could keep them going. The other of the three best movers was the person described in Chapter VII who fenced by
charging TVs, liquor, and other goods and reselling them. In
a sense he was "borrowing" the money. He also spent many
of his waking hours in this activity. As a result of the ability
to move money, there is a delay in, and possibly total avoidance of, personally unjustifiable activity. However, the paradox is that good money-moving ability results in greater
debts.

COMPULSIVE BEHAVIOR

The spiral the gambler experiences is undoubtedly like that of many others with unsharable problems. Alcoholics, woman chasers, drug addicts, status seekers, business failures, and others discussed by Lemert (1967a) and Cressey (1971) in all probability "moved money" and became involved in the enclosed system of options and involvement. From looking at the career of the compulsive gambler, we could predict that drug addicts would use the world of drugs as a primary means of financing their habit, much as gamblers use theirs. If we were in prohibition periods, we would expect bartenders and rumrunners to be infiltrated by alcoholics. We could expect that woman chasers and status seekers, too, may join in subcultural orientation around the values of chasing women and seeking status to such an extent that cosigning loans and talking about "easy" banks may be commonplace happenings. In addition to an increase in financial problems, collateral problems also result at home and work. Woman chasers and status seekers become better liars and are constantly aware of discovery. Changes in self-conception also occur that are products of increasing external pressure. The status seeker, for example, may come to realize that with the heightening front that he puts on for his neighbors comes an ever greater necessity to reaffirm that front and possibly enhance it. With mounting debt, however, can come the realization that he might be the failure he does not want to admit to himself he is. This continues until he eventually accepts a Jekyll and Hyde concept of his personality, much as the compulsive gambler does of himself. Similar comparisons can be made for each of the processes that together make up the spiral of options and involvement.

One question we can pose is: why are our jails and prisons filled with drug addicts rather than compulsive gamblers? It is possible that there are more addicts, but this may not be the case. What is more probable is that imprisoned addicts experienced a need for money at an earlier age. Their needs tend to be more immediate and not delayable, as are the gambler's. The gambler is more able to stall the bookmaker for credit or use another bookmaker as a resource. The young addicts, on the other hand, have no credit established, no home ownership, and no business enterprises that can be utilized for credit purposes. This results in more rapid movement up the spiral and earlier arrest. The criminal record in turn diminishes the possibility that the addict will obtain credit. The gambler, because of established credit, tends to become a master of *precriminal behavior*. By precriminal behavior I mean civil fraud in loan applications, tremendous patterns of lies and deception to keep this fraud going, "borrowing" from checking accounts (often just missing arrest), and engaging in hustles that are perceived by the general public as less serious than "pushing" heroin or other drugs. By and large, the gamblers engaged in lower-risk behavior, which carries lesser punishments. Banks "punish" check writing by withdrawing accounts before the gambler gets arrested. Company officials fire employees rather than subject them to prosecution. Hustlers and cheats are rarely, if ever, prosecuted. Despite these factors, compulsive gambling is much more serious and deserves more attention than criminology and deviance experts grant at present.

This research is the first to ask the question of how the compulsive gambler's world is constructed in his own eyes. Now that we know about the subculture of gambling, I leave it to someone else to investigate it in more detail. Ask about women, professional thieves, and gambling in prison if you will, and do not leave it to neglect as in the past or to the psychiatrists, about whom the gamblers themselves say, "He never had much experience with gamblers obviously . . . from the gems he was pumping out." I hope no one will ever say that about me.

Afterword: Sociologists and the
Medical Model of Pathological Gambling

According to Gambling Commission surveys in 1974, 61 percent of the United States populace gambled. The percentage is probably greater in 1984 because of increased legalization of gambling. The vast bulk of these people are social gamblers. For them, gambling is an enjoyable pastime. The 1974 survey estimated that there are 1.1 million "probably compulsive gamblers" in the population. These are persons who have a chronic and progressive failure to resist impulses to gambling. They cannot resist gambling behavior even though it compromises, disrupts and damages personal, family and vocational pursuits.

In the nineteenth century and until very recently in the twentieth, the dominant view of those who gambled beyond their means was a moral one. The heavy gambler who lost was a sinner or criminal. Moralists used the Protestant ethic as their guide to associate gambling with sloth—with a desire to avoid work. Gradually, beginning with psychoanalytic theorists and continuing to the establishment of Gamblers Anonymous in 1957, this view was challenged. In place of a moral model, a medical model was embraced. At Gamblers Anonymous, for example, members state: "My name is _____, I am a compulsive gambler." The notion of "compulsion" implies illness. It implies that treatment is needed rather than moral condemnation.

In the 1970's and 1980's six distinctive developments occurred which had an impact on the traditional image of the gambler. (1) Legalized gambling increased at record levels. According to the Gambling Commission studies and most experts, this trend will continue and will increase the number of pathological gamblers. An increase in the number has brought more public attention to the issue leading to greater media coverage including interviews with Gamblers Anonymous members and with clinicians attempting to deal with the problem. (2) In April, 1972, at the request of a local Gamblers Anonymous chapter, an inpatient treatment program for compulsive gamblers was initiated by the Veterans Administration at their Brecksville, Ohio Medical Center. This was the first such center anywhere. (3) In the same year, a group of gamblers and professionals initiated the National Council on Compulsive Gambling which has as its prime purpose the education of the public to the view that compulsive gambling is a treatable illness. (4) In 1976, the Commission on the Review of National Policy Toward Gambling gave some attention to the disorder by surveying the population to find out with some degree of accuracy the extent of compulsive gambling. (5) In 1980, the American Psychiatric Association recognized pathological gambling in its Diagnostic and Statistical Manual as a "Disorder of Impulse Control." (6) As a consequence of the above events, treatment programs have been established by the states of Maryland, Connecticut and New York and the state of New Jersey has funded a hotline with an interesting toll free number—(800) GAMBLER.

SOCIOLOGISTS AND THE MEDICAL MODEL

Sociologists have made comments on medical models. For the most part, they are skeptical of the medicalization of deviant behavior. Sociologists point to the "darker side" of the disease model. They raise numerous issues with regards to the medical approach to alcoholism, kleptomania, homesexuality and crime (Conrad and Schneider, 1980). And it should not be surprising that they are currently skeptical of the medical approach to gambling problems.

Four basic methodological and philosophical disagreements with the disease model are voiced by social scientists writing on gambling. The most widely shared concern is with the issue of categorization itself. Sociologists contend that the placement of people into compartments has a distorting effect on reality. The second issue is the determinism implicit in the illness model. This determinism conflicts with a voluntaristic view of social action held by many sociologists. The third concern is that a medical view places biological and individual factors in a position of prominence, hence pushing social considerations aside. Fourth, the disease concept gives a veneer of moral and ideological neutrality which some sociologists maintain distorts reality.

Categorization and the Pathological Gambler—The Issue of Overlap

According to Livingston, gambling compulsively and compulsive gambling are different phenomena (1974). "Gambling compulsively" is what occurs when someone goes to a casino, race track or gambles in some other way. Should the person lose, the gambling can get out of hand. He/she bets more money than intended in order to get even. "Compulsive gambling" on the other hand involves more than just a temporary loss of control. It implies a "career" of gambling and losing and identification of oneself as a compulsive gambler. For Livingston, the difference between the many who gamble compulsively and the few who become compulsive gamblers is a matter of degree. I make a similar distinction in this book, but use the terminology of the gambling world. Gamblers talk about "chasing." Some people chase on a short-term basis while others string together chasing episodes and chase on a long-term basis. Chasing on a long-term basis is what differentiates between pathological and social gamblers. In Chapter I the difference is described. If there are people who become sick, it is because they chase.

A continuum idea is probably a more accurate representation of reality than one which views people who gamble as falling within clearly distinguishable categories. The lines are fuzzy and there are persons who are marginal. They have some problems but not others. Anyone who listens to a GA hotline or answers the phone at the National Council on Compulsive Gambling will understand what is meant by this statement. It is difficult to make a definitive distinction between the person being a social gambler with a problem or two and his being a pathological gambler. This difficulty leads one to be cautious when putting the label of compulsive or pathological gambler on someone who has a problem connected with gambling.

Social scientists who do research on pathological gambling recognize that the disease model is a social construction and hence any dividing line is an artificial one. This does not mean, however, that it is not useful to think of some persons as compulsive or pathological gamblers. The criteria established by the American Psychiatric Association are designed to avoid the sticky problem of overcategorizing persons through the use of medical labels. This is a clearly responsible action, especially when persons contact therapists with depressive and/or suicidal thoughts. I disagree with Herman when he states: "No useful purpose is served by describing a category of compulsive gamblers" (1976:103).

Alfred Schutz calls categories "typifications" (Wagner, 1970:24). They are stereotypes we need in order to engage in interpersonal communication. Categories like "professional gambler," "cheat," "social gambler," "degenerate gambler" and "hustler" are used by persons affiliated with the gambling scene. It is imperative that we realize that these are typifications.

Typifications need to be replaced with a more accurate understanding of everyday life. The word "professional gambler," for example, carries with it connotations of "winner." But the terms are not necessarily synonymous. Even pros have losing streaks. And there is the lure of other gambles which complicates matters. Should these other gambles lead to loans, and other consequences which place the adjective "professional" into question, can we say we now have a "pathological gambler?" There is the possibility of overlap between seemingly opposite terms. Some of the gamblers interviewed for this book classified themselves as "professional gamblers" at points in their careers. In fact, they were *both* professional *and* pathological in their gambling. Gambling was a full time career; they made some money from some of it but lost it in other gambling endeavors. This type of overlap is ironic. As Chapters IV and VII of this book note, these "professionals" exhibit distinctive problems with their occupational pursuits as a consequence of gambling difficulties. These overlaps should not be ignored by proponents of the medical model.

Other forms of overlap include those between alcoholism, overeating, drug addiction, and other addictions and pathological gambling. Since no one has done any systematic research on the problem, we have no idea as to how extensive it is. The "dual addiction" phenomenon is one which needs further research. We should not be surprised if some pathological gamblers show overlap with alcoholism, given the nature of bar culture, bars at race tracks and casinos, and the conjoint occurrence of drinks and cards at most household and mob-rub games. From field experience and interviews however, addiction to other drugs should be less.

Determinism Versus Voluntarism

The second point of philosophical disagreement between sociologists and medical practitioners is the medical emphasis on determinism and the symbolic interaction oriented sociologist's stress on a voluntaristic theory of action (Blumer, 1969): determinism assumes away choice. Symbolic interactionists by and large make the opposite assumption that most people are free to choose within the limits of their position in society and the situational circumstances in which they find themselves.

Psychoanalysts, in general, are criticized for the deterministic idea that compulsive gambling is produced by an unconscious need to lose. The gambler's behavior is therefore perceived to be determined by unconscious masochism which puts him/her in the grips of a compulsion. Oldman (1978) criticizes this view on two grounds. First, he points out that accounts of compulsion are over-represented in those situations where gamblers reach the end of the road. In other words, psychoanalysts failed to look at early gambling. Secondly, the idea of "compulsion" serves an ideological function for society and the gambler. It is only when violations of domestic and economic responsibilities arise that talk of "compulsion" comes to serve a useful purpose for the gambler. In fact, what we have is a situation where gambling is favored over one's domestic hearth.

Oldman, in his critique of the psychoanalytic view, posits a theory of the causation of gambling problems which is similar to the view portrayed in this book.

> Perhaps the most important message for those who gamble, or wish to control gambling, or wish to help those in trouble through gambling, is that this particular mechanism whereby one reaches a crisis point is a consequence not of personality defect but of a defective relationship between a strategy of play on the one hand and a way of managing one's finances on the other (1978:369–370).

What is missing from Oldman's portrayal are some of the following facts (he could call them "symptoms" were he to embrace a medical model). The crisis is actually a series of crises (called closure states in this book). It produces a high degree of psychosomatic complaints such as ulcers, etc. Gamblers who stop gambling, for example, experience withdrawal symptoms (Wray and Dickerson, 1981; Custer, 1982). The rate of suicide attempts is high; there is a high rate of assaults on the gambler by the spouse (a reaction to heavy debts, ruining family finances, etc.) (Lorenz, 1981); and some of the things this book documents—exploitation of family and work setting and crime to support the habit—are also evident. These are clearly pathological behaviors.

Whatever all of the above facts indicate, they demonstrate that more than just a crisis point is involved here. There is a complex of problems produced by the defective relationship. While I would contend that the gambler *voluntarily* enters the gambling situation and thoroughly enjoys it, he/she makes side-bets which commit her/him to a career of gambling. The committed gambler engages in pathological behaviors which are never envisioned in advance and which are regretted after having been done. In a real sense, many feel "compelled" to continue because things have gotten out of control. Consequently, the model depicted herein implies a limited voluntarism (or soft determinism if you prefer). People feel compelled yet still have choices which are limited by socio-economic position, options available and options they are aware of.

The earlier psychoanalytic model of "compulsion" needs to be rejected and a more limited version of soft determinism must replace it. This appears to be what has occurred. Psychiatrists no longer accept compulsive gambling as a "compulsion" and have renamed it "pathological gambling" (Moran, 1970; Bolen, Caldwell and Boyd, 1975; American Psychiatric Association, 1980). Psychiatrists also recognize that pathological gamblers are not masochists. Custer, for example, notes that the first phase of pathological gambling is a "winning phase" (1982). Masochists could not stand the three to five years of winning which is common early in the careers of the pathological gamblers. Therefore, there is widespread rejection by the psychiatric establishment of an "unconscious need to lose" motivation for pathological gambling. This does not mean, however, that they have given up on the principle that pathological gambling can "compel" behavior. The efforts of psychiatrists in courtrooms gives testimony to this. They have testified to "diminished capacity." Basically, they state that gambling has created such torment that the gamblers should not be held fully responsible for their illegal actions.

Minimization of Social Factors

The third area of conflict which arises between sociologists and medical practitioners is the prominence placed on individual versus social causes of problems. According to this view, the true causes of problems with gambling lie in the social arena and are not internal to the individual. Herman states this clearly:

> It is the widespread acceptance of a conventional disease model that is responsible for the notion that the cause of deviance must be inside the individual and that (to return to gambling addiction) the compulsive gambler is under the influence of a special illness (1976:108).

Should sociologists accept this view it would put them in an odd and dishonest situation. First of all, it assumes that pathological gambling is *not* produced by something inside the individual. While I tend to agree (I think it is produced by a defensive strategy called chasing combined with winning at moments determined by chance which reinforce this strategy), it would be unscientific for me to assert that this is so without adequate testing. Secondly, it also assumes, incorrectly from my more recent experience with psychiatrists, that the psychiatrists themselves are all in agreement that the cause of gambling addiction is totally internal to the individual. Most may believe this to be the case, but the Diagnostic and Statistical Manual of the American Psychiatric Association has attempted to put this issue to rest.

> *Predisposing factors.* These may include: loss of parents by death, separation, divorce, or desertion before the child is 15 years of age; inappropriate parental discipline (absence, inconsistency, or harshness); exposure to gambling activities as an adolescent; a high family value on material and financial symbols; and lack of family emphasis on saving, planning and budgeting (American Psychiatric Association, 1980:292).

Each of these predisposing factors is external to the individual and is social in nature.

Moral Neturality: A Functional Analysis of Pathological Gambling

The fourth major area of conflict between sociology and the medical model of pathological gambling is the issue of moral neutrality. This stance takes two forms: an accusation that medical practitioners all too conveniently condemn speculation in games while speculation in business is not condemned, and an overemphasis on the negative side of gambling whilst ignoring gambling's positive aspects.

Condemning gambling serves a useful ideological function. By looking at those who make a "passive submission to fate" as somehow unworthy, we elevate the ideals of hard work and thrift, ideals which serve capitalism well (Oldman, 1978:357). These ideals are at the root of the Protestant ethic.

A theory of compulsive gambling, then, is a necessary component of the work ethic as natural and normal in a well-ordered society. So that the alliance of
protestantism and psychoanalysis is comprehensive
as far as gambling is concerned. The ideology of one
blends easily with the science of the other (1978:358).

Using science, then, we can condemn the practices with
which we morally disagree, practices which produce violations of the ideals of hard work and thrift and put hedonistic
pleasure-seeking in their place.

A collateral issue which questions the neutrality of the
pathological view of gambling is raised by David Hayano
when he points out that the pathological view is one-sided. It
fails to recognize that for some people heavy losing can have
positive effects. He gives the examples of Fyodor Dostoevksy
and Mario Puzo. Both were more productive as a result of
gambling losses (1982:104).

Pathological gambling produces "good"—as an example,
literary art. This is what sociologists call *irony. Functionalism*
recognizes this basic principle (Matza, 1969: Chapter 4). Func-
tionalists search for *both* the positive *and* negative consequences of behavior patterns. They are called functions and
dysfunctions.

Functions are those observed consequences which
make for the adaptation or adjustment of a given system; and *dysfunctions,* those observed consequences
which lessen the adaptation or adjustment of the system (Merton, 1968:105).

A recognition that something can be both beneficial *and*
harmful at the same time is an important idea in sociological
analysis. To focus solely on the negative is a one-sided view.

Robert Merton, the theorist who makes the distinction between functions and dysfunctions, advised sociologists to
search for latent as well as manifest functions and dysfunctions. Manifest functions are intended and recognized while
latent functions are unintended and unrecognized (1968:105).
As a result of Merton's suggestion, sociologists have ex-

amined the manifest and latent functions and dysfunctions of organized crime (Bell, 1962), poverty (Gans, 1971) and other phenomena.

When we ask the question of function, we have to ask "functional for whom?" Pathological gambling, like poverty, is not always functional or dysfunctional for all of society; rather, it is functional or dysfunctional for specific segments of society. In the analysis that follows, I identify the segments of society to which each function and dysfunction specifically applies.

POSITIVE FUNCTIONS

So far in these pages, we have taken a partially pathological view of pathological gambling; we have concentrated on negative consequences, and the following positive functions of pathological gambling must therefore be listed.

(1) Increased part time and overtime work by some pathological gamblers (see page 99) can increase the net productivity of society. (This is providing, of course, that they do not exploit the work setting in some other way which counteracts this increased productivity—see Chapter IV).

(2) The pathological gambler accounts for a large volume of the business of the legitimate gambling industry. We could say that up to 10 percent of employees of the gambling industry owe their jobs to the pathological gambler, though we cannot be exact about the figure. Also, a percent of profits would be due to the pathological gambler. If the gambling industry reinvests this profit in hotels and non-gambling related business, a certain percent of the growth would be tied to the losses incurred by pathological gamblers. If people end up having fun in these hotels and non-gambling related businesses or profit in some other way, this fun and profit would be directly attributable to the pathological gambler.

(3) Sociologists have long contended that organized crime does not have only dysfunctional consequences for society. It also offers an avenue of upward mobility for persons willing to take the risks involved (Bell, 1962). By providing this route of social mobility, potential unrest is channeled out of the system; further stability of the system is thereby assured. To the

degree that the pathological gambler increases the profit in bookmaking, loan sharking and related organized crime activities, s/he aids organized crime in fulfilling its functions. We must add the caveat that we assume the pathological gambler is not exploiting his/her bookie or numbers writer as described in Chapter V.

(4) Pathological gamblers pay more than their fair share of gambling taxes. Any benefits to be derived from these taxes are increased because of the existence of pathological gambling. In New Jersey, for example, the pathological gambler does more for the aged than any other segment of the population does. Politzer *et al.* found that ten out of ninety-two gamblers questioned engaged in tax evasion and sixteen engaged in tax fraud (1981). Quite probably, the fraud and evasion outweigh the underreporting as they typically involve greater sums of money.

(5) Pathological gambling improves the profit picture for loan companies, banks, credit unions and oxies. Again, we have no way of estimating what percent of loans are for gambling. The profit picture increases, providing the gambler pays back the debt. Should s/he commit suicide, file bankruptcy, default on loans, engage in bank robbery, pass bad checks or in some other way victimize these lending institutions, the profit balance may not be as healthy as might be expected.

(6) According to research by Custer and Custer, 66 percent of Gamblers Anonymous members and 90 percent of Veteran's Administration hospital patients surveyed stated they had defaulted on debts (1978). These defaults, while clearly dysfunctional for lending institutions, provide added employment for insurance investigators, auditors, credit agencies, collection agencies, sheriffs and lawyers.

(7) Labeling persons as pathological gamblers allows members of society to reaffirm their moral values of thrift and hard work by comparing themselves with pathological gamblers. These are values which are prime features of the Protestant ethic and the spirit of capitalism. It is because gambling challenges these values that many have opposed its legalization. The idea that gambling discourages thrift holds doubly for pathological gambling. Whether pathological gambling discourages hard work is another matter. This holds, of course, if

we do not conceive of handicapping as hard work—see Chapter II—and avoid all references to part-time and second jobs held by these gamblers. The values of hard work and thrift are reinforced when pathological gambling is condemned.

(8) Should the medical model of pathological gambling take hold in the country, it will provide employment opportunities for professional and peer counselors and administrators, and will increase profits of some proprietary hospitals. As evidence of this, actions are under way in several states to lobby Blue Cross and Blue Shield so they will allow coverage of inpatient care and treatment of pathological gamblers.

(9) Lastly, should the medical model fail to take hold (a highly unlikely occurrence), pathological gambling will continue to benefit those who build prisons as well as extra prison guards and others who must be employed to service the five to ten percent of the prison population with gambling problems (Royal College of Psychiatrists, 1977). Exact estimates of the percent of prisoners involved are still needed as some of the gamblers in earlier studies may have been career criminals who also gamble or have had other problems which caused the crimes.

NEGATIVE FUNCTIONS

It is basically easier to list the dysfunctions of pathological gambling than it is to list the functions. These negative consequences are referred to throughout this book and also in most publications on gambling. In a real sense, this book deals primarily with the dysfunctions of pathological gambling. The negative consequences are not always manifest. There are latent negative consequences as well. A listing and brief discussion of both types of dysfunctions follows.

(1) A disruption of family functioning occurs. This is clearly documented in this book, where patterns of deception, exploitation of family finances, distrust, arguments, separations and divorce threats are documented in Chapter III. The Gambling Commission study also found the family life of the "probable compulsive gambler" to be adversely affected by gambling (Kallick *et. al.,* 1979; Dielman, 1979). "Probable" compulsive gamblers are more likely to report disagreements with spouses

over finances. They were also four times as likely to report that their children had more problems than other people's children. Finally, ten percent reported being married three or more times as compared with two percent for the general population.

Disruption of the family appears to be extensive. Gayford in a study of one hundred cases of spouse abuse found that nineteen husbands were "occasional heavy gamblers" and twenty-five were "frequent heavy gamblers" (1975). Lorenz (1979) notes that twelve percent of a sample of 144 attendees at a conclave of Gamblers Anonymous were physically abusive to the spouse and eight percent to their children. In another study Lorenz found that 61 percent of the (female) spouses physically struck or threw something at the gambler and 37 percent said they were physically and verbally abusive toward their children (1981).

Using a national survey for comparative purposes, we find that 12.1 percent of husbands were physically abusive to their wives and 11.6 percent of wives were physically abusive to their husbands in the last year (Straus, Gelles and Steinmetz, 1980:36). Over the length of the marriage, 28 percent of spouses were physically abusive (1980:32). If anything, these figures reveal that gamblers may be *less* abusive than national survey findings. While this is the case, the spouses of gamblers are more abusive than national norms.

Using the same survey for data on child abuse, how abusive the gamblers are to their children depends on what the respondents meant by "physically abusive." Using lifetime data, Strauss *et. al.* found 73 percent to have used some sort of violence. Seventy-one percent reported slaps and spankings; 46 percent cited pushes or shoves; 20 percent hit their children with an object; nine percent admitted throwing something; and eight percent kicked, bit or punched their children (1980:61). Again, the gamblers' rates are probably lower than the national samples.

These reported rates of violence appear incongruent and deserve discussion. First of all, the gamblers' rates of violence are lower than nationally normed samples. Pathological gambling appears at first glance to have a positive function in lowering domestic disruption. To interpret the rate this way would be to misunderstand the family dynamics. I would suggest that pathological gambling, with its "million miles away" engrossment quite probably removes the gambler from potentially violent situations. Other activities, like financial exploitation, tend to provoke a *reactive* form of violence on the part of the spouse. Lorenz' research provides evidence for this. Pathological gambling is clearly dysfunctional for the family.

(2) Lowered productivity, higher rates of business failure and financial threats to the workplace are detailed in Chapter IV. Custer and Custer found the same thing in their research. In response to the Gamblers Anonymous question "Do you lose time from work due to gambling?" 85 percent of their sample answered "yes" (1978); 70 percent ansered "yes" when I asked this question. These findings are partially contradicted by the Gambling Commission studies which found "probable compulsive gamblers" to be more satisfied with their jobs than the general population. Also, these gamblers reported no days of work missed and fewer days late to work than the general population.

At first glance these results appear incongruous. In actuality, they are not. First, nearly 40 percent of the "probable compulsive gamblers" interviewed by the Gambling Commission were self-employed (Kallick *et al.,* 1979:437). This rate is higher than in the general population and these people should voice greater work satisfaction. Second, I found a high rate of job changes to jobs which would be more convenient for the gambling. Once they were in jobs which could accommodate their gambling, these persons may have been more satisfied with their work than other workers. This result is further bolstered by gambling commission findings that probable compulsive gamblers are more geographically mobile than the general population. Two reasons for such moves can be connected to gambling: job shift or "geographical cure." Third, with respect to time lost at work, since the gamblers need money, they will go to work (perhaps using up more sick days than the average worker—this needs investigation) but, as pointed out in Chapter IV, some time at work is devoted to handicapping and other gambling related activity. The findings on financial exploitation of work are more clear cut. In addition to the material discussed in Chapter IV, Livingston found that thirty-five out of fifty-three compulsive gamblers stole from their employer (1974). A more recent survey by Politizer *et al.* uncovered thirty-three cases out of ninety-two in treatment who reported embezzling from an employer (1981). Self-employed individuals also experience business failure and near failure as a direct consequence of gambling.

(3) Half of the pathological gamblers I interviewed seriously contemplated suicide. Moran found one in five of his sample of fifty attempted suicide (1969); Livingston uncovered eight attempted out of fifty-three questioned (1974); Custer and Custer discovered that 24 percent of Veteran's Administration patients they studied and 18 percent of Gamblers Anonymous members given a questionnaire stated they had attempted suicide (1978). In her study, Lorenz documented that twelve percent of *spouses* of gamblers made suicide attempts (1981). This rate is three times the rate reported in a study of suicide attempts in Los Angeles (Mintz, 1970). Evidently, pathological gambling produces serious stress for spouses as well as gamblers.

(4) Pathological gambling is associated with an increase in the crime rate. The present book (especially Chapters IV to VIII and X) give the clearest documentation to date on this dysfunction. Other researchers have also commented on criminal behavior patterns of pathological gamblers. Sewell, in a probe of 1,058 inmates at Pentonville Prison in London, found five percent of prisoners gambled heavily (n-56), using "more than their family approved" as the definition; another five percent (n-54) were classified as compulsive gamblers; an added two percent (n-18) mentioned having a gambling problem in their past (Royal College of Psychiatrists, 1977). The Sewell study is suggestive of the imprisonment rate while this book fills out the routes to criminality in detail.

(5) An increase in the cost of insurance is a fifth dysfunction. This is connected with different crimes. A survey currently being conducted by the National Council on Compulsive Gambling (under the author's direction) is uncovering patterns of insurance claims and fraud by gamblers which have the consequence of raising insurance premiums for the general public. Included in the early survey results are accounts of getting into accidents because the gambler's mind

was not on driving but on gambling or financial difficulties instead, fraudulent claims elevation, staged accidents, arson for insurance purposes and other activities connected with attempts to raise money. Lest a wrong impression be given, it should be stated that these activities are not common.

A subsidiary dysfunction occurs when over 60 percent of gamblers cash in or surrender policies or when they are lapsed or revoked for nonpayment. The family, other drivers, and accident victims (in apartment as well as auto insurance claims) are victimized in consequence.

(6) Borrowing by gamblers creates potential problems for other borrowers and possibly for the lenders in the case of default. As noted above under functions, lenders gain through borrowing but they can also lose; when gamblers get credit, they obtain money which other borrowers may be denied. It is also possible that defaults and bankruptcies produce increases in lending fees which all consumers of credit end up paying.

(7) Collateral stress is placed on health care delivery services. The vast bulk of the negative consequences of pathological gambling are visited upon the gambler him/herself. Anxiety, depression, psychosomatic illnesses, and suicide attempts are some of the reasons gamblers have gone to psychiatrists, psychologists and others for help. In the process, they have been misdiagnosed as manic-depressive or as having some other form of mental illness; they have been treated for this and released without the practitioner knowing the true cause or without advising the patient to see Gamblers Anonymous. Gamblers have been given shock treatments, drugged and otherwise treated with the assumption that their complaints had a physiological base. In any case, to treat these symptoms is only to mask the trouble. Ironically, as psychiatrists and others become more aware of the extent of the gambling problem and more people are diagnosed as pathological gamblers, further strain will be placed on the system (unless the system expands and provides further employment as noted above).

(8) As the medical model of pathological gambling takes hold and state governments pay for treatment facilities, the citizenry of these states will have to foot the bill. This dysfunction is partially negated however when the bill is paid

through gambling taxes of which the pathological gamblers pay an inordinate share.

(9) Should the medical model not take hold, taxpayers will have to bear the cost of increased prison space, extra guards, and others who will service these persons in prison. This will be the case particularly as more and more states legalize more and more forms of gambling. According to the Gambling Commission, the present 1.1 million probable compulsive gamblers would be inflated to 3.8 million (Kallick *et al.*, 1979:454). This would undoubtedly produce an increase in the crime and imprisonment rates.

Sociologists must come to realize that research on pathological gambling is not the same as critiques of gambling *per se*. One sociologist, Otto Newman, makes the claim that gambling is not a social problem because it has so many positive functions (1975). An implication of this type of writing is that to do research which focuses on the "bad" side of gambling is to take a moral stance which is supportive of the *status quo*.

A thorough examination of the functional analysis described above leads one to the conclusion that pathological gambling has its own functions and dysfunctions. We could also conclude that those who focus merely on the negative side *do* take a moral stance. The moral stance is in the form of an examination of behavior which has many negative consequences for individuals and victims. It is a stance based on a humanitarian concern for those who suffer.

Advice to the Medical Profession

Given the nature of the dysfunctions of pathological gambling just outlined, it is not surprising that medical practitioners, psychologists and others with clinical contact with pathological gamblers (and with their parents, spouses and children) are finally coming to view pathological gambling as an illness. The official recognition of pathological gambling as a "disorder of impulse control" is relatively recent. The realization is a product of the work of Robert L. Custer, M.D., Alida Glen (a clinical psychologist) and of others at the Veteran's Administration hospital in Brecksville, Ohio.

A brief history of the Brecksville team's contacts with compulsive gamblers is in order. According to Dr. Custer, he was treating alcoholics at the Veteran's Administration hospital in 1969 when he was approached by Gamblers Anonymous members. They told him there were some people coming into Gamblers Anonymous that they couldn't help. Some were suicidal; others were on the verge of committing some crime to get themselves out of a jam; still others were mentally confused and needed psychiatric help. Custer brought in to his hospital troubled gamblers using already existing diagnostic categories.

It is a credit to this clinical team that they listened to Gamblers Anonymous members rather than assume an all-knowing and superior stance. They examined the psychoanalytic model and found it to be seriously deficient because Gamblers Anonymous members recounted stories of early winning histories in their careers. (Masochistic personalities could not stand three to five years of winning.) The Brecksville team also found that individual therapy was not effective; group therapy worked because it enabled the gamblers critically to counterfoil the dishonest facade most pathological gamblers erect. This facade impedes the treatment process. It is also to the credit of Custer's team that they recognized the value of Gamblers Anonymous in treating the gamblers. The American Psychiatric Association's recognition of pathological gambling as a disorder of impulse control (1980) was primarily a product of the work described above. It was used by the American Psychiatric Association. The diagnostic criteria are as follows:

A. The individual is chronically and progressively unable to resist impulses to gamble.

B. Gambling compromises, disrupts, or damages family, personal, and vocational pursuits, as indicated by at least three of the following:

1. arrest for forgery, fraud, embezzlement, or income tax evasion due to attempts to obtain money for gambling.
2. default on debts or other financial responsibilities.
3. disrupted family or spouse relationship due to gambling.

   4. borrowing of money from illegal sources (loan
      sharks).
   5. inability to account for loss of money or to pro-
      duce evidence of winning if this is claimed.
   6. loss of work due to absenteeism in order to pur-
      sue gambling activity.
   7. necessity for another person to provide money
      to relieve a desperate financial situation.
   C. The gambling is not due to Antisocial Personality
      Disorder (American Psychiatric Association,
      1980:292–293).

Since these criteria are going to be used in the future as an
increasing number of gamblers seek treatment, it is imperative
that the categorization reflect, as nearly as possible, a complete image of the world of pathological gambling. The research in this book and elsewhere leads to questioning of several points in the diagnostic criteria.

According to *Diagnostic and Statistical Manual: III, American Psychiatric Association,* arrest for forgery, fraud, embezzlement or income tax evasion due to attempts to gain money
for gambling are the criminal offenses which are characteristic
of pathological gamblers. Not everyone who commits a crime
will be arrested! Additionally, the four offenses chosen have a
middle class bias. The arrest criterion also overlooks bookmaking, fencing stolen goods, burglary, robbery and other
crimes cited in this book. Discounting questionable loans involving civil fraud as well as Shylock loans and early patterns
of juvenile delinquency involving burglaries and other property theft, forty-four out of fifty-three compulsive and borderline compulsive gamblers committed crimes which fed their
habits (see Table on pages 224–225 and Appendix C on
pages 263–265). This criterion should be replaced with the
term "committed a crime in order to support the gambling
habit."

The second DSM III criterion requires default on debts or
other financial responsibilities. This is characteristic of some
late stage pathological gamblers. The existence of two or more
loans not directly traceable to household and other "legitimate" purposes would probably be a better trigger especially

if the loans are connected with payment of gambling debts. In my interviews with social gamblers who lose, I found that adventurous borrowing occurred but no borrowing to get even. Money borrowed was meant to continue an evening's entertainment or to have money to splurge on vacation. In no case did any of these gamblers have more than one loan. To extend the DSM III criteria to borrowers may bring in extra cases but these people will also have to meet other criteria.

Criterion three is on the mark. In fact, the disruption of family functioning produced by pathological gamblers is extreme, as demonstrated by the discussion above under dysfunctions.

The fourth criterion is borrowing money from illegal sources. This criterion is valid; more than half of my sample borrowed from illegal sources. The fifth and seventh criteria are also indicative of pathological gambling and I have no complaint with them either.

Criterion six is overly restrictive and assumes that the gambler is an employee. This study and the Gambling Commission survey both found high rates of self-employment among the gamblers. Both time and financial resources are exploited by the pathological gambler. Jobs are changed to be more convenient to gambling and the Commission survey found higher than average rates of geographical mobility among probable compulsive gamblers, which appears to support the findings presented here.

The last diagnostic criterion: "The gambling is not due to Antisocial Personality Disorder" deserves some comment. To a certain extent this criterion was added in order to make it easier for psychiatrists to go on the stand in courtroom trials where pathological gamblers are charged with forgery, fraud, embezzlement or income tax evasion—the classic middle class offenses. Its additional function was to gain some support from the general public, legislatures, and clinicians for the view that pathological gambling is truly a disease not affiliated with the criminal element. Overcoming that prejudice was perceived to be a major undertaking. To these ends, the following statement was made in explanation of the rationale for excluding the antisocial personality disorder.

Problems with pathological gambling are often associated with Antisocial Personality Disorder and in Pathological Gambling antisocial behavior is frequent. However, in Pathological Gambling any antisocial behavior that occurs is out of desperation to obtain money to gamble when money is no longer available and legal resources have been exhausted. Criminal behavior is rare when the individual has money (1980:292).

Clearly, the twenty-four out of fifty pathological gamblers in this volume who made book, wrote numbers or chopped the pot, the eleven who hustled suckers, the pimps, some of those who fenced stolen goods, the card and dice cheats, and the two systematic check forgers who passed checks as an occupation do not fit the above description. Whether they fit the criteria for "antisocial personality disorder" is another matter. What is clear to me however, is that *àll* of them had gambling problems. To say that even one of them is "basically" an antisocial personality rather than a pathological gambler is to distort reality.

While it would be nice to have compassion for "the working stiff" and not for the "rounder" (someone with an illegal source of income and life style to match), psychiatrists will have to face the fact that professional thieves and others with different sets of values can become pathological gamblers. David Maurer's study of the American confidence man is worth quoting here:

Gamblers, because of their natural grift sense and their wide knowledge of people, fall naturally into the routine of the big con . . . the Postal Kid says: "You become hungry for dough to gamble with. Then you go out looking for a mark you can trim. You take the chances and the gamblers take the dough away from you." [Talking about con men in general Maurer says:] most con men gamble heavily with the money for which they work so hard and take such chances to secure. In a word, most of them are suckers for some other branch of the grift . . . within a few

weeks, or even a few days, a $100,000 touch has gone
glimmering and the con men are living on borrowed
money or are out on the tip or the smack [short cons]
to make expenses.

Con men are well aware of this weakness, yet few of
them it seems, are able to curb their gambling instincts. . . .

This indulgence of the gambling instincts becomes
more than relaxation; their gratification is the only
motive which many con men have for grifting. . . .
They win and lose, win and lose, always losing more
than they win, until they come away broke and full of
reasons why their systems didn't work that time
(1974:150–155).

Living on borrowed money, being unable to curb gambling
instincts, losing more than one wins, and being full of reasons
why "systems" don't work that time are clear signs of addiction to gambling. Given this fact, it should not be surprising
that many con games have a gambling motif including the
classic depicted in the movie *The Sting*.

While con men and other thieves can be pathological gamblers, it is unlikely that Gamblers Anonymous or clinicians
will be able to deal with them. Both treatments utilize main-
stream middle class values in the rehabilitation process. For
example, providing restitution to those who have been victimized is one of the major requirements placed on gamblers in
treatment. This is not something career thieves wish to do.

RESEARCH ON PATHOLOGICAL GAMBLING: AN AGENDA FOR THE FUTURE

Four types of research are needed. First, and most important, are ethnographic studies of subpopulations of gamblers.
Secondly, more solid epidemiological research is required to
find out the incidence and prevalence of pathological gambling. Thirdly, research is needed which will examine the diagnostic criteria and make it more detailed than it is. Fourth,
evaluation research into treatment programs is needed.

Ethnographic studies are still needed on women (the author is conducting one such study), prisoners, and professional thieves. The action setting described in Chapter VII remains unresearched. Existing studies of poolrooms (Polsky, 1969), bowling alley hustling (Steele, 1976), and card and dice hustlers (Prus and Sharper, 1977) distinguish between hustlers and suckers, and include backers but overlook the pathological gamblers on the scene. According to the Gambling Commission, Hispanics and "race-other" (namely Asians and American Indians) are overrepresented in the ranks of pathological gambling but there are no current studies which examine the phenomenon (Kallick *et al.,* 1979:434–436). Ethnographies are needed. In addition, intensive ethnographic interviews are lacking which look into the family system and how gambling interacts with it at different phases.

As for epidemiological studies, the only one conducted to date was done by the Gambling Commission. As of 1974, they estimated that 0.77 percent of the U.S. adult population were "probable compulsive gamblers" (Commission on the Review of National Policy Toward Gambling, 1976:73). This survey has come under fire for asking the wrong questions. According to Larry Nadler (forthcoming), the Commission survey made an estimate of 1.1 million probable compulsive gamblers and 3.33 million potential compulsive gamblers. It is the 1.1 million figure that is always referenced but the procedures for differentiating the probables from the potentials were subjective. Also, there have been temporal changes since 1975 when the survey took place. States have legalized gambling and this should have an impact on the number of pathological gamblers. The final major point made by Nadler is that the DSM III criteria need to be included in any future survey.

The third form of essential research needed are studies which will examine the DSM III criteria and uncover instances of overlap with other pathologies as well as overlaps with criminal behavior systems, professional gambling, and "social gambling." In the process, different types of pathological gamblers will surface as types of alcoholics and substance abusers have already surfaced. This research will cover some of the same ground as ethnographic studies but much will probably take a questionnaire and/or clinical assessment format. Clinicians will perhaps be in the best position to search alcoholic populations to see what percent of alcoholics are dually addicted to alcohol and gambling, for example. Sociologists will be in a better position to examine prison populations.

Finally, we need research which will assess the value of existing treatment programs. At the present time we seem to know the following: individual therapy is probably not so effective at breaking down the resistance that most pathological gamblers have to recognizing they have a problem with gambling. Group oriented approaches help to overcome the pattern of lying to oneself and others about the issues involved. Additionally, Custer and his associates found that conjoint marital therapy (where gambler and spouse are talked to together) is potentially hazardous early in the treatment process because pent up stresses rise to the surface. This can produce situations where the spouse engages in reactive violence against the gambler. For this reason, Custer recommends conjoint marital therapy only after the initial phase. The final thing we know about treatment is that Gamblers Anonymous appears to be the most successful mode and should probably be used as a baseline measure against which other treatment modes should be compared. At this juncture, top priority should be geared to determining how successful Gamblers Anonymous actually is.

Social scientists would do well to examine what is currently happening in the clinical area. They can learn much about pathological gambling from the enquiring believers in the medical model. While some psychoanalysts still "pump out gems" and some psychiatrists are convinced that they really don't need to examine social relations, others have come to realize that we can learn much from each other by not being blind to alternative views.

References

American Psychiatric Association
  1980   *Diagnostic and Statistical Manual: III*. Washington, D.C.:
          American Psychiatric Association.

Bell, Daniel
  1962   "Crime as an American Way of Life: A Queer Ladder of
          Social Mobility." Pp. 127–150 in *The End of Ideology*. New
          York: Free Press.

Blumer, Herbert
  1969   *Symbolic Interactionism: Perspective and Method*. En-
          glewood Cliffs, N.J.: Prentice-Hall, Inc.

Bolen, D. W., Caldwell, A. and Boyd, W. H.
  1975   "Personality Traits of Pathological Gamblers." Paper pre-
          sented at the Second Annual Conference on Gambling.
          Lake Tahoe, Nevada (June).

Commission on the Review of the National Policy Toward Gambling
  1976   *Gambling in America*. Washington, D.C.: U.S. Government
          Printing Office.

Conrad, Peter and Schneider, Joseph W.
  1980   *Deviance and Medicalization: From Badness to Sickness*.
          St. Louis: The C. V. Mosby Company.

Custer, Robert L. and Custer, Lillian F.
  1978   "Characteristics of the Recovering Compulsive Gambler: A
          Survey of 150 Members of Gamblers Anonymous." Paper
          presented at the Fourth Annual Conference on Gambling.
          Reno, Nevada (December).

Custer, Robert L., M.D.
  1982   "An Overview of Compulsive Gambling." Pp. 107–124 in
          Pasquale Carone, Stanley Yoles, Sherman Kieffer and
          Leonard Krinsky (eds.), *Addictive Disorders Update: Al-
          coholism, Drug Abuse, Gambling*. New York: Human Sci-
          ences Press.

Dielman, T. E.
  1979   "Gambling: A Social Problem?" *Journal of Social Issues* 35
          (Number 3):36–42.

Gans, Herbert
  1971   "The Uses of Poverty: The Poor Pay All." *Social Policy* 2
          (July/August).

Gayford, J. J.
  1975   "Battered Wives." *Medicine, Science and the Law* 15
          (Number 4, October):237–245.

Hayano, David M.
  1982   *Poker Faces: The Life and Work of Professional Card Play-
          ers*. Berkeley, CA: University of California Press.

Herman, Robert D.
    1976   *Gamblers and Gambling.* Lexington, MA: Lexington
            Books.

Kallick, Maureen, Suits, Daniel, Dielman, Ted and Hybels, Judith
    1979   *A Survey of Gambling Attitudes and Behavior.* Ann Arbor,
            MI: Survey Research Center, Institute for Social Research,
            University of Michigan.

Livingston, Jay
    1974   *Compulsive Gamblers: Observations on Action and Absti-
            nence.* New York: Harper Torchbooks.

Lorenz, Valerie C.
    1979   "Dysfunctional Family Life Among Pathological Gam-
            blers." Presented at 87th Annual Convention of the Ameri-
            can Psychological Association. New York, NY (Septem-
            ber).
    1981   "Differences Found Among Catholic, Protestant and Jewish
            Families of Pathological Gamblers." Paper presented at the
            Fifth National Conference on Gambling and Risk Taking.
            Lake Tahoe, Nevada (October).

Matza, David
    1969   *Becoming Deviant.* Englewood Cliffs, NJ: Prentice-Hall,
            Inc.

Maurer, David
    1974   *The American Confidence Man.* Springfield, IL: Charles C.
            Thomas Pub.

Merton, Robert K.
    1974   *Social Theory and Social Structure.* New York: Free Press.

Mintz, R. S.
    1970   "Prevalence of Persons in the City of Los Angeles Who
            Have Attempted Suicide." *Bulletin of Suicidology* 7:9–16.

Moran, E.
    1969   "Taking the Final Risk." *Mental Health* (London) (Win-
            ter):21–22.
    1970   "Varieties of Pathological Gambling." *British Journal of
            Psychiatry* 116:593–597.

Nadler, Larry
    forthcoming   "The Epidemiology of Pathological Gambling: Cri-
            tique of Existing Research and Alternative Strategies."
            Journal of Gambling Behavior and Pathology.

Newman, Otto
    1975   "The Ideology of Social Problems: Gambling, A Case
            Study." *The Canadian Review of Sociology and Anthropol-
            ogy* 21 (November):541–550.

Oldman, David
    1978   "Compulsive Gamblers." *The Sociological Review* 26
            (May):349–371.

Politzer, Robert M., Morrow, James S. and Leavey, Sandra B.
    1981   "Report on the Societal Cost of Pathological Gambling and
            the Cost-Benefit/Effectiveness of Treatment." Paper pre-

sented at the Fifth National Conference on Gambling and Risk Taking. Lake Tahoe, Nevada (October).

Polsky, Ned
  1969   *Hustlers, Beats and Others.* Garden City, NY: Doubleday Anchor.

Prus, Robert and Sharper, C.R.D.
  1977   *Road Hustler: The Career Contingencies of Professional Card and Dice Hustlers.* Lexington, MA: Lexington Books.

Royal College of Psychiatrists
  1976   "Social Consideration and Recommendations on Legalized Gambling." Evidence Prepared for the British Royal Commission on Gambling (May).

Steele, Paul D.
  1976   "The Bowling Hustler: A Study of Deviance in Sport." Pp. 86–92 in Daniel M. Landers (ed.) *Social Problems in Athletics.* Urbana, IL: University of Illinois Press.

Straus, Murray A., Gelles, Richard J. and Steinmetz, Suzanne K.
  1980   *Behind Closed Doors: Violence in the American Family.* Garden City, NY: Anchor Press/Doubleday.

Wagner, Helmut (ed.)
  1970   *Alfred Schutz on Phenomenology and Social Relations.* Chicago: University of Chicago Press.

Wray, Ian and Dickerson, Mark
  1981   "Cessation of High Frequency Gambling and 'Withdrawal' Symptoms." *British Journal of Addictions* 76.

The Research Process

Starting with the Gamblers Anonymous group I had first studied in 1971–72, I began attending GA meetings again, only this time using the meetings as a possible resource for interviews and snowballing [asking a person to ask another person, etc.] from there to non-GA sources. I had decided on the interview because of past experience with compulsive gamblers. Because of negative reactions to their behavior, they often hide the full extent of their gambling losses from others. Even for group-oriented gamblers, money acquisition is typically accomplished alone.

After twenty-two interviews I was stumped. There were no other gamblers I could interview. I had run through the local GA cluster I was working out of, which included two GA chapters. My attempts to get into a third group failed. I was denied access to meeting attendance because several members did not want outsiders there. I ended up interviewing only one member from that group, who also attended one of the groups I frequented. In addition, attempts to interview gamblers who were still "in action" also failed. I interviewed only two gamblers through snowballs: one compulsive gambler in a period of abstinence and one card cheat. The snowball rolled but it never grew.

Several gamblers attended meetings only once or twice a year. They would come and say they had been gambling and then leave. Attempts to contact two of these gamblers foundered. For one, I drove to a location fifty miles away three different times and he failed to show up. I finally got the message.

Out of sheer desperation I decided to go to University of Massachusetts classrooms and ask if anyone knew gamblers who were "losing more than they were winning." With this effort I hoped to interview some budding compulsive gamblers and snowball from them. As a result of this effort I interviewed thirteen college students: three borderline compulsive gamblers, three with persistent problems but who did not chase losses constantly, six who were "holding their own," and one winner. In addition to these thirteen, there were two students who consistently failed to make appointments; one of these was the only black I had asked for an interview.[1] Efforts to snowball away from college students to their nonstudent friends failed. The college students refused to introduce me to their home-town friends.

TWO EFFORTS THAT FAILED AND SEVERAL BLIND ALLEYS

At about the time I had run out of interviews from the first GA group and the students were gone for the summer, I decided to venture out and look for compulsive gamblers in the community. One of the GA members—a bowling hustler who did not want to contact his friends because he feared their influence on him—suggested I try observing an alley and talking to the men there. For several afternoons and evenings I watched the hustlers hustle others. I had very little money, so could not afford to bowl all the time or drink. About the third time I went, I struck up a conversation with one of the hustlers. I was asking about how the game went when all of a sudden he asked me what I was doing there in the alleys. I made the mistake of saying I was just watching, rather than introducing myself as someone who was "thinking of doing a study for a sociology paper." After that, he asked me if I was in a bowling league. I replied no, and he became defensive about the situation. "These guys are just hustling, that's all." After this, he wandered away, and I later saw him talking to the manager, and the manager occasionally looked at me. He also followed me as I left the alley and got in my car and took off.

Realizing what a stupid thing I had done, I went back to the alley looking for the hustler, to explain my presence. All I saw there was the bowling-alley manager, who gave me a strange look. I observed the bowlers and then some pool hustlers for a while. I was so nervous at that point that I left, never to return. I had been told that the manager was a bookmaker and that loan sharks hung around the alley. The combination scared me too much, because, at the time, I saw the situation as one in which I was being defined as a busybody where busybodies equal police. To top all this off, when I left I thought I saw a car following me. The result was extreme paranoia and interrupted field work. From all this, I have one major recommendation for researchers. If you are going to do research in an organizational setting and are not going to participate (the role I was taking was constrained by finances to that of a "busybody"), approach the people at the top first. It reduces paranoia and may end up costing less.

From this lesson I decided to try another place where hustlers hung out. Through a non-GA source, I found out that a local golf course was used by hustlers. I went there and talked to the manager, thus lowering suspicion (I told him I was interested in hustling) and hung around the clubhouse talking to hustlers and watching them play gin rummy. I got to know several of the players and eventually interviewed two of them: one hustler who was winning and one who was holding his own. Through them I interviewed a compulsive gambler who was in a period of abstinence. The other person, whom they identified as a "sickie," was still in action and "too busy" to see me.

At about this time I realized that it would take a very long time to achieve rapport with this compulsive gambler and others that may show up. I was faced with the dilemma of attempting to use other avenues for getting information or else commit myself to a potential blind alley. I chose the former.

EXPERIENCE WITH THE CRIMINAL JUSTICE SYSTEM

I had early decided to attempt entry into county houses of correction and state prisons. The first thing I did was to try county houses of correction in Massachusetts. I first sent letters and failed to receive any replies. After this I went to the county prisons in person. Efforts to gain entry into two of these failed. In one, the sheriff, who was in the midst of a re-election effort, was never around to be consulted, and I was told, "You'll have to get his permission first." In the second, the sheriff also was not around, but he later told me over the phone that he didn't think there were any compulsive gamblers there.

Because of some earlier contact with one of the sheriffs (as a teaching assistant for Edwin Driver at the University of Massachusetts I had set up visits for undergraduates), I achieved access there and interviewed the one prisoner who was known to be a compulsive gambler. If there were more compulsive gamblers, they weren't talking to the counselors or prison officials about it. When I interviewed the prisoner (a systematic check forger), he confirmed the opinions of the counselors. He said there was a lot of card playing for cigarettes but that there were no other compulsive gamblers.

After I had finished the interview, the respondent asked me about Gamblers Anonymous. I gave him a GA phone number, but he said that was inadequate because he could call out but no one could call him (GA uses an answering service). He still wanted a phone number, so I gave him the first name and phone number of a GA member along with some GA literature. About a week later the GA member whose number the prisoner had, called me up and said that he was being badgered by the guy with collect phone calls and there was nothing he could do. He was rather upset. When he told me this, I realized I had partially violated the anonymity of the GA member by giving out the phone number. I made two mistakes: first, I failed to ask the GA member if it was OK to release his number to someone else; secondly, in order to achieve reciprocity with one of the interviewees, I jeopardized the good rapport I had developed with the GA group. Luckily nothing was said at future GA meetings. Reciprocity was eventually effected by going to meetings with the prisoner on his release.

My next experience with the criminal-justice system involved several Rhode Island probation officers. Despite much help from the people there, they did not know the people on their caseload outside of the offenses they committed. This was a product of having caseloads of 100–150 people at a time. Two gamblers were contacted by the caseworkers; one refused, and I interviewed the other, an ex-GA member now in abstinence. After about two full weeks of effort I stopped wasting the caseworkers' time.

At the probation office I was told that I might be more successful at the state prisons. After talking to the warden I was denied access, with the inference that I would be bothering people in Massachusetts.

At approximately the same time, I set in motion the paperwork that had to go through the Massachusetts and federal prison systems in order to satisfy laws regarding research on human subjects in the prisons. The effort was successful in the federal system but was bogged down in the state system. The permission of each prison warden had to be obtained to conduct research; much of this was withheld due to uprisings at Walpole and Concord prisons. As for the federal system, I eventually interviewed eight prisoners: six compulsive gamblers, one bookmaker, and a card hustler.

At Danbury Federal Correctional Institution I talked with a counselor who was helping to set up a GA chapter. I went to the second meeting and advised him on how it should be run (mainly anonymously, voluntarily, and without his being there). I also helped establish contacts with local GA chapters for members to attend those meetings in rotation. It was at the meeting I attended that I contacted most of the prisoners to be interviewed. Two of them were interviewed by mistake; they were "playing the system" by going to GA meetings. But their interviews were helpful in illuminating other facets of the gambling world.

While reciprocity with the prison officials was maintained by the help in setting up the GA chapter, reciprocity with the prisoners was another matter. Two of the gamblers asked that I write letters for them. One had a sentence review coming up and wanted me to write a letter to the judge. I wrote a letter describing what compulsive gambling is and noted that the prisoner in question was one. I also sent GA literature to the judge and stated that GA attendance may possibly be a condition of early release. The other prisoner asked me for a letter to put in his files. I did this by stating that he had helped me in the interviewing. Both these interviews were of good quality and went far beyond what you would assume by looking at the criminal records.

GOING HOME AND NEW GAMBLERS ANONYMOUS CONTACTS

At the time I had obtained the contacts in the Rhode Island probation system (summer 1974), I decided to see if some friends I had known at the gas station where I worked during college could help me out. I ended up interviewing five people: three who were "holding their own" and two bookmakers. Again, despite help from these friends, the "degenerate gamblers" they knew did not want to talk about gambling. The bookmakers were interviewed for purposes of comparing them with the compulsive-gambling bookmakers I had already interviewed.

Contact with Gamblers Anonymous was opened again in August, when I received a reply from a letter I had sent to an eastern New England GA group. There is ideological disagreement between eastern and western New England groups that has its basis in how to run GA meetings.[2] This disagreement and the distance that has to be traveled to reach meetings reduces interaction between groups in the two areas.

A result of the lessened contact and subsequent delay in interviewing more compulsive gamblers was a theoretical sidetracking produced by interviews with those who were "holding their own." In this case I became involved in an analysis of becoming a regular gambler and not the more narrowed focus of becoming a compulsive gambler. The sidetracking proved useful, however. I found that those who were holding their own were also impressed with winning and with the action. These interviews (especially those with students) demonstrated the lack of clear boundaries between compulsive and non-compulsive gambling.

I started attending GA meetings all over eastern New England and eventually interviewed twelve GA members from four groups. This was made possible because one of the members from the first group I went to "sponsored" me by taking me to meetings and telling others that I was out to help GA. He was an old, established hand in GA and had been active in regional group organization.

REINTERVIEWS AND GAM-ANON MEMBERS

After conducting seventy interviews, I had analyzed much of the data and still had some unanswered questions. Some I could ask at GA meetings, but others required reinterviews. Finances restricted the number of reinterviews to four GA members (all of whom were group-oriented gamblers).

In addition to reinterviewing the four gamblers, I interviewed six wives and attended four Gam-Anon meetings (Gam-Anon is a therapy group for spouses of compulsive gamblers).

In March 1975 my 1972 Chevy Vega wagon started making

a loud noise (it had fifty thousand miles on it). I had put on at least twelve thousand miles during the research process and burnt out the engine on a cheaply made car. Between March and June I went to only three GA meetings, due to my car, but by this time data analysis was consuming most of my waking hours.

SAMPLE DESIGN

Given the unsharable nature of the problem, compulsive gamblers do not typically come out of hiding for all to see. They exist within the gambling world, which is immoral to some members of the general public. Also, the behavior is illegal if they bet through the bookmaker or at an illegal club. In addition to

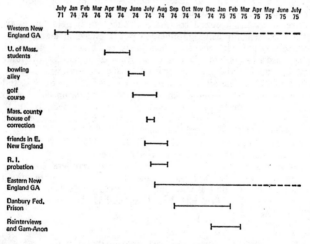

Time Periods Involved in the Different Phases of the Effort to Gain Interviews

being part of a deviant subculture, they are known as "sickies," fools, stupid, idiots, and guys who cannot control themselves. They may gamble in isolation as a result. It was an awareness of this feature, garnered from attending GA meetings, which made me decide to use the intensive interview as a major source of material for this study.

It is my essential belief that data should be gathered from as many sources as possible, given the defects inherent in each research method. In order to overcome this I used the technique of *triangulation* (Webb et al., 1966; Denzin, 1970). This tactic requires the use of overlapping research strategies to improve the validity and reliability of the research process. To accomplish this, meetings of eight Gamblers Anonymous groups (two much more intensively than the others) were attended during a one-and-a-half-year period. It soon became evident that the interviews provided a much more adequate source of information about things the interviewees wished to hide from the group than were the meetings themselves. Several cases of gambling relapse were recounted as well as offenses for which the statute of limitations had not yet run. In turn, the meetings provided double checks on information obtained in interviews. In therapy, members recounted their stories. If a person recalled something he had forgotten about at interview time, I probed further after the meeting was over and recorded it later. Additional cross checks occurred as GA members were used as sounding boards for ideas. Copies of chapters were given to various members; their comments were requested and in several cases were incorporated into the final results.   -

This research relied upon *theoretical sampling* (Glaser and Strauss, 1967) as a source of systematic information about the relation between gambling and getting money. With this sampling procedure, the researcher starts with a general knowledge of the subject matter and decides to sample based on this. Following the initial sampling, the researcher continues to sample but guides future interviews (or observations) in an attempt to develop theory as it emerges. A general knowledge of the subject matter (through the eight months of GA-meeting attendance for my master's thesis) indicated that the GA members might possibly be different from those who failed to join, especially insofar as the illegal behavior patterns were concerned. At first I had visions of interviewing fifty GA members and fifty non-GA members in and out of prison. The first focus of the theoretical sample was to be threefold: get GA members on all ranges of illegal activity, obtain non-GA members as a hedge against the bias of sampling captive populations (Polsky, 1969: 110–11), and finally interview prisoners as a third route to coverage—to counterbalance the possible middle- and working-class bias of the GA sample.

Problems with the criminal-justice system, naïveté about the willingness of compulsive gambling respondents who are presently "in action" to talk, late entry into GA chapters in other portions of New England, as well as finances, reduced the actual number of interviews to seventy gamblers and six wives. Of these seventy-six interviews, fifty were with compulsive gamblers (three of the fifty were "borderline," and three others were "questionable," fifty-three "problem" gamblers in all; see footnote 3, Chapter I for a discussion of this).

The attempt to interview GA and non-GA sources was not as successful as I would have liked. There were thirty-seven GA people (thirty-one active members and six ex-GA members) and thirteen non-GA compulsive gamblers. The following table indicates the sources of these interviews as well as the twenty other interviews with gamblers.

Interview Sample Source and Types of Gamblers

	C.G.	Persistent problems	"holding own"	non-c.g. winners, hustlers, bookmakers	Total
Gamblers anonymous	37				37
Snowball from GA	1			1	2
University students	3	3	6	1	13
Golf course	1		1	1	3
Personal connections			3	2	5
Prison	7			2	9
Probation	1				1
Total	50	3	10	7	70

The second focus of theoretical sampling was to obtain individuals who had used varying methods of getting money to gamble with. It became evident during the research process that while GA membership was important, what appeared to be more important was the intensity of membership in gambling groups and the involvement in different forms of illegal activity. In order to find out whether a prospective interviewee was involved in certain illegal activities, I had to ask informants. Often, informants did not know who had done what. The first person I interviewed, for example, had never told *any* GA members that he had run a whorehouse and stolen meat for sale on the black market during World War II and later fenced for boosters and acted as a tipster and then wheelman for burglars.

This problem was further accentuated in the prison sample, in which it appeared that the gamblers did not associate with one another to a great extent, and if they did, did not discuss their past life. It was also a problem with the second GA cluster, in which the twelve steps of the GA recovery program were accentuated rather than past-life stories as in the first GA cluster.

A result of the informants' lack of knowledge of the past actions of others, some individuals were interviewed who had used different methods of getting money than were reported, and others were less involved in the gambling subculture than was thought by the informants.

Of the two major dimensions of theoretical sampling, I feel I was fairly successful in sampling across the range of group involvement from loner to action-system oriented. Future studies should focus on the subculturally oriented gambler, as I feel that full saturation was not reached on this group in the present study.

These efforts should be based on observation as well as interviews of members as they abstain for short periods of time. (I am skeptical as to whether the full truth would emerge while the gambler is in action.)

The second dimension of theoretical sampling posed the most serious problems. There was a wide dispersion of possible means of getting money to gamble, which was much greater than originally anticipated. It is felt that achieving saturation in each of these categories would be a never-ending process as new methods of getting money are constantly discovered in the research process, as illustrated in the table below.

Frequency of Various Efforts to Obtain Finances

	Number of Cases
Loan fraud	45
Systematic loan fraud (over and beyond forgery or false statements)	14
Shylock loan	27
Bookmaking and other gambling entrepreneurship	24
Check forgery	21
Embezzlement (money or checks)	15
Employee theft (items)	7
Larceny	14
Fencing stolen goods	11
Pool, golf, and bowling hustling	11
Burglary	8
Card and dice cheating	6
Swindling suckers	8
Armed robbery	3
Pimping	2
Selling marijuana	2
Selling cocaine	1

THE INTERVIEWS

In all, I conducted seventy-six intensive interviews. Each was tape-recorded and lasted anywhere from one to four hours (up to eight hours with several reinterviews), with an average of approximately two hours. They were conducted in the home or room of the respondent, at the place of business, in a park, and in prison. In each case special care was taken to conduct the interview in privacy. Because of the potentially embarrassing nature of some of the questions and possible reluctance to talk in the presence of others, this was deemed essential for a free-flowing interview.

The interview guides were separated into five basic sections:

Career-history Sheet

Education	Married	Occupations
		1934—delivery boy, cleanser
1936—high school		1938—42—brewery truck driver
	1940—marry 2 children wife worked in factory	1942—45—Navy seaman, till Aug. '45
		1945—47—unemployed
		1947—returned to brewery
		1948—49—iceman delivery man
		1949—(accident) no work for 8–9 mos.
		1949—50—bookmaker—50% partner, then alone
		1950—present—large supermarket chain (warehouse)
		1952—62—driver (bookmaking part time)
		1962—present—supervisor in warehouse
	after 1968 separation— after GA	(part time unloading trucks)

background information, life history with gambling emphasized, Gamblers Anonymous "20 questions," history of financial indebtedness, and history of illegal activities. The guide was constantly being changed and added to and questions were deleted as I found out more about compulsive gambling.

Gambling	Loans	Crime
1928—9 yrs. old played 7½ (card game like blackjack)		1928—stole from sister and mother's friend
1930-31—11, 12 yrs. old craps, poker (watched father)		
1938—horses (summer after high school)		
via bookies, setback craps and cards in Navy		
	1947-48—first loan, bank	
horse rooms		
horses	—easier to borrow money	1949—books, horses and numbers
(get deeper, *numbers*, heavier)	—credit union	
1950s—quit for few months	loans through friends	early 1950s—fooled with wife's check-book deposits
		writer
	1964-65—constant crisis; tried to borrow way out of debt (22 loans)	
		1967—bad checks via friends
	1968—Aug. 3, 1968, joined GA	

The background-information section consisted of questions about age, ethnicity, education, marital status and history of separations (probed later), occupational history, income of self and wife, class consciousness, religiousness, and parental background. This basic information and "important" dates were used to start a *career-*

history sheet, which was used later on in the interview as a guiding mechanism. One of those sheets appears on pages 250–51.

The gambler's life history in gambling was then queried. Each individual was asked *how* he first became involved in gambling, who influenced him, whom he gambled with and how the stakes rose and the time consumed increased, frequency of wagering and numbers, and how the forms of gambling changed. The career-history sheet proved invaluable in aiding recall, as certain points in the gambling history could be related to "before I was married . . . ," "just after I quit that job . . ." and other such comments. The sheet was used to help probe. For example, using the enclosed sheet as a guide I asked, "What was a typical week of gambling like when you were with the iceman?" "What was a typical day?" Throughout I asked about relations between gambling and work and home and about periods of abstinence and relapse. The gamblers' perceptions of certain actions and people were constantly sought: "What did you think of that?" "How did you feel about him [her] when he [she] did that?"

The third section of the interview included the Gamblers Anonymous "20 questions." These originally acted as an early measure of a person's involvement compared with others. I soon found out that these questions did not accurately measure involvement but were quite useful for probing dimensions that the gamblers tended to skirt around in the discussion of their gambling histories. For example, pawning watches, engrossment in gambling to the exclusion of all else, and suicide discussions were elicited in this section but rarely in a previous one. The interviewees were asked to comment on their answers rather than answer merely yes or no. A common probe here was to simply ask "How?" and "How else?" Those items also served as a preliminary introduction to the other portions of the interview. All fences discussed their fencing in question 11, for example.

The fourth section of the interview—the history of borrowing habits—was used to further fill in the gaps in the gambler's life and attempt to gather sequential information in as systematic a fashion as possible. Loans from friends, relatives, other gamblers, loan companies, credit unions, Shylocks, and oxies were probed again, using the career-history sheet as a guide. (For example, What was the first loan-company loan like? What did you do? How does that work? What was a typical month of loans like, when you were a truck driver in the '50s? How was it different from when you were working for the iceman?) After asking about loans, I probed for tactics used, stalling and avoidance procedures, and help received from others.

The fifth section probed for specific illegal activities that had not been mentioned in the previous segments of the interview. I originally started out with nine categories that were in the literature on compulsive gambling and that I had encountered in attending

GA meetings for the master's thesis. These categories were bookmaking, loan fraud, bad checks, employee theft, embezzlement, robbery, burglary, fencing, and shoplifting. During the interview process I added on con games, swindles, hustles, prostitution, selling drugs, income-tax evasion, insurance fraud, and helping out thieves as a tipster, shill, or stall. I also asked about how these things worked, what they thought of them, and whether concerns other than gambling were involved at the time (drugs, alcohol, women). After this, I asked about their experience with the criminal justice system.

Throughout the interview process, various additions, deletions, and changes were made in order to encourage serendipity. For example, a two-page addition to the guide was made up for bookmakers which included organization of bookmaking, working practices, and customer-bookmaker conflict. As the research progressed, closure was achieved on several processes, and these areas were de-emphasized in future interviews. For example, after about thirty interviews the patterns of relations at home appeared to be fairly set while those with friends were still cloudy. As a result, more time was spent probing relationships with friends.

During the process of getting better at interviewing, I learned from several mistakes. The earlier interviews were filled with my cutting in on free flow of conversation to probe more about something the respondent had just discussed. Later on, I just jotted down the probes on a separate sheet of paper. This also reduced failure to follow up on information. Since I never knew whether an interviewee would be back in action and hence "too busy" for a reinterview, the first interview had to be as good as possible.

Another problem was the failure at first to talk in their language. This was eventually resolved. I knew quite a bit about horses and some about sports but was not an "insider" to all forms of gambling. I made the mistake in several of the early interviews of letting this go by, thinking that it would resolve itself. As a result, it took me longer to learn what "bird cage," "middling," and other jargon meant. Later on I took a "I know quite a bit about gambling but am not sure exactly what that is" attitude. Thus I used the respondents as informants about the system. Instead of allowing "I am sure you know what that is all about" to go by, they proceeded to teach me.

Along similar lines, I was fascinated by some of the jargon and became hooked on some of it rather than the process that it represented. One mistake concerns the term "moving money." Cases numbers four and seven had both used the term. After they used it, I began to ask: "Have you ever heard of the term 'moving money'?" It was not until case number 46 that the following interaction took place.

Q. Have you ever heard the term "moving money"?
A. No.

Q. It is taking money from one source to cover money from another source.

A. We call it "juggling." Scheming.

At this point I realized the error. All the time others had been talking about moving money, manipulating, juggling, scheming, and wheeling and dealing, they were talking about the same thing. This mistake had cost me several months of conceptual confusion. Now, instead of focusing on this term I focused on the *process*. Many previously unrelated activities became related. The person who said he "juggled" his checkbook was similar to the one who wheeled and dealed in order to get a loan consolidated. In a similar vein, Polsky's pool hustler who "dumped" was doing the same thing as the bowling hustler I interviewed who was involved in a "bag match." After interview 46 I started asking about processes.

TAPING

During the course of the interviews, I came upon some rather useful methods for using a recorder and maintaining sanity at the same time. I used the tape recorder in two fashions: first of all, I recorded my recollections of GA meetings in the car going home. Since the drive home averaged over an hour and fifteen minutes (some took two to two and a half hours each way), I used this period to recall as much as possible about the meeting and what was said informally before and after. I found it useful to remember the last things that happened and then recall them in reverse order, with the most clear memories first. I found that this enabled me to remember much more detail than trying to obtain chronological order. After attending many meetings, I found that I had to record only new information rather than the routine. The second use of the recorder was during the interview itself. For the home interviews, I first entered the room and asked where the plug was. This often was answered with a reply something like the following: "Oh, you are going to use a tape recorder?" My answer was an informal reply to the extent that it would be impossible for me to remember everything. If the respondent balked at the idea, I told him that I would like to use it just for basic information and he could tell me to stop the recorder if I asked a question he did not want to answer on tape. All the respondents agreed to this, and several had me stop the tape at various junctures.

Having the interviewees tell me to stop the recorder proved quite productive. Two of the prisoners stopped at income. One had an income of one hundred thousand dollars per year in check forgery; the other had a forty-thousand-dollar income half of which was derived from cheating at cards. While they did not want their income on tape, each discussed his occupation in great detail on the recorder. Three other gamblers told me about offenses for which the statute of limitations had not yet run: armored-car heist; muggings, hijackings, burglaries; and bookmaking. Two respondents told me about offenses but were reluctant to go into detail, on or off the tape. One concerned a situationally induced theft of over ten thousand dollars. The FBI was involved at one point. The other told me all the details of how he used his job as car salesman to obtain loans on fictitious automobiles but balked when I asked him how many loans he had. Finally, one person stopped when I asked him about early occupations (he worked in a speakeasy during prohibition) but then described his daily actions as a bookmaker.

One of the prisoners agreed to being taped only after he searched my wallet. He was evasive in several places but eventually told me about fencing, as well as his occupations: pimp and card cheat. On his compulsive gambling and legal efforts to get money, his interview flowed fairly freely.

Finally, I caught one interviewee in a lie. At a GA meeting he had mentioned helping a professional burglar, but when he talked about it in the interview he said that he didn't go on any jobs with him. I then asked him if he was the one who mentioned a hammer breaking. He then discussed the activity. He also talked about insurance fraud (he and his brother took a sledge hammer to his car) and other illegal activities. I feel this reluctance was more a product of an attempt to manage respectability in my eyes than of reluctance in regard to the recorder.

In using and transcribing the tapes, I found (through a process of trial and error at times that cost bad tapes and missing sections of tapes) that it is worthwhile both for personal sanity and to avoid embarrassment over recording difficulties to do the following:

1. Use a recorder with a built-in microphone. Mikes are a pain; they can be in the OFF position without your knowledge, and they make respondents edgy.
2. Bring extra Duracell batteries, an extension cord, and a hookup to plug into the car cigarette lighter for auto interviews. Low batteries should be avoided at *all* cost; they make the voices sound like Donald Duck, only faster.
3. Stay away from air conditioners, TVs, dishwashers, washer-and-dryers, and typewriters. The noise they make overrides the tape.
4. Use a recorder that makes a loud click at the end of each side of the tape. I "recorded" for one-half hour after one side of the tape had stopped, much to my embarrassment.
5. Use a pedal in transcribing. It's faster than hand operation and worth *much* more than its original cost.
6. Make sure the tapes are of good quality. "Bargain" tapes are *not* a bargain when they break and drag, which is most of the time. They are good for only one interview. After that you may hear two interviews at once, as the old interview is not fully erased when a new one is recorded over it.

In order better to systematize the data that were obtained, I decided to utilize a combination of analytic induction (Becker, 1958) and the constant comparative method of data analysis (Glaser and Strauss, 1967). Analytic induction is a process that includes a search for universals in data analysis. Through this process it was determined that *all* the compulsive gamblers chase losses, are enamored of action to such an extent that they become engrossed in it to the detriment of other spheres of their lives, and rationalize losses.

I found the method of analytic induction to produce a rather sterile image of the gambler. It placed the chase, action, and rationalization out of context. There is no semblance of "being there." In order to offset this tendency, I utilized ethnographic description of the process of gambling along with Glaser and Strauss's constant comparative method of data analysis.

The constant comparative method of analysis involves the comparison of categories of data for similarities and differences. Loners were compared with subculturally oriented gamblers, single men compared with the married, track gamblers with sports bettors, handicappers with systems players, less supervised workers with more supervised workers; other comparisons were also made on all conceivable cross categories whether seemingly logical or not. In order to do this effectively, analytical files were set up. Interview transcripts and observational notes were typed up on ditto master sheets. The original transcripts were typed on purple ditto and then my conversation was underlined with red ditto to highlight the different speakers. I also used red to make marginal comments.

Fifteen copies of each sheet were run off. Two full sets were stapled together—one stored at home and the other in the file for the person or place (all were dated and coded to preserve anonymity). Other copies were stored in various analytical files. Since each page went into several files, a Magic Marker was used to circle the pertinent points for a specific file. With use of this method, entire pages did not have to be reread every time I looked in a file. Later, while I was writing up the chapters, some files were combined and others separated further when I put them into looseleaf binders.

Within the files

There were several general categories, each with subsections; I list some: role relations (wife, children, priest, psychiatrist, work setting); gambling itself (professional gambling, gambling friends, hustling, cheating, "doing gambling"—typical week, chasing); borrowing (bail-outs, borrowing from gambling friends, borrowing from non-gamblers, first loan, refinancing, oxies); crime (checks, employee theft, burglary, fencing, bookmaking, closure, threat). In all, there were over one hundred analytical files. Many of the above categories were subdivided. For example, work setting was divided into personal business, hustling, occupational hassles, and part-time jobs.

In addition to the files, various information was coded and put on a master sheet. This included such categories as age, sex (all the gamblers were male), race (all were Caucasian), religion, social-class origin, and predominant occupation.

Each of the coded categories and each file served as a source of information for comparative purposes. I found out, for example, that middle-class gamblers tended to be loners, married gamblers have special problems that single gamblers do not, and some illegal actions are easily rationalized while others are not.

Throughout the process, I allowed the gamblers themselves to describe their world as they see it. In this fashion, moving money, chasing, and engrossment were recognized as major aspects of compulsive gambling. In some cases, the traditional variables proved to be inadequate, and this showed forth in interviews. For example, it became evident that the degree of job supervision was the most important feature in the occupational sphere for the gambler. A person with less occupational prestige but more "free time" could do more gambling than one with a higher degree of prestige, while the self-employed person was the most free of all. The traditional "white-collar"-"blue-collar" distinctions, while of some relevance, were not as important as the degree of job supervision.

As indicated in several of the comments throughout this excursus on methods, the main objective throughout the task at hand was to be as phenomenologically true to the world of the compulsive gambler as possible. While it is realized that *no* effort can be true to the world, I wished to point out some of the tasks and shortcomings in this attempt.

Gamblers Anonymous Pamphlet

GAMBLERS ANONYMOUS

Gamblers Anonymous is a fellowship of men and women who share their experience, strength and hope with each other that they may solve their common problem and help others to recover from a gambling problem.

The only requirement for membership is a desire to stop gambling. There are no dues or fees for GA membership; we are self-supporting through our own contributions. GA is not allied with any sect, denomination, politics, organization or institution; does not wish to engage in any controversy; neither endorses nor opposes any causes. Our primary purpose is to stop gambling and to help other compulsive gamblers do the same.

Most of us have been unwilling to admit we were real problem gamblers. No person likes to think he is different from his fellows. Therefore, it is not surprising that our gambling careers have been characterized by countless vain attempts to prove we could gamble like other people. The idea that somehow, some day, he will control his gambling is the great obsession of every compulsive, gambler. The persistence of this illusion is astonishing. Many pursue it into the gates of insanity or death.

We learned we had to concede fully to our innermost selves that we are compulsive gamblers. This is the first step in our recovery. With reference to gambling, the delusion that we are like other people, or presently may be, has to be smashed.

We have lost the ability to control our gambling. We know that no real compulsive gambler ever regains control. All of us felt at times we were regaining control, but such intervals—usually brief —were inevitably followed by still less control, which led in time to pitiful and incomprehensible demoralization. We are convinced to a man that gamblers of our type are in the grip of a progressive illness. Over any considerable period of time we get worse, never better.

Therefore, in order to lead normal happy lives we try to practice to the best of our ability certain principles in our daily affairs.

The word spiritual can be said to describe those characteristics of the human mind that represent the highest and finest qualities such as kindness, generosity, honesty and humility.

THE RECOVERY PROGRAM

Here are the steps which are suggested as a program of recovery.

1. We admitted we were powerless over gambling—that our lives had become unmanageable.

2. Came to believe that a Power greater than ourselves could restore us to a normal way of thinking and living.

3. Made a decision to turn our will and our lives over to the care of this Power of our own understanding.

4. Made a searching and fearless moral and financial inventory of ourselves.

5. Admitted to ourselves and to another human being the exact nature of our wrongs.

6. Were entirely ready to have these defects of character removed.

7. Humbly asked God (of our understanding) to remove our shortcomings.

8. Made a list of all persons we had harmed and became willing to make amends to them all.

9. Made direct amends to such people wherever possible, except when to do so would injure them or others.

10. Continued to take personal inventory and when we were wrong, promptly admitted it.

11. Sought through prayer and meditation to improve our conscious contact with God as we understood Him, praying only for knowledge of His will for us and the power to carry that out.

12. Having made an effort to practice these principles in all our affairs, we tried to carry this message to other compulsive gamblers.

THE UNITY PROGRAM

In order to maintain unity our experience has shown that:

1. Our common welfare should come first; personal recovery depends upon group unity.

2. Our leaders are but trusted servants; they do not govern.

3. The only requirement for GA membership is a desire to stop gambling.

4. Each group should be self-governing except in matters affecting other groups or GA as a whole.

5. GA has but one primary purpose—to carry its message to the compulsive gambler who still suffers.

6. GA ought never endorse, finance or lend the GA name to any related facility or outside enterprise, lest problems of money, property and prestige divert us from our primary purpose.

7. Every GA group ought to be fully self-supporting, declining outside contributions.

8. Gamblers Anonymous should remain forever non-professional, but our service centers may employ special workers.

9. GA, as such, ought never be organized; but we may create service boards or committees directly responsible to those they serve.

10. GA has no opinion on outside issues: hence the GA name ought never be drawn into public controversy.

11. Our public relations policy is based on attraction rather than promotion; we need always maintain personal anonymity at the level of press, radio, films and television.

12. Anonymity is the spiritual foundation of the GA program, ever reminding us to place principles before personalities.

TWENTY QUESTIONS

Most compulsive gamblers will answer yes to at least seven of these questions.

1. Do you lose time from work due to gambling?

2. Is gambling making your home life unhappy?

3. Is gambling affecting your reputation?

4. Have you ever felt remorse after gambling?

5. Do you ever gamble to get money with which to pay debts or to otherwise solve financial difficulties?

6. Does gambling cause a decrease in your ambition or efficiency?

7. After losing do you feel you must return as soon as possible and win back your losses?

8. After a win do you have a strong urge to return and win more?

9. Do you often gamble until your last dollar is gone?

10. Do you ever borrow to finance your gambling?

11. Have you ever sold any real or personal property to finance gambling?

12. Are you reluctant to use "gambling money" for normal expenditures?

13. Does gambling make you careless of the welfare of your family?

14. Do you ever gamble longer than you had planned?

15. Do you ever gamble to escape worry or trouble?

16. Have you ever committed, or considered committing, an illegal act to finance gambling?

17. Does gambling cause you to have difficulty in sleeping?

18. Do arguments, disappointments or frustrations create within you an urge to gamble?

19. Do you have an urge to celebrate any good fortune by a few hours of gambling?

20. Have you ever considered self-destruction as results of your gambling?

NEW MEMBERS

To all GA members, particulary the new GA members, here are some additional suggestions.

1. Attend as many meetings as possible. (You, yourself, can be the only judge of how sincerely you attend.)

2. Telephone other members as often as possible between meetings. Use the Telephone List!

3. Don't tempt or test yourself. Don't associate with acquaintances who gamble. Don't go in or near gambling establishments. Don't gamble for anything—this means buying a raffle ticket, flipping a coin, or entering the office sports pool. If you don't make the first "tiny" bet, you can't make any big ones.

4. Read The Recovery Program often. Try to follow it! These 12 steps are the basis for the entire GA program.

5. When you are ready, ask the Trusted Servants for a Pressure Group meeting, for you and your wife.

6. Be patient! The days and weeks will pass soon enough and as you continue to abstain from gambling, your recovery will really accelerate.

For further information write to:

National Service Office
Gamblers Anonymous
P.O. Box 17173
Los Angeles, Calif.   90017

Local chapters are usually listed in the telephone book.

Order in Which Offenses Were Committed by the Gamblers

On the next page is a table that represents the fifty-three gamblers who were "problem gamblers." Fifty of these I have classified as compulsive gamblers. This table should be compared with the table on pages 224–25, as it is that table in long form. The numbers in the left column represent gamblers one to fifty-three. The numbers inside the table represent the rank order in which the gamblers engaged in the activities in question. These numbers should be read across. Case #1, for example, first engaged in juvenile delinquency (burglaries and other thefts in this case) in order to finance his gambling. He then took out a loan from a Shylock. Thirdly, he engaged in burglaries, and so on until he passed checks as the ninth activity he engaged in. I present this table in order to represent the vast differences among gamblers. Ties, as in Chapter X, are represented by the same score (e.g., 8.5 for case #1 means that systematic fraud, fencing, cheating suckers, and tax evasion were engaged in at about the same time or the interviewee forgot exactly which had come first). Alternatively, such a score as 3.5 was given for items that occurred at the same time. For 3.5, this means that two things tied, and as a result, there is no score of 3 or 4 but two scores of 3.5.

Case	Loans	Shylock Loan	Making Book	Checks	Embezzlement	Larceny	Hustling Suckers	Systematic Fraud	Fencing
# 1	6	2	4.5	11		boost 4		8.5	8.5
# 2	2		4				1	6	
# 3	2	5.5	3.5	5.5			1		7
# 4	2	7	1	4.5				7	7
# 5	4	2	3	5.			1	6.5	6.5
# 6	4		10	7.5	2	petty 3 grand 5	1		7.5
# 7	3	5	2	6.5	6.5		1	4	
# 8	5	5	8	9		grand 5	1.5	5	
# 9	2	6	3	5		grand 7	1		
#10	6		5	7	4		2		
#11	3	2			4				
#12	1	2			5	3.5			
#13	2	1			4	petty 3			
#14	1			2	3	petty 4			
#15		1	3	2		grand 4			
#16	1	4.5	2		3				4.5
#17	1	3		2	4			5	
#18	1	2		5	3.5			3.5	
#19	4	1		2.5	5				
#20	2		1	3	4.5				
#21	1	2	3	4				5	
#22	1	3		2					
#23	4	3	2						6.5
#24	1	2	3						
#25	1	3	2						
#26	1	3	2						
#27	1		3			petty 5			6
#28	2		1						
#29	2	4			3		1		
#30	1	2			3			4	
#31	1	2				petty 3			
#32	1	2						3	
#33	1.5	3						1.5	4
#34	1	2							
#35	1			2				3	
#36	1			2				3	
#37	1			3					
#38	2				1				
#39	1					2			
#40	1								4
#41	1								
#42	1								
#43	1								
#44	1								
#45	1								
#46	1								
#47			2			1			3.5
#48			2				1		
#49			1						
#50						1.5			
#51						1			
#52									
#53									

Swindling Suckers	Cheating Suckers	Employee Theft	Armed Robbery	Burglary	Juvenile Delinquency	Pimping	Selling Drugs	Income Tax Evasion
	8.5			3	1			8.5
6	6	3						
8	3.5							
4.5	3							
8								
		7.5		7.5				
			8					
			5		1.5			
4								
	2.				2			
				3.5				
2.5								
		4.5						
5			8	6.5	1		8	
		2		4				
				4				
		4		5				
7	5.5					5.5		
		3						
								2
		2		5		3		
							3.5	
					1.5			
							2	

List of References

Amir, Menachim
  1967   "Forcible Rape," *Federal Probation*, 31 (March): 51–58.

Becker, Howard S.
  1958   "Problems of Inference and Proof of Participant Observation," *American Sociological Review*, 23 (December): 652–60.

  1960   "Notes on the Concept of Commitment," *American Journal of Sociology*, 66 (July): 32–40.

  1963   *Outsiders*, New York: Free Press.

  1970   "Personal Change in Adult Life," pp. 583–93 in Gregory P. Stone and Harvey A. Farberman (eds.), *Social Psychology Through Symbolic Interaction*, Waltham, Mass.: Xerox (reprinted from *Sociometry*, 27 [March 1964]: 40–53).

Bernie P. (as told to William Bruns)
  1973   *Compulsive Gambler*, Secaucus, N.J.: Lyle Stuart.

Bergler, Edmund, M.D.
  1970   *The Psychology of Gambling*, London: International Univsities Press.

Bloch, Herbert A.
  1951   "The Sociology of Gambling," *American Journal of Sociology*, 57 (November): 215–21.

Bloch, Herbert A.; and Geis, Gilbert
  1970   *Man, Crime, and Society*, New York: Random House.

Blum, Richard H.
  1971   *Deceivers and Deceived: Observations on Confidence Men and Their Victims, Informants and Their Quarry, Political and Industrial Spies and Ordinary Citizens*, Springfield, Ill.: Charles C. Thomas.

Camp, George
  1968   "Nothing to Lose: a Study of Bank Robbery in America," unpublished Ph.D. dissertation, Yale University.

Cicourel, Aaron V.
  1970   "Basic and Normative Rules in the Negotiation of Status and Role," pp. 4–45 in *Recent Sociology No. 2*, Hans Peter Dreitzel (ed.), New York: Macmillan.

Cressey, Donald R.
1969   *Theft of the Nation,* New York: Harper & Row.

1971   *Other People's Money,* Belmont, Calif.: Wadsworth.

Denzin, Norman
1970   *Sociological Methods: a Sourcebook,* Chicago: Aldine.

Devereux, Edward C., Jr.
1949   "Gambling and the Social Structure," unpublished Ph.D. dissertation, Harvard University.

Dodds, Brian
1974   "Compulsive Gamblers as Sick as Alcoholics: at Last a Treatment Center Is Prepared to Help Them," *Midnight* (July 8): 14.

Dostoevsky, Fyodor
1972   *The Gambler,* Chicago: University of Chicago Press.

Drake, St. Claire; and Cayton, Horace
1945   *Black Metropolis,* New York: Harcourt, Brace & World.

Drzazga, John
1963   *Wheels of Fortune,* Springfield, Ill.: Charles C. Thomas.

Edgerton, Robert
1967   *The Cloak of Competence: Stigma in the Lives of the Mentally Retarded,* Berkeley and Los Angeles: University of California Press.

Egen, F.
1952   *Plainclothesman,* New York: Greenberg.

Freud, Sigmund
1961   "Dostoevsky and Parricide," in James Strachey (ed.), *The Complete Works of Sigmund Freud,* Vol. 21, London: Hogarth Press.

Gamblers Anonymous
1964   *Gamblers Anonymous: Big Book,* Los Angeles: GA Publishing Company.

Gamblers Anonymous
n.d.   *Gamblers Anonymous* (pamphlet), Los Angeles: GA Publishing Company.

Garfinkel, Harold
1967   *Studies in Ethnomethodology,* Englewood Cliffs, N.J.: Prentice-Hall.

Gauthier, Maurice
1959   "The Psychology of the Compulsive Forger," *Canadian Journal of Corrections,* 1 (July): 62–69.

Gibbons, Don C.
1973   *Society, Crime, and Criminal Careers,* Englewood Cliffs, N.J.: Prentice-Hall.

Glaser, Barney G.; and Strauss, Anselm L.
1967   *The Discovery of Grounded Theory: Strategies for Qualitative Research,* Chicago: Aldine.

Goffman, Erving
1959   *The Presentation of Self in Everyday Life*, Garden City, N.Y.: Doubleday.

1967   *Interaction Ritual*, Garden City, N.Y.: Doubleday.

Henslin, James M.
1967   "Craps and Magic," *American Journal of Sociology*, 73 (November): 316–20.

Herman, Robert (ed.)
1969   *Gambling*, New York: Harper & Row.

Hindelang, Michael J.
1971   "Bookies and Bookmaking: a Descriptive Analysis," *Crime and Delinquency*, 17 (July): 245–55.

Hirschi, Travis
1969   *Causes of Delinquency*, Berkeley: University of California Press.

Hoffman, William, Jr.
1968   *The Loser*, New York: Funk & Wagnalls.

Horning, Donald
1970   "Blue Collar Theft: Conceptions of Property, Attitudes Toward Pilfering, and Work Group Norms in a Modern Industrial Plant," pp. 46–64 in Erwin O. Smigel and H. Laurence Ross (eds.), *Crimes Against Bureaucracy*, New York: Van Nostrand-Reinhold.

Hughes, Everett Chevrington
1958   *Men and Their Work*, New York: Free Press.

Ianni, Francis; with Reuss-Ianni, Elizabeth
1972   *A Family Business*, New York: Mentor.

Irwin, John
1970   *The Felon*, Englewood Cliffs, N.J.: Prentice-Hall.

Joey (with Dave Fisher)
1974   *Killer*, New York: Pocket Books.

Klockars, Carl B.
1974   *The Professional Fence*, New York: Free Press.

Kusyszyn, Igor
1973   "The Psychology of Gambling: Unrelated Facts and Fancies," Address to Annual Meeting of the Rocky Mountain Psychological Association (May 11), mimeo.

Lemert, Edwin
1967a   "An Isolation and Closure Theory of Naive Check Forgery," pp. 99–108 in *Human Deviance, Social Problems, and Social Control*, Englewood Cliffs, N.J.: Prentice-Hall (reprinted from *Journal of Criminal Law, Criminology and Police Science*, 44 [September–October 1953]: 296–307).

1967b   "The Behavior of the Systematic Check Forger," pp. 109–18 in *Human Deviance, Social Problems, and Social Control*, Englewood Cliffs, N.J.: Prentice-Hall (reprinted from *Social Problems*, 6 [Fall 1958]: 141–48).

Lesieur, Henry R.
1973   "Compulsive Gambling—Quitting Gambling Through Gamblers Anonymous," unpublished M.A. thesis, Department of Sociology, University of Massachusetts, Amherst, Mass.

Livingston, Jay
1974   *Compulsive Gamblers: Observations on Action and Abstinence*, New York: Harper & Row.

Lofland, John
1969   *Deviance and Identity*, Englewood Cliffs, N.J.: Prentice-Hall.

Mahigel, E. Louis; and Stone, Gregory P.
1971   "How Card Hustlers Make the Game," *Trans-Action*, 8 (January): 40–45.

Malinowski, Bronislaw
1948   *Magic, Science, and Religion*, Glencoe, Ill.: Free Press.

Martinez, Thomas M.
1970   "Gambling, Gamblers, and Self," Stanford University, unpublished Ph.D. dissertation.

Martinez, Thomas M.; and La Franchi, Robert
1969   "Why People Play Poker," *Trans-Action*, 6 (July–August): 30–35 and 52.

Matza, David
1964   *Delinquency and Drift*, New York: John Wiley & Sons.

1969   *Becoming Deviant*, Englewood Cliffs, N.J.: Prentice-Hall.

Maurer, David
1974   *The American Confidence Man*, Springfield, Ill.: Charles C. Thomas.

McCall, George J.
1963   "Symbiosis: the Case of Hoodoo and the Numbers Racket," *Social Problems*, 19 (Spring): 361–71.

McKenzie, David
1970   "Poker and Pop: Collegiate Gambling Groups," pp. 161–78 in Glenn Jacobs (ed.), *The Participant Observer*, New York: George Braziller.

Mead, George Herbert
1934   *Mind, Self, and Society*, Chicago: University of Chicago Press.

Merchant, Larry
1973   *The National Football Lottery*, New York: Holt, Rinehart & Winston.

Miller, S. M.
1964   "The American Lower Class: A Typological Approach," *Social Research*, 31 (Spring): 1 to 22.

Morehead, Albert H.
1950   "The Professional Gambler," *Annals of the American Academy of Political and Social Sciences*, 269 (May): 81–92.

National Council of Churches
1966   *Report on Legalized Gambling: Guidelines for Study and*

Action (pamphlet), New York: Council Press for Commission on Social Welfare.

Polsky, Ned
1969   *Hustlers, Beats, and Others,* Garden City, N.Y.: Doubleday Anchor.

Ray, Marsh
1961   "The Cycle of Abstinence and Relapse Among Heroin Addicts," pp. 163–68 in Howard S. Becker (ed.), *The Other Side,* New York: Free Press.

Reckless, Walter C.
1973   *The Crime Problem,* New York: Appleton-Century-Crofts.

Robinson, W. S.
1951   "The Logical Structure of Analytic Induction," *American Sociological Review,* 16 (December): 812–18.

Roebuck, Julian
1963   "The Negro Numbers Man as a Criminal Type," *Journal of Criminal Law, Criminology and Police Science,* 45 (March): 48–60.

1967   *Criminal Typology,* Springfield, Ill.: Charles C. Thomas.

Scarne, John
1961   *Scarne's Complete Guide to Gambling,* New York: Simon & Schuster.

Scott, Marvin
1968   *The Racing Game,* Chicago: Aldine.

Scott, Marvin; and Lyman, Sanford
1968   "Accounts," *American Sociological Review,* 33 (December): 46–62.

Smigel, Erwin O.
1956   "Public Attitudes Toward Stealing as Related to the Size of the Victim Organization," *American Sociological Review,* 21 (June).

Spector, Malcolm
1973   "Secrecy in Job Seeking Among Government Attorneys: Two Contingencies in the Theory of Subcultures," *Urban Life and Culture,* 2 (July): 211–29.

Sutherland, Edwin H.; and Cressey, Donald R.
1970   *Criminology,* Philadelphia: J. B. Lippincott.

Sykes, Gresham M.; and Matza, David
1970   "Techniques of Neutralization: a Theory of Delinquency," pp. 292–99 in Marvin Wolfgang, Leonard Savitz, and Norman Johnston (eds.), *The Sociology of Crime and Delinquency,* New York: John Wiley & Sons (reprinted from *American Sociological Review,* 22 [December 1957]: 664–70).

Tec, Nechama
1964   *Gambling in Sweden,* Totowa, N.J.: Bedminster Press.

Thomas, W. I.; and Thomas, Dorothy
1928   *The Child in America,* New York: Alfred A. Knopf.

Trice, Harrison M.
1966   *Alcoholism in America,* New York: McGraw-Hill.

Trippett, Frank
1970   "The Suckers," *Look,* 34 (May 19): 34–41.

Turner, Ralph H.
1953   "The Quest for Universals in Sociological Research," *American Sociological Review,* 18 (December): 604–11.

Webb, Eugene J.; Campbell, Donald T.; Schwartz, Richard D.; and Sechrest, Lee
1966   *Unobtrusive Measures: Nonreactive Research in the Social Sciences,* Chicago: Rand McNally.

Wolfgang, Marvin
1957   "Victim-Precipitated Criminal Homicide," *Journal of Criminal Law, Criminology and Police Science,* 48 (June): 1–11.

Zola, Irving Kenneth
1967   "Observations on Gambling in a Lower-Class Setting," in Robert Herman (ed.), *Gambling,* New York: Harper & Row (reprinted from *Social Problems,* 19 [Spring 1963]: 353–61).

Zurcher, Louis A., Jr.
1973   "The 'Friendly' Poker Game: a Study of an Ephemeral Role," pp. 155–74 in Arnold Birenbaum and Edward Sagarin (eds.) *People in Places: the Sociology of the Familiar,* New York: Praeger (reprinted from *Social Forces,* 49 [December 1970]: 173–86).

Notes

AUTHOR'S NOTE

1. Most common in this vein are criminology texts. Some of the more glaring in this respect are Gibbons, *Society, Crime and Criminal Careers* (1973); Reckless, *The Crime Problem* (1973); and Sutherland and Cressey, *Criminology* (1970). The only exception is Bloch and Geis, *Man, Crime, and Society*, where sparse mention is made of gamblers (1970: 199).

INTRODUCTION

1. See Becker (1963: 24) for a discussion of career contingencies as the term is used in this book.

2. Essentially, I follow the dictates of ethnomethodology. The activity that is produced (compulsive gambling) can be understood only in terms of the methods that go into producing it. Gamblers "do" compulsive gambling much as Agnes "does" femininity (Garfinkel, 1967); people "do" status (Cicourel, 1970); and passing and denial are accomplished by the mentally retarded (Edgerton, 1967).

3. For definition see p. 128. Definitions are also referenced in the index.

4. Oxies are credit-union-like organizations that were originally established by Jewish businessmen to enable them to help other Jewish businessmen obtain credit. Mostly, Jewish gamblers used oxies, but use was not restricted to them alone. Some of these oxies have heavy financial backing from bookmakers, who regularly send customers. There are loan companies that have similar arrangements as well.

CHAPTER I

1. For the purposes of this study, I will define "lower class" as a low-income group generally and the unstable in particular, who comprise a category of unskilled, irregular workers, broken and large families, with a residual bin of the aged, physically handicapped, and mentally disturbed (Miller, 1964: 12). The major characteristic of the lower class is a crisis-life existence generally equivalent to poverty. This is distinguished from "working class" by income and occupation. Working-class workers "get by" on their generally semi-skilled and skilled blue-collar jobs.

2. See Marvin Scott's *The Racing Game* for a more thorough discussion of this pattern at the race track (1968: 124–25).

3. Six of the college students straddled the border. Three were definitely over the borderline and on to a disastrous career, while I could not make a determination for three others. Hence, there are fifty compulsive gamblers and fifty-three "problem gamblers." The three extras are the three college students for whom I could not make any deter-

mination. These three lost control periodically but gained it again. The loss of control had repercussions for living as they had to borrow heavily (relative to how much money they had) to pay creditors. In addition, one of these stole a lottery check, the second shoplifted, and the third shoplifted and "sold pot" to finance gambling and pay debts. While gambling had these effects, they were engaged in short-term chases but not involved in the long-term chase.

4. In this section I agree with and follow Lofland's framework and agree with Livingston's usage of it. Utilizing Lofland's theoretical framework in *Deviance and Identity* (1969), Jay Livingston perceives the long-term chase (which he calls "encapsulation," after Lofland's usage) as a product of threat (1974).

5. Lofland defines closure as a principle of action: "Among the class of proximate and relatively immediately available social acts, the act which is most proximate and performable in terms of the facilitative states of places, hardware, Others and Actor himself will be the act chosen" (1969: 61). This differs from Lemert's definition of closure, which will be used in later chapters. According to Lemert, closure is "a process whereby the tension initiated by a situation is resolved and the configuration (whether of behavior or of mental process) tends to as complete or 'closed' a condition as the circumstances permit." (1967a: 105)

CHAPTER II

1. Several previous researchers have done excellent, systematic studies of betting strategies. The most comprehensive in this fashion are "Gambling and the Social Structure," by Edward C. Devereux, Jr. (1949); *The Racing Game,* by Marvin Scott (1968); and "Observations on Gambling in a Lower-Class Setting," by Irving Zola (1963). These three works all concern the horseplayer, and the reader is directed to these sources for information on strategy and social structure at the race track and the bar.

2. Much of the gambling does not involve handicapping. Cards are not "handicapped"; they are played with varying degrees of skill. The winners typically utilized percentages and "systems" of betting as well as reading facial expressions and cheating. Such games of skill as pool, bowling, and golf involved "hustling" and being hustled. The techniques involved in hustling are more than adequately discussed by Ned Polsky (1969). The same activities occur in bowling and golf but under different names. A "backer" may be called a "banker," and a "dump" may be called a "bag match" (that is, the game is in the bag or will be dumped), but the tactics involved are quite similar.

3. Zola discusses the "hedge" as a *verbal* form of insurance to maintain status within the betting group. (1967).

4. Malinowski, in *Magic, Science and Religion,* noted that magic and ritual often serve the instrumental function of reducing anxiety about uncertain future events (1948).

5. The conclusions of Zola (1967) as to the hierarchy of betting structures are confirmed. Status decreases as we move from handicapping to tips to hedges to hunches (and superstition-oriented betting).

6. See "Craps and Magic," by Henslin (1967); *Black Metropolis*, by Drake and Cayton (1945); and "Symbiosis: the Case of Hoodoo and the Numbers Racket," by McCall (1963).

7. None of the people in this sample had this firsthand. The few who knew had been calling a betting service every day prior to the games being played. In those cases in which betting services were called, several gamblers would get together and share the telephone and betting-service costs.

8. To be a loner in one form of gambling does not necessarily mean one will be a loner in another. Card players, golfers, and bowlers cannot gamble alone. Many of those who were loners at the track also were card players or involved in some other group-oriented gambling at the same time. They would typically use the group-oriented gambling to help them out of the rut created in their loner activities.

9. The *line* is the term used by those who bet with bookmakers for "point spread" in football, basketball, and hockey, and for the odds on baseball and other sporting events (golf and boxing, for example). *Point spreads* are a way of balancing bets. For example, the line on a New York Giants–Dallas Cowboys football game may be "New York by 6." In this event, if I bet New York the Giants must win by 7 or more points. If I bet Dallas, then the Giants must win by 5 or fewer points or the Cowboys must win. If the Giants win by 6, there is no bet (thus 6½ and 5½ are favored by the bettors). *Odds*, on the other hand, are based on win-or-lose situations. How much a team or person wins by does not matter. In a game in which the New York Yankees are favored over the Boston Red Sox, the "line" may read 6–7. If I bet on the Yankees I must "lay out" $7 if the Yankees lose. If they win I get only $5. If I bet on the Red Sox, the bookmaker must lay out $6 if the Red Sox win, but if they lose I pay only $5. It costs me less to bet on the Red Sox, because they are the underdogs. These odds change (ranging from 5½–6½ to 13–15) depending on the varying strengths of each opponent. The closer the opponents the lower the odds. Odds are used for sporting events other than football, basketball, and hockey, and also for elections. See note 11, Chapter V.

10. See Livingston for an explanation of why this is so (1974).

11. Eight of the compulsive gamblers I interviewed were involved in this type of twenty-four-hour-a-day, seven-day-a-week action system. Two were involved in the particular complex described above; one was in another, similar complex; and five were involved in systems surrounding a gambling "club" (whether organized as such or not).

12. See Marvin Scott's *The Racing Game* for the structure of track social organization (1968).

13. The action component of life is discussed by Goffman in "Where the Action Is." For Goffman, action consists of "activities that are consequential, problematic, and undertaken for what is felt to be their own sake." (1967: 185)

14. Psychoanalysts, Bergler in particular (1970), see this physiological state of "pleasurable-painful" tension as important, yet invoke unconscious motives for achieving the painful state. They conveniently forget the pleasurably fearful aspects of life: for example the police officer, career serviceman, race-car driver, and skydiver who hope and wait for action. One Gamblers Anonymous member told me that a Dr. Robert Custer is doing autopsies to find out the causes of compulsive gambling (see related story on Custer by Brian Dodds, 1974).

15. A similar focus on action is described by Thomas Martinez (1970:

source used by Kusyszyn, 1973). Martinez uses cognitive dissonance to describe five mood stages in the process of becoming a compulsive gambler. The five mood stages are 1) risk-taking, 2) here and now, 3) fantasy, 4) euphoria, and 5) mysticism. With each mood state comes a heightened drive to achieve the ultimate high (euphoria). He explains compulsive gambling as the desire to "enhance these pleasurable states rather than playing the game in the usual way."

16. Half of those interviewed followed this particular pattern of movement between different events to continue streaks or break them. Two of those interviewed used amphetamines to extend their gambling time; others used coffee and cold water splashed in their faces to keep them awake for as long as possible.

17. Several procedures are possible in establishing a gambling club, whether at a person's house or in a hotel, a garage, a bar, or a club specifically set up for gambling. There are tremendous variations in these procedures. The game may be relatively small, with a fee applied to refreshments and some for the house man. Alternatively, there may be a "sit-down" fee along with a certain fee per hour. The higher the stakes, the greater the fee. The highest fee I encountered was a twenty-five-dollar-per-hour fee per person. If the game is chopped (more likely with poker), the variety explodes. In a chopped game a certain percentage is taken (chopped) out of the money that piles up in the game (the pot) and after every raise (after each time people add more money to the pot). Organized games typically charge a straight 5 per cent out of every pot. These games are guaranteed "on the square" (as one card hustler put it, "Shit, man, you don't cheat them games; they'd fuckin' shoot you"). House men deal and the cards are changed often. In non-organized games, typically the dealer pays a fee to deal. Major variations include the percentage that is taken out of the pot (it is often equal to the ante), how often it is taken out (e.g., it may be 25 per cent when a certain person—usually the house man—deals), and whether the dealer pays to deal.

18. Eleven of the compulsive gamblers interviewed were pool, golf, or bowling hustlers, six were card and dice cheats, at least seven were good card players that did not cheat, twenty-four were gambling entrepreneurs at some point in their career, and six were constantly privy to "inside information" (these figures overlap). All of them compensated for their winning by being losers at the track, with the bookmaker (bookmakers typically gamble with other bookmakers), or at card or dice games run "on the square."

19. For further discussion of rationalization, see: Marvin Scott, *The Racing Game* (1968: 90); Livingston (1974: 61); Scott and Lyman (1968); Zurcher, "The 'Friendly' Poker Game: a Study of an Ephemeral Role" (1973: 169–70); Larry Merchant, *The National Football Lottery* (1973); Zola (1967); Dostoevsky (1972).

CHAPTER III

1. Out of the fifty gamblers I interviewed, thirty-four were married once, eight were single, five were divorced, and three had been divorced and remarried.

I interviewed no female gamblers. This is a product of three separate facts: gambling is predominantly a male-oriented subculture, credit is less available to females, and as a result, once the female is committed to gambling she has fewer resources with which to get into debt, and females have less money with which to get into gambling debt in the first place. All are products of sexism in North American society. When females do gamble, it is likely to be bingo, cards, casinos, and horses, rather than sports. No one that I know of has done a study of females in the gambling setting. I attempted to interview three women. The first was a bingo addict who worked two jobs and went to Gamblers Anonymous meetings seven nights a week. She was almost impossible to track down. The other two were track nuts. I saw one of these at the only GA meeting she ever showed up at. She never returned. The other was from Florida and too mobile to interview. These facts, and the fact that I write this chapter from the perspective of the male, make this study more sexist than I would like.

2. Devereux (1949) would contend the influence of the Protestant ethic is important—an interesting note because all but six in the sample were either Catholic or Jewish and two out of the six who were brought up Protestant, became agnostics. Historically, those groups condemning gambling in the United States have been Protestant. The National Council of Churches specifically has waged all-out propaganda campaigns against legalization in those states where it has been proposed (see, for example, National Council of Churches: 1966).

3. Rumere is a Greek card game similar to rummy.

4. Three gamblers filed personal bankruptcy (three others were contemplating it), and four sold their houses.

5. Edwin Lemert describes *closure* of financial resources as "a constriction of behavior alternatives held as subjectively available." (1967a: 101)

6. The term "bail out" is used quite frequently by different gamblers but has two different meanings: for some it means a total clearance of debt, and "it would take an atomic bomb to bail me out"; for others it means getting out of a jam. It is the second meaning that is referred to above.

7. Three of the gamblers interviewed remained single for precisely this reason. One did not get into any serious relations because he was afraid of facing the music, and the other two had girl friends who dropped them when they found out about the loss of money.

8. Livingston found the same pattern I did (1974: 46).

9. Unbeknown to the wife, stag parties are gambling havens where card and dice hustlers ply their trade on people who gamble only once or twice a year. Also, people typically sell tickets to the parties in gambling circles, knowing that the gamblers will be only too glad to come. Hence there are three types of people there: friends and relatives (the suckers), hustlers, and gamblers.

10. See Erving Goffman, *The Presentation of Self in Everyday Life* (1959).

11. For further information on various routes to Gamblers Anonymous see Lesieur (1973) and Livingston (1974).

12. Eight of the gamblers had previous divorces or were presently divorced, but only three attributed the divorces to gambling. The others had "we were too young" or "military marriage" types of explanation.

13. These amounted to 40 per cent—a low figure because of differing conceptions of the meaning of separation. Some may have felt that one

or two days didn't count. After a while I became aware of this and probed, but that was after half the interviews had been conducted.

CHAPTER IV

1. In this regard, the general public would tend to confer less seriousness on an action committed against a larger victim organization (Smigel, 1956). There is no reason to believe the gamblers would disagree.

2. Originally, this research was organized along class lines. It soon became apparent that it was not class but freedom on the job that was a major factor in determining the extent of exploitation. There are class connections in that working-class jobs tend to have greater supervision.

3. Teachers are supervised by their students and via them by the community they teach in, as well as by the supervisors assigned to them in the school system.

4. The two amphetamine users slept on jobs: one held many supervised jobs and was fired for sleeping several times; the other had no problems as the manager of a local telephone-company office.

5. Four of those I interviewed held jobs with immense free time: one was an entertainer, the second was a pimp and card cheat, and the two others were check forgers. For these four, the occupation they held was like having no job at all. They were free to gamble almost full time. Car salesmen also have a lot of free time. According to several interviewees who have been car salesmen, gambling and woman chasing are frequent sidelines.

6. One had a banker who was rarely present at the business office. The other was in partnership with his brothers in a pizza house. This business dissolved and he went on his own.

7. On the career-history sheet (see Appendix A), they were forced to put "many jobs" or "10–12 jobs from '60 to '62" or the like.

8. Fifteen of those interviewed have quit work and gambled full time with the intention of continuing to gamble for a living.

9. Car salesmen are notably absent from the list of employee thieves also, but their opportunities lie elsewhere: in the loan department.

10. Donald Horning, in "Blue Collar Theft: Conceptions of Property, Attitudes Toward Pilfering, and Work Group Norms in a Modern Industrial Plant," contends that the amount of theft is almost directly related to the degree of surveillance and the categorization of items that are pilferable (1970).

11. Only 10 per cent mentioned this in interviews, but I feel it was higher, as this was not probed until late in the interview process.

12. Those most prone to talk about this are persons in positions of financial trust. They are also the most prone not to tell their boss they have joined Gamblers Anonymous. Only one gambler told me he had borrowed from his boss; he received a sermon. When the fact of gambling was made known to several other employers, two members were fired for no other reason than that they were gamblers, and the others said the boss made stigmatizing statements after it was revealed that

they had loans or were involved in shady deals in connection with the gambling.

13. Donald Horning, in a study of pilferage at an industrial plant making television tubes, found that only five out of eighty-eight interviewed had stolen for resale (1970). The discussion in the text borrows from Horning.

14. Two persons reported "scalping" and padding expense accounts. One "scalped" in order to pay off a loan so he wouldn't have to "pay for" his "mistake." He would go without meals in order to do it. In a sense, he was pilfering money of uncertain ownership and had the same rationale as those who stole small items for personal use. One can envision a whole series of items of uncertain ownership that white-collar employees pilfer for personal use, from paper clips to paper to pens and so on, *ad infinitum.*

15. Of those who stole at work, six were in supervised jobs (two cooks, a meatcutter, a clerk in stores where other clerks and supervisors were around, an electrician, and an unemployment-compensation worker), while fourteen were in jobs with less supervision, such as sales clerk with no one else on duty, salesman on the road, manager of stores and motels, and supervisory personnel.

16. Of the twenty employee thieves, eight were short-run thieves (four of the "hit and run" type, four with restricted opportunity). The other twelve were habitual thieves: five "jugglers," six outright thieves, and one who was both.

17. Another person (a guest speaker from a distant GA chapter) spoke of doing the same thing; only, he said, "they didn't have a bowling banquet that year." GA members who have been put in positions of trust such as treasurer for a hockey league have worried about the possible consequences of those positions if they should have a "slip" (relapse).

CHAPTER V

1. Putting all the entrepreneurs together (compulsive and noncompulsive), there were nineteen who held jobs as bookmakers, runners, or writers at various times; eleven sold parlay cards; five ran numbers; one was a New York-style runner; and six ran card and dice games (two of these had "clubs").

2. Card and dice games pose relatively few problems for the entrepreneurs. The major problems in this connection are hustlers and cheats who may want in on the game, police, partners who may want to "subway" the profits for themselves, and robbery of the game.

3. Egen describes these three variations in *Plainclothesmen* (1952). He calls them the wire room (telephone), handbook (personal transaction), and horse room (impersonal betting in a location with information on blackboards and a cashier's cage). See also Marvin Scott's *The Racing Game* (1968).

4. This notion is perpetrated by the mass media and was commonly voiced by middle-class gamblers early in their careers.

5. This strategy was reported by four gamblers and used by three

who reported it. When I reinterviewed two of the four, both said that it was an exceedingly common practice among their friends.

6. One person reported another scheme for past-posting, which involved changing the starting time of college sports events on the sheet that bookmakers use for starting times.

7. See Merchant (1973) for an excellent discussion of the early line and the outlaw line.

8. Hindelang, in "Bookies and Bookmaking," mentioned that the vice squad let one of the bookies he interviewed copy his records prior to their confiscation (1971). None of the bookies I interviewed who had been raided mentioned this.

9. There is a fourth suggestion, theft, but this is rare. Several cases were reported through Gamblers Anonymous grapevines.

10. An excellent autobiographical account by a "Mafia hit man" describes this and provides further corroboration for the results of this study. "Joey" (pseudonym) states, "You don't have to use violence. You just have to remind people it's there." (Joey, 1974: 139)

11. Baseball and odds betting in general are difficult to explain. 5½–6½ is not equivalent to 11–13 because the odds are balanced against $5.

The various bets you can make in baseball are "pick": Here the gambler picks his team. The odds are 1–1. It is bet at 5–6. The gambler, as in football, picks his own team, but there is no point spread. If the team he chooses wins, he collects $5. If the team he selects loses, he pays out $6. After this, things get complicated.

| | gambler selects favorite | | selects underdog | |
| | favorite wins | favorite loses | underdog wins | underdog loses |
odds	he collects	he pays	he collects	he pays
5½–6½	$5	$6.50	$5.50	$5
6–7	$5	$7.00	$6.00	$5
6½–7½	$5	$7.50	$6.50	$5
7–8	$5	$8.00	$7.00	$5
8½–2 (2 to 1 odds)	$5	$10.00	$8.50	$5
9–11	$5	$11.00	$9.00	$5
11–13	$5	$13.00	$11.00	$5
13–15 (3 to 1 odds)	$5	$15.00	$13.00	$5

Generally, this is as high as it goes. The bookmaker will move the odds in order to get more customers interested in the payoff on the underdog. This is especially the case if the favorite is the home-town team.

12. Marvin Scott has an excellent discussion of this in *The Racing Game*. Included also are strategies used by trainers in competing with the bookmaker (1968).

CHAPTER VI

1. The border line between legal and illegal use of checks is quite thin. At some banks, "rubber" (alternatively called "bouncing") checks are covered by automatic high-interest loans, while at other banks the

same activity is called illegal (typically if the check is not covered in seven days).

2. Of the six gamblers who had no loans, two were college students, two used up personal resources from large businesses, one borrowed from wealthy friends, and the sixth dealt solely with loan sharks.

3. When the gambler who held the record for the number of loans finally quit gambling, he recounted not knowing how many loans he had. He went to his garage and took out a shopping bag in which there were hundreds of payment books, twenty-two of which were active at the time.

4. See Wolfgang (1957) and Amir (1967).

5. This finding needs further verification, with a larger sample.

6. Three gamblers mentioned using similar ploys during periods of unemployment, while this avenue of funding was closed to several others who were unemployed or between jobs because they had failed to think of the scheme or were loners.

7. It was related by several sources that some oxies had at least 75 per cent of their customers brought to them by bookmakers.

8. Francis Ianni, in *A Family Business* (1972), relates that some finance companies are used to "launder" money from bookmaking and Shylock rackets. The finance companies mentioned by the interviewees may have had this function, but none of those I spoke with were certain of organized-crime connections in the loan company.

9. Recently it has become much harder for *anyone* to get a loan, because of the tightening money market. Finance companies have been hit especially hard, and as a result, some have stopped giving confidential loans. In addition, credit bureaus are being used to a greater extent because of the fear of default.

10. When I was stationed in Vietnam as a company clerk and mail clerk for USARV Trans. Det. (United States Army Vietnam Transient Detachment—a replacement company that processed an average of five thousand men per day in and out of Vietnam), we used to receive between two and three *mailbags* full of letters *per day* from Public Finance Company, Signature Loans, Ace Finance, Gem Loans, etc., to "Commanding Officer, USARV Trans. Det. APO SF 96384" notifying the commanding officer that GI Joe owes fifty dollars or so to them. The implication of these letters was that the C.O. would act as a collecting agent (which many C.O.'s did). At one point we forwarded these letters, but the aggravation grew so much that we threw them away.

11. In a phone interview, a loan-company official states that it is up to the discretion of the officers of the company whether to add on new interest when rewriting the loan in this fashion. He said that he makes his decision based on the sincerity of the lendee.

12. None of the gamblers had criminal proceedings brought by banks because of forgery on a loan. While one was caught, the "cosigner" (his wife) refused to sign a statement indicating forgery.

13. Twenty-seven of the compulsive gamblers have borrowed money from loan sharks and loan-shark-like people or institutions. Three of these interviewed have engaged in loan-sharking at various times.

14. Twelve out of the twenty-nine who went to Shylocks fell in this category. All four gamblers who had four or more concurrent loans with four different loan sharks "produced" in some fashion.

15. Seven of those I interviewed who wrote checks had been gambling entrepreneurs prior to writing checks. At the time they wrote the

checks, some had quit for a while. For example, one had quit being a bookie's writer in order to placate his wife. This avenue of funding was closed off. For others, the entrepreneurial activity, along with other sources of funds, were not bringing in enough money.

16. For three, there had been previous check passing; and for one, the stolen checks were a logical extension of embezzlement.

17. The reader must be cautioned about extending these conclusions beyond the small sample.

18. Supposedly this is what happens to the "average" check user who gets charged a fee by the bank for processing an NSF (non-sufficient funds) check.

CHAPTER VII

1. The college-student poker players I interviewed talked about "going light in a pot"—an institutionalized form of borrowing in college circles that does not exist among older players. In this form of borrowing, the player borrows money from the table—in a sense, getting a loan from the future winner.

> Like, if I have to go light in a pot or something like that, like, say I'm out of money. So instead of putting money in I still want to stay in so we allow people to go light. So if the bet's a dollar they pull a dollar out of the pot and put it in front of them, until the hand's over. Then that money there they owe double. Instead of putting a dollar in they take it out and put it in front of them and say I owe this dollar plus a dollar of my own money when I get it. So after the hand's over they might have four dollars or five dollars to them and they owe the winner the five dollars plus the five dollars they would have thrown in.

This occurs only in games in which all the players are friends; otherwise the college students borrow only from close friends in the game; if there are no close friends, they will bring enough money to last the night.

2. Several of the gamblers had credit at Las Vegas and Puerto Rican casinos. There was no problem for any of them, because if you "stiff" (don't pay) one casino, the others are not informed. One "guest speaker" at a GA meeting (he was from New York) mentioned owing twenty different casinos in Vegas ten thousand dollars each. It is quite possible that a person could eventually get "desperate" after owing enough places. Organized crap and poker games and casinos also give credit via the in-house loan shark. This operation is definitely not in the same league as using casino money to play in the casino itself or failure to pay the bookmaker (unless the book is "wacked out" [crazy and violent] or organized, which most appear *not* to be), although some casinos have the reputation of dealing with "collection agents."

3. Eleven of the gamblers I interviewed fenced stolen goods. Eight of these obtained their contacts through gambling circles. Those who did not fence had practical reasons for not fencing: lack of opportunity; their wives would not allow bought stolen goods into the house, never

mind goods intended for resale; and the profit to be gained was "peanuts compared to what I owed."

4. See *The Professional Fence,* by Carl B. Klockars (1974), for a
discussion of the tactics used by a highly skilled fence in analyzing the
market and taking advantage of the sellers and buyers of the goods he
fenced. Some of the gamblers used similar methods but none were
nearly as sophisticated as Vincent, the professional fence.

5. See Polsky (1969: 42) for an excellent discussion of hustling. The
comments here are made only to elaborate on that analysis as it relates to those hustlers who were interviewed.

6. Much has been written on the activities of card and dice cheats
(see as a small sampling Mahigel and Stone, 1971; Drzazga, 1963;
Morehead, 1950; Scarne, 1961). Most of this material is geared toward
the instruction of naïve gamblers in the trade. Several, notably Mahigel
and Stone and Morehead, discuss the social organization of card and
dice hustling.

7. Six of the compulsive gamblers I interviewed were card and dice
hustlers. All these were shills, and only one was a mechanic and even
he was a shill most of the time. Of the cheats, three had been pool hustlers, four became or were bookmakers, and two hustled in other ways
(one was a pimp, the other fenced).

Since five out of six compulsive gamblers involved in card and dice
hustling were shills and not mechanics, I have limited the following discussion to this aspect of cheating.

8. The different hustles thought of were so varied that closure in the
research-oriented sense was never achieved for this aspect of the research. See *Deceivers and Deceived,* by Richard Blum (1971), for a
discussion of some of the swindles possible.

CHAPTER VIII

1. In using the term "professional thief" I only mean that the people they learned certain tactics from received all (or virtually all) of
their income from theft as conventionally defined. I exclude card and
dice cheats from this discussion, as they have been dealt with in a previous section.

2. This type of activity appeared to be easily forgotten, as it was of a
fleeting and situational nature. As a result, I would expect that it was
more common than recalled.

3. Hirschi, in *Causes of Delinquency* (1969), calls this "attachment."
While Hirschi discusses attachment as a form of internal moral supervision, the gamblers did not speak in these terms.

4. Twenty-six of the gamblers who engaged in these activities justified them. I use the term justification in the sense of denying there is
anything wrong with the action. The basis of the justification is the
ideological beliefs the gamblers hold. They have never had to rationalize or neutralize a pre-existing personal belief against these acts, because, for the most part, they have always thought these actions to be
morally OK.

5. This structure of defenses and apologies for their behavior is almost exactly like that of Vincent, the professional fence in Carl

Klockars' case study *The Professional Fence* (1974). The systems of rationalization are so alike that I would agree with Klockars when he says they are "more than the mere rationalizations of one particular man with a particular life history."

6. I did not ask the gamblers if they neutralized *pre-existing* personal beliefs by doing so. One can only guess that in some cases they did (e.g., burglary) and in others they did not (e.g., loans). This point should be taken up in future research.

7. Their rationalizations are similar to those used by Cressey's trust violators in *Other People's Money* (1971).

8. Lemert, in "An Isolation and Closure Theory of Naive Check Forgery" (1967a), discusses closure in subjective terms. Behavior alternatives are constricted by factors that are subjectively determined. Lemert discusses closure only in terms of check forgery.

9. In several interviews, the interviewees told me that I was the first person to ever know the full extent of everything about them that they were ashamed of. For some there were things "it would be better if my wife *never* knew about," and for others there was trust in my statements of confidentiality (I had known a few going on three years). I knew more than other people only because I probed into sensitive areas.

10. Only four of the compulsive gamblers referred to themselves as thieves: two were systematic check forgers and the third stole from every job he ever had. The fourth looked at himself as a thief with reference to bank robberies he had committed. Only the two check men saw their *occupation* as thief.

11. In a sense, he was much like George Camp's bank robbers in *Nothing to Lose* (1968).

CHAPTER IX

1. "Getting caught" by the police, FBI, or other forces of the law occurred to fourteen out of fifty compulsive gamblers. Three others were arrested by the police but released because of insufficient evidence. They had committed a variety of offenses: burglary, embezzlement, bad checks, armed robbery, selling cocaine, pimping; and one maintained he was falsely accused. Six were interviewed in prison. Six others were apprehended by their employers for various forms of employee theft; two of these were remanded to police authority for prosecution.

2. On the "sad tale," see Scott and Lyman's "Accounts" (1968).

3. Recently the emergence of Gamblers Anonymous has given judges a place to send compulsive gamblers who appear before them. GA members have appeared in court to testify to the sincerity of the defendant. I have been witness to several attempts by bookmakers to "use" GA in this fashion. In one case where the bookie was also a compulsive gambler, it succeeded; in another, it failed because the GA members saw through his tactics. They knew him by reputation.

4. The argument could be made that the compulsive gambler needs an authoritative-type probation or parole officer but one that will revoke the gambler's probation or parole *only* for evidence of gambling or hanging around gambling settings. See John Irwin's *The Felon* (1970) for a discussion of types of parole officers.

5. Marsh Ray found a similar pattern among heroin addicts (1961). He discusses the disgust-and-reflection pattern as a form of treating oneself as an "object" in Meadian terms. (See Mead's *Mind, Self, and Society*, 1934.) Since his sample was small (seventeen), he found only the "disgust" pattern that leads to voluntary abstinence. It is possible that with a larger sample he would have found patterns similar to those I found and discussed.

6. The person that succeeded went to the track once, bet one race, and has not returned to this date. Other than that, he has not gambled for three years. He thanks Gamblers Anonymous for his initial "strength" but says he now relies on Silva Mind Control. He hasn't attended GA in over two years.

CHAPTER X

1. The degree of skill was low compared to the big-con men discussed by Maurer (1974) and even most of the short-con men in Roebuck's (1967) and Blum's (1971) work. (Big and short con refer to the time involved in its performance.)

2. Possibly changes in friendship patterns occur among group-oriented compulsive gamblers. As the gamblers gamble with heavier compulsive gamblers, they may change their ideology to match that of the group they now hang around with. This has been found to be the case with alcoholics (Trice, 1966: Chapter 4).

3. Only four gamblers filed bankruptcy (two personal and two business), and four others seriously contemplated it.

4. Four gamblers never experienced it (the two self-employed gamblers who depleted their bank accounts and the two systematic check forgers who did not have trouble obtaining money). Others spoke in terms of "every time, before I went to get a new loan," or "before the checks," they did not know where to go to get money.

5. The most prominent reasons for insomnia were unknown West Coast scores, unknown race results, tension engendered by the excitement, thinking about their handicapping, and not knowing where money was going to come from the next morning to make a loan payment or pay the bookmaker. The only way many could sleep was to think of how they could get the money necessary for the morning.

6. GA members frequently state that GA is the only way to stop gambling. Livingston has a good discussion of this phenomenon (1974: 124–26).

7. See Livingston (1974: Chapter 3) for a clearer delineation of the influence of social class on the career of the compulsive gambler.

8. The freedom of a belief structure that allows for free spending and living it up has only rarely been touched on (Maurer, 1974, for example).

APPENDIX A

1. There were several black hustlers at a bowling alley I went to. The encounters there are described below.

2. Those in eastern New England run their groups using the twelve steps of recovery as the basis for organized therapy, while western New England and New York groups run "horror story" sessions. From my observations, horror stories appear to be more successful in attracting new members, while the twelve steps of recovery serve to keep old ones, as the meetings are less repetitious.

Index and Glossary Reference

Because many of the terms used in the text are technical and part of the gambler's argot, these terms are referenced in the index.